*The Valley's Legends and Legacies VI*

# THE VALLEY'S
# Legends
# &
# Legacies VI

*By Catherine Morison Rehart*

To Sandi,
Best wishes
Cathy Rehart
4-12-06

**Word Dancer Press**

*Sanger, California*

Published by
Quill Driver Books/Word Dancer Press, Inc.
1254 Commerce Avenue
Sanger, CA 93657
559-876-2170
800-497-4909
QuillDriverBooks.com

Word Dancer Press books may be purchased for educational, fund-raising, business or promotional use. Please contact Special Markets, Quill Driver Books/Word Dancer Press, Inc. at the above address or phone number.

Quill Driver Books/Word Dancer Press, Inc.
Project Cadre:
Doris Hall, Stephen Blake Mettee

ISBN 1-884995-50-0

Rehart, Catherine Morison, 1940-
    The valley's legends & legacies VI/ by Catherine Morison Rehart.
        p. cm.
    Scripts of the KMJ radio program, The valley's legends & legacies.
    ISBN 1-884995-50-0(pbk.)
    1. Fresno County (Calif.)--History--Anecdotes. 2. Fresno County
    (Calif.)--Biography--Anecdotes. 3. San Joaquin Valley (Calif.)-
    -History--Anecdotes. 4. San Joaquin Valley (Calif.)--Biography--Anecdotes.
    I. Valley's legends and legacies (radio program)
    II. Title.
    F868.F8R44          2005
    979.4'82--dc21                              CIP

In Memoriam
Elizabeth Brown Morison
My Grannie-Ma
You continue to light my path


To
The people of Fresno and Merced counties
As they celebrate 150 years of history

# Contents

# Contents

# Contents

# Contents

# Contents

# Contents

# *Foreword*

As the child of Greek immigrants who came to California and settled in Fresno, I am the first to acknowledge the importance of the people who make the San Joaquin Valley unique and special. Many of them are responsible for opening doors and hearts to families like mine and for allowing dreams to be realized. In her books, Catherine Rehart shares the history of ordinary people, whose extraordinary lives and commitment to the region offer legends and legacies for future generations to relive and appreciate, cherish and remember.

I was born, raised and educated here in Fresno County. As a child, parent, and educator for more than forty-four years, I know firsthand the value of preserving the rich history of our Valley. From the very personal family stories that share my family's arrival to the opportunities that ensued to help us grow and prosper, we are indeed a living example of how our valley is blessed and rooted in rich diversity. Our agrarian roots and our ability to work the fields and cultivate the land have made this land—our field of dreams—an oasis for nourishment and prosperity. The richness of our soil is truly symbolic of the promise and potential that grows and resides here. We have bred famous athletes, writers, statesmen, scholars, artists and astronauts.

Catherine Rehart's books take us back in time and, in doing so, reveal the intricate and delicate tapestry of people and stories that have made a permanent and lasting imprint on this important region of California.

As a former history teacher, I have often reminded my students of the importance of knowing and understanding their past. The people, the politics, changes, and challenges all shape the Valley we know and love today.

Ms. Rehart's ability to provide a glimpse into the past is indeed her gift. She is a talented writer and historian, and I know you will celebrate the heritage of the Valley when you read this book. I hope it will also serve as a springboard for conversation in your own family and circle of friends, to share, discuss, document, and record your own special stories. They, too, are the legends and legacies of this great place we call "home."

—Dr. Peter G. Mehas
Fresno County Superintendent of Schools

## *Preface*

A nother amazing journey completed and the hope of more to come—that's what I am thinking about as I begin to write this preface. Fifteen years ago, when John Broeske of KMJ Radio called and asked me to write this series, *The Valley's Legends & Legacies*, I never in my wildest imaginings thought where this journey might lead. It has been a fascinating and joyful ride.

Here we are with volume six—more new stories of the people, places, and events that played a role in the history of our great Central Valley. In this book you will revisit some old friends and meet some new ones. You will read the stories of two local men who knew Abraham Lincoln; and, you not only will learn more about the Chinese who settled in Chinatown, but more about that part of Fresno as well.

Some very interesting people have visited Fresno. In these pages you will be present at evening events that featured Carry A. Nation, William Jennings Bryan, Jack Benny, and Isaac Stern. You will also be a guest at a meeting of the West Park Thursday Club.

In January 2004, I was invited to be the first author to appear at Merced's brand-new Barnes & Noble store. When I arrived, a crowd of people was waiting. Their first question was, "When will you come to Merced and write about us?" A gentleman in the group gave me a card for the Merced County Historical Society. Who could refuse such a heartfelt request? I called Sarah Lim, director of the society, and made an appointment. My visit to Sarah and the marvelous museum and organization she oversees was a highlight of the last two years. I will be returning there in the future because I feel like my Merced journey has just begun. Within these pages you will find stories that were gleaned from research there.

I hope in the future to visit the south Valley. I feel like everywhere I look, rich history awaits—my frustration is that there aren't enough hours in the day to do all I dream of doing.

I spend many hours perusing microfilm of early newspapers. One hundred and twenty years ago, everything was in the newspaper. If someone took a trip, there was a story about it. If someone had a party, it was written about. Every event in the early history of our Valley cities was written about in the newspaper. When a holiday, such as July Fourth, was celebrated, the entire list of parade entrants, with descriptions of the floats, was in the paper. Every speech was printed in its entirety. This is invaluable for the historian. It places her right in the center of the event and makes her feel like she was watching the parade go by and listening to the speeches. It allows her to accurately portray the event for her readers and listeners.

These snippets of Valley life are some of the pieces that go together to make up the whole fabric of who we are in the twenty-first century. Because the population of our Valley cities has grown so much and because there are more stories for reporters to cover, today's newspapers can't give the kind of detail they gave one hundred years ago. This will make it harder for future historians. We do need to look back to our past, before we can envision the future.

I hope you enjoy these stories about our Valley. It is my joy and privilege to bring them to you.

Cathy Rehart

# Acknowledgments

A work of history requires not only the patience of Job when seeking out the truth that only diligent research can provide, but also the assistance of many, many people.

First and foremost I must turn to the staff of the California History and Genealogy Room at the downtown branch of the Fresno County Free Library—my second home. Ray Silvia, Melissa Scroggins, Bill Secrest, Sr., and Bill Secrest, Jr.—thank you all for your help, your expertise, and your friendship—you are all the bright spot in many a day.

A second thank-you goes to Bill Secrest, Jr., for scanning several photos from the library's collections onto disks. The picture of the three different courthouse domes was his creation. I watched with increasing fascination as he created this stunning visual illustration for my story.

To Sarah Lim, director of the Merced County Historical Society—thank you for opening your archives to me, for proofreading many of the Merced scripts, and for sharing photos from the society's collections. Thank you also for granting me the honor of speaking at the Merced County Historical Society's annual meeting as you began your celebration of Merced County's Sesquicentennial—it was an afternoon I will never forget. I look forward to continuing my work with you.

A huge thank-you to Zoe Bishop, docent coordinator for the Merced Historical Society, for your informative tour of the Merced Courthouse Museum. I learned so much that day not only about Merced County, but also about the Merced community's successful efforts to preserve and restore their historic courthouse.

Karana Hattersley-Drayton, historic preservation resource manager for the city of Fresno, always graciously answers my questions and provides information on historic buildings that prove invaluable. Thank you, Karana.

Ever since my children were very small, our favorite Friday night dining experience was at a restaurant in Clovis. The owner, and the lady who presided over the kitchen, is Seferina Franco. The delicacies that she made warmed our tummies and delighted our palates week after week. She is retired now and Franco's Restaurant is managed by her daughter Rosalie Franco Sandoval. It is still our favorite eatery…as soon as my son gets home from Michigan, we drive directly from the airport to Franco's. After a taco, an enchilada, and a chile relleno, Bill knows he's home. I spent a wonderful afternoon with both ladies and, for the first time, learned Seferina Franco's amazing story. It a story of determination, love, and commitment to her family and to her community—it warmed my heart. Thank you for sharing your story with me, Mrs. Franco, and thank-you for giving my family so many delicious meals and memories.

One morning an e-mail from my cousin Rob McKay appeared in my mailbox. Famous baseball player Bobby Bonds had just died and Rob wanted to tell me that, in 1966, he and my dad went to Euless Ballpark in Fresno and watched Bonds play. Rob still had the ticket stub. None of the newspaper articles reporting on Bonds death, including those in *The Fresno Bee*, reported that Bobby Bonds had ever played baseball in Fresno, even though *The Bee* reported on Bonds playing the morning after the 1966 game. When the story ran on KMJ Radio, we had the fun of knowing we had scooped everyone. Thanks, Rob, for remembering and for sharing this story with me.

During the last two years, some institutions in Fresno have celebrated noteworthy anniversaries. The First Chinese Baptist Church has served the Fresno community for more than 120 years. Fresno Pacific University celebrated its sixtieth birthday and the Fresno Philharmonic Orchestra turned fifty years old.

I am so grateful to the Reverend Danny Jack and Dr. Dennis Chinn for preparing materials on the history of the First Chinese Baptist Church for my use, for giving me a tour of their church and gardens, and for inviting me to the church's annual Fun and Fellowship event. Thank you for your warm hospitality and graciousness in answering my many questions.

A meeting with Kevin Enns-Remple, archivist at Fresno Pacific University, and Dr. Arthur Wiebe, former president of the university, in the library of the university turned into a fascinating afternoon. They told me the history of the school's beginnings as a Bible college and its gradual evolution into a fine liberal arts university with a strong emphasis on Biblical teachings. Thank you, gentlemen, for sharing your school's history with me.

My neighbor and good friend Ann Vermel, then development director for the Fresno Philharmonic Orchestra, told me about the orchestra's birthday and provided information about the orchestra's history. Thank you to Ann and to the members of the Philharmonic board of directors for your assistance so that the story of the orchestra could be told accurately.

The ladies of the West Park Thursday Club invited me to lunch. Over a delicious meal they reminisced and shared their club's history with me. They allowed me to bring home scrapbooks, program books, and other materials so I could write about their organization, which has lasted more than 100 years. I also learned about West Park Colony and their memories of growing up there. A very special thank-you to Helen Bixler, Ida Blackburn, Harriet Pervier Burleigh, Eleanor Harden, Harriett Harkness Holgate, Mary Jane Burleigh McCullough, and Nancy McNeil—all members of the West Park Thursday Club. Thank you also for loaning me photos for this book.

Two delightful mornings were spent at the Arne Nixon Center at the Henry Madden Library at California State University, Fresno. Curator Angelica Carpenter gave me a tour of the center, discussed their collections, and told me how and why the center was established. Another morning I had the great joy of interviewing Dr. Maurice Eash, a director of the center and a close friend of the late Dr. Arne Nixon. If a luncheon appointment had not intervened, we probably would have visited all day. Dr. Eash's stories about Nixon helped to flesh out the person for me and provided insights into his life and his vision for the center. I am eternally grateful to you both. Thank you also to Dr. Eash for allowing me to borrow photos for this book. An afternoon visit with Denise Sciandra, president of Arne Nixon Center Advocates, provided additional insights into this fascinating gentleman, Arne Nixon.

One cold January afternoon, I met two of my Fresno High School classmates, JoAnn D'Ambrosio Woodward and Buddy Arakelian, in front of Royce Hall on the Fresno High School campus. We went into Principal Robert Reyes' office and had a visit about Fresno High School, the International Baccalaureate Program that is being implemented there, and the restoration of Royce Hall after a terrible fire. A tour of the newly restored Royce Hall followed. When JoAnn, Buddy, and I went into the auditorium and sat where we had sat as seniors, many memories came flooding back. It was an incredible moment that I'm grateful we could share together. Thank you, Mr. Reyes, for the information you provided and for giving us that special tour. Also, a large thank you to J. Martin Temple, whose architectural firm—Temple-Andersen-Moore—oversaw the restoration of the building. Thank you for allowing me to interview you and for all the details you provided that allowed me to write a more accurate story.

These pages contain the stories of two dear, departed friends—Healey Tondel and Pat Fey. Healey's story was drawn from a lifetime of memories and helped along by articles from *The Fresno Bee*. Pat Fey's daughters, Sarah and Ellen Fey, invited me over for a visit one Saturday afternoon. As we began to talk about their mother I thought, "I wrote a script about her husband, Russ. I must write one about Pat, too." The visit turned into an interview and opened up wonderful memories for all three of us. It was a most memorable, teary afternoon of sharing about a very talented lady who contributed so much to her community. It was with joy that I wrote about my dear friend Pat whom I miss so much. Somehow, having her story in this book brought her closer to me than ever. Thank you Sarah and Ellen for sharing your memories and for providing photos for this book.

Dave Phillips gave me a copy of a memoir that his grandfather, William Walker Phillips, wrote for his grandchildren. It is an amazing document—filled with the stories of a fascinating life journey. I am deeply grateful for your generosity in sharing this document with me and for the photographs of your grandparents that you have allowed me to use for this book.

A delightful afternoon in the home of Cathy and Gary Craycroft provided me with photos and with the story of Craycroft Brick Company, the business that, quite literally, built Fresno. Thank you both for your warm hospitality and for opening up your archive of information about both your family and the business. Thank you for proofreading the scripts and for teaching me about the finer points of brick making. As is the case with so many of the people I have the honor to meet in this job, I came away feeling that I had made two new friends whom I look forward to visiting with again.

Thank you also to Joyce Gibson and Beverly and Earl Knobloch for sharing photos of the Craycroft Brick Company with me.

I want to thank Barbara Roe, Ed Dunn, and DeWayne Zinkin for providing material about Harold Zinkin's life and for allowing me to use photos for this book.

I want to thank my superlative editor and dear friend Bobbye Temple for catching my glitches before anyone else can see them and for continuing to make me a better writer. Thank you to my good friend Doris Hall who does such a beautiful job with the layout and final proofing of the book.

Thank you to Steve Mettee and his team at Quill Driver Books for your publishing skills and for your continuing enthusiasm for this project. To Josh Mettee, my companion at many a book signing, thank you for your marketing skills.

A very large thank you to Al Smith who, even though he is retired, remains a most important part of *The Valley's Legends & Legacies* radio program. It is he who brings the scripts to life every day. Thank you, Al, for the partnership we have shared for fifteen years and for your commitment to this program. What a joyful journey it has been!

Thank you to John Broeske, Ray Appleton, and to all the KMJ staff for your continuing support of *Legends*. A special thank you to Robert Wilson, owner of Fresno Lincoln-Mercury, for your long time sponsorship of this program. I am so grateful for your enthusiasm for local history and for your belief in the importance of *The Valley's Legends & Legacies* to our community.

As always, my heartfelt gratitude goes to you, dear reader and listener, for picking up these books and for turning on your radio so you can read or hear the latest story about our Valley. Your interest in the history of our Valley community and your curiosity about what other stories may yet be unearthed, motivates me to dig deeper and to find more tidbits about our past to share with you.

C.M.R.

The Valley's Legends and Legacies VI

# Roeding's Olives

Our stories of the Valley have chronicled many of George Frederick Roeding's achievements. One that has not been discussed is his early success in the growth and production of olives.

Although Frank Locan, who lived near Roeding, and James Jameson and E. W. Gower, who were farmers in the Fowler area, had experimented with growing olives, it was Roeding who was the pioneer. By 1890, he had sixty acres of olive trees that were flourishing. He had pickled some of the olives at his ranch, but he decided he wanted to go into this phase of the business on a larger scale.

In October 1898, Roeding opened an olive pickling plant in a building on Front (H) Street in downtown Fresno. His plan was to use 1,500 gallons of the olives that his orchards produced each year and, in addition, to buy olives from other local growers. He hoped that his plant would stimulate the expansion of olive groves in Fresno County.

The visitor to Roeding's plant witnessed the process firsthand. Each stem was removed from the fruit by hand. Next, the olives were sent through a chute and separated according to size. The olives were then dropped into a lye solution to remove their bitterness. Then, after being removed and thoroughly washed, they were placed in barrels to soak in salt brine that was gradually made stronger until it reached the maximum strength. When the process was complete, the olives were placed in smaller containers for shipping.

In addition to pickling olives for consumer tastes, Roeding was experimenting with curing some of the fruit using only the salting process. These olives would be sold to saloons for use in beverages. Dried olives were also made at the plant. The production of olive oil would follow later. George Roeding was a man who was not afraid to experiment, and his innovative ideas broke new ground in many areas and added significantly to agriculture in Fresno County.

# Wellington Pilkinton

The story of one of Fresno County's pioneers begins in 1833 on the Wyatt Plantation near Richmond, Virginia. It was in that year that one of the Wyatt's slaves gave birth to a son. She named him Wellington. When Wellington was eighteen, he was sold to a wealthy miller named Robert Pilkinton who took him to Georgia. Pilkinton gave his slave opportunities to learn two trades—Wellington became a master blacksmith and also a miller. He took his master's surname.

When the Civil War broke out, Wellington went to war as the servant of Monroe Pilkinton, his master's son. The two men served together at Shiloh, Lookout Mountain, Vicksburg, and Richmond. Wellington not only fought in these battles, but also protected the young man in every way he could. At the war's end, both men returned to Georgia. Wellington received his freedom, but had nowhere to go. He loved his master's family and suddenly was faced with not only leaving them, but also with losing the protection they had given him.

Wellington rented a piece of land on a plantation nearby and raised peaches, cotton, wheat, and corn. He married Doris Caldwell and the couple had a son, Wellington, Jr. The former slave continued to run Mr. Pilkinton's mill and made his own farm a success.

In 1903, Wellington Pilkinton's son headed west to California. Wellington, Sr., Doris, and their other children joined him. The family began to farm near Bowles, growing peaches and grapes—when late summer arrived, many of the grapes were made into raisins.

On January 30, 1927, at the age of ninety-four, Wellington Pilkinton died far from the cotton fields of Georgia, but within close proximity to the cotton fields of the great Central Valley. He died surrounded by his children and grandchildren and was honored as one of the African-American pioneers of our Valley.

In the early days of our city, the Fourth of July was generally celebrated with a parade, literary exercises, and fireworks. On July 4, 1889, those in Fresno who espoused the cause of Prohibition decided to hold their own literary exercises. Nichols' Hall was the site of their festivities.

The meeting began with a prayer given by the Rev. Judy, followed by choral selections, the reading of the Declaration of Independence, and the delivery of a number of short speeches by men who were active in the local temperance movement. A resolution honoring the work of the late Captain Ewing in the "cause of temperance and sobriety" was adopted.

The program ended with a social hour featuring ice cream and lemonade.

The following day, one of the courtrooms in the Fresno County Courthouse was filled to overflowing. Many arrests had been made the night before, all of them with the same charge—drunk and disorderly behavior—and now these men were brought, one by one, before the judge to receive their punishment.

Most of them were either fined five dollars or sentenced to five days in jail, depending on their answers to the judge's questions. Those who appeared to be genuinely remorseful were given the lighter sentence.

Two of the men brought some levity to the proceedings. Thomas Forrester, who was found on Front (H) Street sleeping off the effects of his celebrations, was asked by the judge if he had been in Madera on the previous day. "No, your Honor," Forrester loudly answered, "I have never been guilty of that crime, sir!" Fred Meyers, trying to gather some semblance of dignity about him, stated that he had walked fifteen miles to get into town. It was the walk rather than beer, he stated, that caused him to walk in a crooked manner. Although the spectators were amused, the judge was not. Both men were sent to jail.

For all those in court that day it might have been a wiser choice to have attended the temperance meeting and limited their liquid refreshment to lemonade.

As soon as gold miners began to swarm into our foothills, businesses were established to supply their needs. Saloons and general stores, along with a hotel or two, were found in most of the gold mining camps. Food, however, had to be brought on wagons from Stockton or over the Pacheco Pass—a long, hard trip, indeed.

Some of the miners, finding their luck in the gold fields was running out, decided to do something about providing food for the people pouring into California. Yank Hazelton was one of the men who left the gold fields and began raising cattle on the valley floor. Soon, sheep and hogs were also being raised.

With the advent of Moses Church's canals in the early 1870s, water was carried from the Kings River to individual farms and to the colonies that developed all around the new town of Fresno Station. Vineyards were planted; orchards were set out—every type of agricultural product one could think of was soon grown somewhere in the Central Valley. The once arid desert was transformed. Soil that, without irrigation, had produced only tumbleweeds and wildflowers was found to be incredibly fertile. The wild elk and antelope that had roamed our Valley for centuries disappeared. In their place were farms producing crops that transformed the Central Valley into the richest agricultural valley in the world. Agriculture supplanted gold and cattle to become the basis of the economy of Fresno County.

Today, our great Central Valley is the nation's food basket—it is the richest agricultural area in the country. The amazingly diverse bounty of crops grown here allows us to say that this Valley truly feeds the nation.

# Baseball & Bobby Bonds in Fresno

A faded ticket for a Fresno Giants baseball game stamped June 18, 1966, holds special memories for Robert McKay of Oakland, California. He was eleven years old that summer and was spending a week in Fresno with his aunt and uncle, Catherine and Scotty Morison.

John Euless, a close friend of Rob's late grandfather, Henry McKay, invited Rob and his Uncle Scotty to attend a Fresno Giants game and sit with him in his box at Euless Park. As the game progressed, Euless explained the finer points of the game and talked about some of the players. The Giants' right outfielder was the third man at bat. He was new to the team. As he walked up to the plate Euless said, "Watch this young man, Rob. He is a real prospect for the big leagues." The pitcher threw the ball. The bat connected with the ball, sending it flying. Rob remembers that "he was really fast running down the first base line." The young player's name was Bobby Bonds. He would hit twenty-six home runs during that 1966 season.

After one season with the AA Fresno Giants, Bonds played with the Eastern League in Waterbury, Connecticut, and then with the San Francisco Giants' farm team in Phoenix. In 1968, he signed with the San Francisco Giants.

In June of 1968, Rob was spending another week with his aunt and uncle in Fresno. On June 25, he and his Uncle Scotty decided to listen to the Giants' game on KMJ Radio. Giants' announcer Bill Thompson was calling the play-by-play. It was an exciting game. In the sixth inning the bases were loaded. Thompson said that a player who had just been signed to the team was coming up to bat—his first moment at the plate in the major leagues. The crowd in the stadium held its breath—the fans listening on the radio held their breath. The ball was pitched; the bat was swung—it connected with the ball, sending it soaring out of the ballpark. Six-foot-one Bobby Bonds had hit a grand slam, tying a record set in 1898 by a pitcher named Duggleby in his debut with the Philadelphia Nationals.

Bobby Bonds went on to play for seven seasons with the San

Francisco Giants. He was a three-time all-star during his fourteen-year major league career.

On August 24, 2003, the day after Bonds' death from cancer, Rob McKay turned on the radio to listen to the Giants' game. In tribute to Bonds they replayed the broadcast of his 1968 grand slam. It sounded just like Rob remembered it all those years ago and brought back wonderful memories of a magical summer night in Fresno when he watched as Bobby Bonds sped down the first base line.

A walk down Pollasky Avenue in Clovis, a couple of blocks south of Bullard Avenue, will take the traveler past a large brown building on the west side of the street. Delicious aromas emanate from within—she has no choice but to go inside and enjoy the best tacos this side of Heaven—for she has arrived at Franco's Restaurant. Celebrating forty-five years in business, the story of this eatery is also the story of a family and a remarkable woman, the matriarch of the clan.

Seferina Herrera Franco was born in Frontenac, Kansas, in 1916. Her father worked for the Southern Pacific Railroad. In 1919, the family moved to Clovis and, in the early 1920s, built a house in the 800 block of Fulton Avenue, which today is Clovis Avenue. She remembers the dirt streets and the horse drawn water wagon that would periodically water the streets to keep the dust under control.

In 1939, Seferina married Luis Franco. Luis worked as a foreman for Earl Smittcamp at Wawona Farms. In 1954, seeking work that was year-round rather than seasonal, Luis went to work for the Southern Pacific Railroad. Seferina and Luis were blessed with four children.

Early in their marriage, a relative who owned a restaurant in Gardena became ill and asked Seferina to run the restaurant for her. She taught Seferina how to prepare her special dishes. When Seferina returned to Clovis, she decided she wanted to open her own restaurant. In 1944, a real estate agent told her about property he had for sale on Pollasky—ironically, just a block west of the home she grew up in. It was a good-sized parcel and was on the market for two hundred dollars. She gave him twenty-five dollars and paid the loan off at ten dollars a month. When the loan was paid, she and Luis moved an old house onto the property and moved into it with their family. On December 19, 1945, it burned down. They moved to a railroad section house—their only cost here was one dollar a month for electricity. Seferina saved every penny she could and, in 1948, they built a twenty-by-twenty-five-square-foot building on their property. It was vacant for ten years until they could save enough to open the restaurant she dreamed of. They also built another building on the property for their home. During these years, Seferina would wrap her two young children in a blanket, board the truck that would take them to Wawona Farms, and spend the day picking berries.

On Clovis Day in April 1958, Franco's Restaurant opened. At first it was strictly a take-out kitchen, but soon she purchased three or four tables and enough chairs for dine-in customers. They had a large Coke machine on one wall—the customers helped themselves to a soft drink and would often go to the refrigerator to get ice for their drinks. As business increased, the building was enlarged. Two more times, over the years, this would prove necessary. The second addition took over Luis and Seferina's driveway.

In 1994, Seferina Franco was inducted into the Clovis Hall of Fame in recognition of her contributions to the business community. She is the only Hispanic woman to receive this honor.

The story does not end here. Seferina's other contribution is the exceptional family that she has raised. Each generation has grown up working in the restaurant. Today, her daughter, Rosalie Franco Sandoval, manages the operation. Her daughter-in-law, Maria Franco, also works in the business. Her grandchildren and great-grandchildren perform the necessary tasks that a business like this requires. In every sense, this is a family operation.

For forty-seven years Franco's Restaurant has been a part of the Clovis community. Its story is the story of a family, the dream of an incredible woman, and the hard work that made the dream a reality.

The planets must have been in a bizarre alignment on September 12, 1865, for on that day William Parker Lyon, one of the most incredible showmen ever to grace the streets and hallowed halls of Fresno, was born. The event took place in Fayetteville, New York. John, his father, was a preacher; his mother had a penchant for chamber pots. When Lyon was three years old, he fell out of his crib and landed upside down with his head firmly lodged in one of his mother's granite pots. A trip to the blacksmith, who used a chisel to dislodge the boy's head, was a landmark event in Lyon's life.

In 1868, John Lyon decided to head for San Francisco—in its heyday as a colorful Gold Rush city. He had heard it was full of sinners and he felt he could "save" them. A few months later Parker and his mother followed. They boarded a steamer in New York with only a suitcase and a large china chamber pot decorated with red roses. The steamer took them to the Isthmus of Panama where they boarded a train to the Pacific coast. They took another boat to San Francisco. John Lyon took them to the seedy hotel where he was living. It was not an auspicious beginning.

For a young boy, San Francisco was a magical place. Mark Twain, Robert Louis Stevenson, the Silver Kings of the Comstock Lode, exotic Chinese men, ladies of unacceptable social standing—a whole host of colorful characters walked its streets. Gold was the medium of exchange. There were swindlers on every corner. Their stock-in-trade was to see how quickly they could talk the miners out of their gold.

The Lyon family was just struggling to get by. Mrs. Lyon finally talked her husband into turning his flair for preaching into something more lucrative. "John," she said, "you could talk the angel Gabriel out of his horn. Go out and become an auctioneer." He did and became a great success selling furniture to people whether they needed it or not. His son, Parker, who later became a partner in his father's business, inherited his gift of gab. Our story will continue.

# William Parker Lyon—The Saga Continues

As we continue the story of young Parker Lyon we find him singing in the saloons of San Francisco for a few cents a day. His golden voice was heard by a Baptist preacher who hired him to not only sing in his church, but also to pump the organ.

All was well until one day when, during the baptism of a very hefty young lady, the rather diminutive preacher and the lady, who were both standing in the baptismal pool, lost their footing. The fall resulted in the dislodging of the lady's wooden leg, which shot out of the water and upset a collection plate filled with gold coins causing much shock and merriment among the congregation. Amid all this uproar, Lyon forgot to pump the organ, which died with a loud shriek. Lyon was laughing so hard he fell over the organ rail and was fired by the preacher for his trouble.

In the late 1870s, the Lyons moved to Oakland and opened the Centennial Auction House. Every morning before they opened for business, Parker and his father would move as much furniture out on the sidewalk as they could. This was the showroom. There was more inside. Anyone who stopped to look at the outside offerings was quickly approached by either father or son and treated to a smooth sales pitch. On auction days, the place would fill with people hoping to find a bargain. They also came for the whiskey.

John Lyon may have given up fulltime preaching, but he still gave sermons on any available street corner against the evils of drink. While he was out preaching, his son, Parker, was in the basement doctoring up a barrel of whiskey with tobacco juice and red pepper. The reputation of his whiskey spread quickly—it was considered the hottest in California. Men flocked to the auction house and down to the basement for a glass of the fiery drink. Poet Joaquin Miller was a frequent visitor—the libation usually brought on a recitation or two. The business flourished. The Lyons finally had plenty of money coming in.

In 1889, W. Parker Lyon married Clara Elsey, a girl he had met during his school days in Oakland. Clara was a member of a prominent family. During the reception following the wedding ceremony the gifts were on display. Prominently placed amid the offerings was the china chamber pot decorated with the large red roses that had made its way from New York, over the Isthmus of Panama, and on to San Francisco. It was a gift from Parker's mother. Our story continues.

W. Parker Lyon was Fresno's most colorful mayor and furniture entrepreneur.

# W. Parker Lyon
## Says

Is about the right price for Saturday
___
1134-1140 I Street

# William Parker Lyon—The Saga Ends

In 1892, W. Parker Lyon and his wife, Clara, moved to Fresno. He opened a furniture store on I (Broadway) Street. He was determined to make a million dollars. Using creative advertising, his business increased so rapidly that he had to expand his store twice during an eighteen-month period. By 1908, he had easily reached his million-dollar goal.

Lyon was a born showman—Fresno's version of P. T. Barnum. He had a zest for life that was contagious. He was a great booster of Fresno and did all he could to put Fresno on the map.

His bravado masked a deep sadness. The flamboyant public figure was, in his home, a devoted husband and father. In February of 1898, the Lyons' only children, seven-year-old Gladys and four-year-old Elsie, died of diphtheria within two weeks of each other. The grieving parents were inconsolable. The couple would later have two more children, a son, Parker, Jr., and a daughter, Mildred.

In 1905, Lyon was elected mayor of Fresno on an "open town" platform. Three years later, citing the health of his children, he resigned his position and moved away. They came back to Fresno, later moved to the Bay Area, and then to southern California.

An enthusiastic collector of everything under the sun that dealt with the history of the West, Lyon opened his Pony Express museum in Arcadia. He filled his museum with everything from a bustle purported by have been worn by Jenny Lind to a huge number of cigar store Indians to a complete railroad station donated by the president of the Southern Pacific Railroad. Visitors were overwhelmed not only by the sheer size of the collections, but also by the incredible anecdotes told by Lyon as he led them through his museum.

In addition to running the museum, Lyon, with his son, Parker, Jr., founded the Lyon moving company.

Clara Lyon died in 1946. On December 14, 1949, Lyon mailed his Christmas cards, visited with his son, Parker, Jr., and Parker's wife, and returned to his home. He awoke a little after midnight coughing. He called his doctor who came to the house immediately. Lyon said to Dr. Howard Scott, "I guess this is it, Doc." He died of a heart attack a few minutes later.

That afternoon, the front page of *The Fresno Bee* featured a story on Fresno's former mayor. For those who remembered him, it was a day to mourn, but it was also a day to smile as vivid memories of the colorful showman who truly loved Fresno replaced thoughts of sadness.

During Mayor W. Parker Lyon's term in office, he received a number of threatening letters. Written in a scrawling hand, these letters would either come by regular post or would be left on his front porch in the middle of the night. It was a frightening thing for the whole family and Lyon chose to tell only his most intimate friends about them.

After his resignation as mayor in the spring of 1908, Lyon and his family moved away. Because he had so many business interests in Fresno and he and his wife had so many friends here, they returned and bought a home on San Joaquin and J (Fulton) streets. All seemed to be well, now that he was out of office.

Lyon sold the house on San Joaquin Street, moved his family to a home on Van Ness Avenue, purchased a large parcel of land next to the Herman Brix home on Fresno Street, and began to design a large home for his family. He also became an investor in the new Hotel Fresno that was being built at Merced and I (Broadway) streets. It seemed as though the Lyon family was home to stay.

Then, one night, a letter was left on the porch. Other letters came by post—all written in the same scrawling hand as before. The message in the letters was very clear—if you don't leave Fresno, your home will be burned to the ground and your children will be taken away. As horrifying as this was, Lyon was prepared to stay and fight. Mrs. Lyon, however, was so worried about her children that she insisted they leave Fresno.

W. Parker Lyon purchased a home in Redwood City and moved his family there. They would later move south to Arcadia. Lyon kept his business interests in Fresno and visited from time to time to check on his properties.

The letters were turned over to the police, who could find no clues. Lyon felt that his political enemies were behind them. It was another sad leave-taking for the man who had done so much for the city he loved.

W. Parker Lyon's first visit to Fresno, in 1892, was in his capacity as a fire insurance adjuster. He liked the climate and the look of the new city. He talked his wife into moving to Fresno.

Soon after they arrived, he decided that the local furniture dealers didn't understand how to market their product. Having grown up at his father's furniture auction house, he knew all the tricks of

# Asbestos Coffins!
## Fresno's New Industry.

—⚮—

### A La Vleleau, we have thee Now!

☛ Guaranteed to pass one through the fiery ordeal unscathed.

—⚮—

Factory address,  - - -  Shelbyville.

### W. Parker Lyon,

Inventor and Manufacturer.

Fresno address,

## Mammoth Furniture Department Stores,
### 1126·1128·1130·1132 I Street.

W. Parker Lyon advertisement from *The Fresno Morning Republican* in 1894. *Courtesy of California History and Genealogy Room, Fresno County Free Library.*

the trade. He met a woman who was recently widowed. She wanted to get rid of her furniture because of the memories it evoked. He bought the whole lot for twenty-five dollars, and he opened a furniture store on I (Broadway) Street. His goal was to make a million dollars.

Lyon paid a visit to Dr. Chester Rowell, owner and editor of *The Fresno Morning Republican,* and made a proposition. He would take out a column for ads for his store that would run directly across from the editorial page. If the ads doubled the paper's circulation, Lyon would get them for free; if they didn't, Lyon would pay double for the ads. Lyon's ads were so clever and so funny that the *Republican's* circulation did go up. They became a feature of the paper for many years. They were so funny, in fact, that, according to Lyon, the *San Francisco Chronicle* paid him five dollars each for the right to reprint them.

Lyon's first ads used the chamber pots that he had dutifully collected over the years. Another ad that appeared in 1894 featured asbestos coffins that were guaranteed to pass through the fiery ordeal unscathed. An ad that appeared several years later in the same vein was entitled "Hades Cooling Off." It should be noted that oil had been discovered near Coalinga. The real oil boom was yet to come, but some oil already was being taken out of the ground. The ad continued: "I've got rich selling my patent fireproof asbestos coffins to Fresno's wicked, but this oil well business gave it to me in the neck, and makes my coffin factory look like thirty cents. Why? Because all the oil is being taken out of the earth, and when exhausted no more will the flames of purgatory be fed with petroleum. The devil will skate on the ice and when W. Parker Lyon...[takes] the Hades special [he] will have to carry a big roll of blankets along and a Bolton frost alarm." W. Parker Lyon, college chum of Peter the Great.

A man of many gifts...W. Parker Lyon.

# Lyon's Last Christmas Card

The death of W. Parker Lyon, ex-mayor of Fresno, on December 15, 1949, brought back many memories for those had known him during the Gay '90s era of Fresno history.

Just a couple of days after his death, many of his friends were surprised to find his Christmas card in their mailboxes. He had mailed them just hours before he died of a heart attack. The card with its sincere, yet simple, message said: "On this, my eighty-fifth Christmas, my friendship, like my antiques, take on the rich patina of years. My heartiest wish for you—Merry Christmas." He signed his name with a flourish that ended in a drawing of a chamber pot—Lyon's favorite collectible and advertising logo.

An article in *The Fresno Bee* on December 18, 1949, was filled with the reminiscences of many of his close friends—all recipients of his Christmas card. Judge Ernest Klette remembered that one day while he was watching a fire engulf a building, Lyon came running up to watch, too. There was nothing odd about that except that, under one arm, Lyon was carrying a stuffed crane. Klette also recalled a day when Lyon stretched out on a pallet in the middle of Courthouse Park and proceeded to take an afternoon siesta.

Ben Levy of Levy Brothers Insurance remembered Lyon's unique advertisements. He also remarked on Lyon's opportunism as a businessman. The day after a fire across the street, a "Fire Sale" sign graced the window of Lyon's store that had been cracked by the heat of the fire. He did lots of business that day.

His lasting accomplishments—Fresno's first city hall, modern sewer system, and the subway on Fresno Street—were all talked about. So, too, were his visits to the halls of government many years after he had left Fresno. He would always appear wearing his black frock coat, a loud paisley vest and silk top hat. He would tell the city commissioners that he had just "dropped by" to see if they were running Fresno properly. He would stay awhile and listen to their deliberations. Then he would take out his two-pound pocket watch that had once belonged to Tom Thumb, check the time, and leave the chambers. Later, no one would remember what had been discussed, but those present never forgot Lyon's visits.

# The Parrot of the Diamond Palace

The 1890s were turbulent years in the Fifth Ward of Fresno. Better known as Chinatown, it also included a triangular area of downtown Fresno that encompassed I (Broadway) Street from Merced to Tulare streets. The area was growing faster than the rest of downtown. It had a colorful flavor—it was home to a large variety of ethnic groups, a cross section of retail businesses, many of the city's poorest citizens, and a great number of saloons. The corrupt police force patrolled it even less regularly than it did other parts of the city. To a great extent lawlessness prevailed.

City government at the time was in the hands of the Triangle Gang—three members of the Board of Trustees who ran the city. The gang, businessman Bart Alford, hotelman William Fahey (known as "Boss Fahey"), and realtor Stephen Cole, kept a tight rein on city government. Boss Fahey represented the Fourth Ward (an area south of downtown) and often wore a gilded triangle on his lapel to denote his power.

Among the major political forces in the Fifth Ward was a woman named Mollie Livingstone. She operated a dance hall at Tulare and E streets named the Diamond Palace. She also owned a dozen other businesses nearby that all fell under the heading of "bawdy houses." She was an acquaintance of everyone in town. When John Daly petitioned the trustees to grant a liquor license for his saloon on F Street, her name, which was placed on the petition in support of Daly's request, assured that his license would be granted.

In January 1894, the gentlemen of Fresno were shocked to learn that Mollie's parrot, that graced the main room of the dance hall, had been stolen. The parrot, it seems, had a facility with language and could easily pronounce the names of all Mollie's customers.

Mollie was devastated. Then she remembered a handyman who had done some work for her and gave the police his name. They tracked him down. The parrot was returned to Mollie unscathed. The patrons of Mollie's establishment could breathe a collective sigh of relief and probably raised their glasses in a toast to the parrot.

# The First African-American Pioneers

Researching the earliest African-American pioneers in Fresno County is challenging—information is limited. It appears that the first African-American man to set foot in what is now Fresno County was Jacob Dodson. He was a servant of John C. Fremont and is listed on the roster of the California Battalion. As a part of that battalion, Dodson took part in the Mexican War of 1846–1847 and played his role in winning statehood for California. Fremont later took an anti-slavery position, but, in the mid-1840s, it is unclear whether or not Dodson was a slave. It is known that he received neither rank nor pay for his service.

The Gold Rush brought people of every ethnic and racial background to the foothills of California. The 1850 census of Mariposa County lists three African-American families. Two years later another census tells us that there were fifty-seven African-American men and two African-American women in the foothill mining camps of what are today Mariposa, Merced, Madera, and Fresno counties. One of the men listed his birthplace as Africa; the others stated that their homes were in the northeastern states or in the south. Some may have been runaway slaves, but, since California had come into the Union as a Free State, all of these new residents were counted as United States citizens.

In the census of 1860, Fresno County was home to three African-American men and one woman. Jane and Tom Dermon's stories have been told in earlier tales of our Valley. They became important and valued citizens of the Millerton community. There was also a man named Tom McCray at Millerton who was a servant in the home of John and Mary Blackburn. Blackburn served as a member of the Fresno County Board of Supervisors.

As limited as our information is about the lives of the earliest African-American pioneers of our county, their names are listed in the legal records. They were here and made their own contributions to the beginnings of Fresno County.

# Gabriel Bibbard Moore

There is an old cemetery near the Trimmer Springs Road in the community of Centerville. It is here that many of the pioneers of this part of Fresno County are buried. Near the fence, a broken white headstone, with the name of the occupant of the grave missing, marks the final resting place of the first African-American stockman in the Kings River area.

There is no written record of the early life of Gabriel Bibbard Moore, who was born in Alabama in 1812, until 1853, when he arrived in the Upper Kings River area with the Akers wagon train. Richard and William Glenn, who traveled with the Akers party, brought Gabriel Moore with them. It is not known whether or not he was their slave. All records list him as a stockman.

Soon after his arrival, Moore got into trouble with the law. He was accused of flirting with some of the many Native American wives of William Campbell, the superintendent of the Kings River Indian Reservation. The Glenn brothers spoke in his defense and he was cleared of the charges.

Even though Moore could neither read nor write, he became an important stockman. By 1860, he was listed in the census as a taxpayer in Fresno County and had holdings worth $3,000. He hired a number of his white neighbors to herd his cattle on the Valley floor and take them into the mountains during the summer months.

Gabriel Moore had a wife, Mary, and a son, Ephraim. When he was drowned on May 25, 1880, while driving his cattle across the Kings River, his wife and son were named administrators of his estate. Moore and his wife had also adopted four children with the surname Baker—they were siblings.

Gabriel Moore was a man who was respected by his community and appreciated for his sense of humor as well as for his abilities as a stockman and citizen. Like other pioneers, he blazed an important trail in the history of our county and will be remembered in the tales of our Valley.

The boxing fans of the Central Valley were in for a real treat for on the night of February 15, 1949, a gathering at the Hotel Fresno brought some of the greatest pugilists of all time to Fresno. The occasion was a heartwarming one. They had come to pay tribute to one of Fresno's most cherished heroes—Young Corbett III, known to his family and friends as Ralph Giordano.

Following Corbett's winning of the Welterweight Championship of the World on February 23, 1933, he was greeted to a true hero's welcome in Courthouse Park. Fresnans not only valued Corbett for his achievements, but also for his humility and graciousness.

In 1946, Corbett had suffered a serious skull fracture in a car accident near Delano. He was still trying to recover. The dinner was to honor him and also to raise funds for the Young Corbett Foundation.

Three hundred people filled the elegant dining room of the Hotel Fresno. As they feasted on roast turkey, the master of ceremonies began the evening's entertainment. Max Baer, the 1934 Heavyweight Champion of the World and one of Corbett's closest friends, was a perfect choice to fill this role. He began by regaling the guests with some very funny stories from the days of his boxing career. Then he introduced the man of the hour. He said, "You've honored one of the greatest men we've had in boxing—Young Corbett…and the tremendous turnout of people is significant of the high regard in which you hold your local hero."

Corbett thanked everyone for their friendship and for the confidence they had placed in him. He told the audience that their very presence made him "feel as though I am getting better already." When asked by Baer to name his toughest fight, he said without a pause, the fight with Fred Apostoli. Apostoli, the former Middleweight Champion of the World, was seated nearby with movie star Victor McLaglen, a Fresno County resident and former boxer.

Many congratulatory telegrams, including one from boxing great Jack Dempsey, were read. Corbett's nephew, Dick Contino, who at nineteen was already becoming a famous accordion player, entertained the gathering.

The event raised over six thousand dollars for the Young Corbett Foundation. More importantly, it gave not only Fresnans but also major figures from the world of boxing an opportunity to once again shine the spotlight on one of the most deserving heroes in the tales of our Valley.

Fresno school children were used to celebrating the lives of the great presidents of their country, but on November 22, 1898, something new was in store for the grammar school students. Their teachers planned a special event that would celebrate the life of one of the great poets of the nineteenth century—Alfred, Lord Tennyson, who had been England's poet laureate. Literature teacher Mary Stewart was the principal organizer of the program.

On the afternoon of November 22, the auditorium of Fresno High School began to fill with parents, students, teachers, administrators—even the members of the board of education were present. The program began with a piano solo by Aline Edwards. The roll was called—every student had to respond with a quotation from Tennyson. Bertha St. John entertained the audience with a piano selection.

Miss Margaret Baird read her composition on the life of Tennyson. Then Lloyd Crow strode to center stage and recited "The Charge of the Light Brigade." As he uttered the immortal words of the poem's first stanza, "…Into the Valley of Death rode the six hundred…," the crowd burst into applause. When all was silent, he completed the poem. More applause followed.

Each recitation was followed by a piano or vocal solo. Clara Gearhart's composition on "Enoch Arden" was well received. Myrtle Dreman recited "Lady Clara Vere de Vere." Elsa Einstein, Florence Clapp, and Herman Levy entertained on the piano and mandolin.

Perhaps the best was saved for last. Ned Prescott, a lad with poetic talent, recited a poem he had written titled "A Memorable Day." It was a parody on "The Charge of the Light Brigade" and involved the children of the grammar school. Amid loud applause, Tennyson Day came to an end. It was truly a memorable day in the tales of our Valley.

# Thursday Night at the Bodega Saloon

The evening of September 9, 1898, was a rather busy one at the Bodega Saloon. Even though it was a Thursday night, the barstools and tables were filled with customers. Everyone seemed to be having a good time. Barkeep James Bray was having all he could do just to keep the patrons happy and the glasses filled. The last thing he needed was trouble. However, life often seems to dish up whatever it is we don't want and, on this occasion, it outdid itself.

At exactly 7:00 P.M., the front door swung open and a rather suspicious looking man entered the Bodega. He stood very quietly for a moment or two, observing the room and its inhabitants. Then his eyes brightened. He noticed a number of unopened bottles of whiskey sitting at one end of the counter. About that time Barkeep Bray saw the man gaze longingly at the bottles he had not had time to put away. Bray knew he didn't have time to watch the man, so he politely asked him to leave the premises.

Sitting at one of the tables was prominent attorney and sometimes troublemaker Walter D. Grady. He had been at the Bodega for some time and was feeling rather wonderful. He saw Bray motion to the man to leave. Then he saw the man pick up one of the bottles of whiskey, tuck it inside his coat, and walk toward the front door.

Bray ran after the man, called to him to stop, and, when he would not give up the whiskey, Bray knocked the man to the floor. The bottle broke and its contents spilled everywhere.

Grady, not one to miss a good fistfight, was on his feet in a flash. He reached Bray just as the thief dropped to the floor. Grady threw a punch that hit Bray on the forehead and almost knocked him out—not exactly an appropriate gesture toward a man who was only trying to retrieve his property.

When Policeman Morse arrived and heard about the three-cornered fight, he couldn't believe it until he saw who was involved. He arrested the thief and walked out the door, shaking his head.

# The Evangelist's Big Mistake

Although the governmental climate of Fresno in the 1890s was still a matter of concern, the majority of Fresno's citizens were upstanding members of the community. Fresno was a community of families who, for the most part, were trying to raise their children in the best way possible.

In March of 1896, the K Street Methodist Church invited the Reverend I. T. Johnson, an evangelist, to conduct a series of revival meetings. All went fairly well until the night of March 24, when he proclaimed from the pulpit that two-thirds of the girls of Fresno were "ruined by the time they were fourteen." He blamed the schools of the city for this situation.

The community outcry was immediate. A reporter from the *Republican* met with the evangelist and asked him where he obtained these statistics. Johnson refused to tell him, saying only that a man from Brown University gave him the information. Johnson left this interview and visited the office of the *Expositor* newspaper, hoping for their support. He climbed the stairs to the editorial office and was hustled back down the stairs and shown the door by William T. Osburn.

A meeting was called of all the leading citizens of Fresno in the office of the First National Bank. The impressive gathering was focused on how to demand a retraction from Johnson and how to get him to leave town. They drafted a statement for Johnson to sign. Johnson was brought before them and, under pressure, he signed a statement to the effect that his accusation reflecting on the chastity of Fresno's girls was untrue and that he would apologize to the community. Johnson signed the paper, but showed no real contrition. When he tried to leave the bank from the I (Broadway) Street door, he suddenly realized there were hundreds of people waiting for him outside with vengeance in their hearts. He quickly closed the door and, with Sheriff Jay Scott at his side, exited on Mariposa Street.

The meeting continued with a discussion of how to persuade the unwilling evangelist to leave town. A gentleman named Sibley offered to provide a large number of feathers; O. J. Woodward said he would gladly donate a barrel of tar. It was not certain whether or not these offers were in jest. A subcommittee consisting of J. P. Meux, T. L. Heaton, and John Reichman was appointed to draft a resolution concerning Johnson. When completed, it condemned the slanderous statements made by Johnson and advised him to depart from Fresno and never return.

Late that night, Reverend Johnson and his wife left Fresno. The men of the community had spoken in defense of their daughters, their families, and their schools. It had been quite a tempestuous few days in the tales of our Valley.

# The Man with the Very Long Beard

In 1891, a rather interesting looking man could be seen on the streets of Fresno. His demeanor was serious and he was very tall, but his outstanding feature was a beard that was so long it reached below his knees. The man's name was Dr. J. R. Sutton. Those who saw him on the street were awestruck—the beard was so long and so full that it almost had a life of its own.

Two months after his arrival, everyone in town knew who he was. The beard, having accomplished its mission, was now carefully plaited and assumed a secondary role in Sutton's appearance. Although he had a wife, who had come to Fresno with him, word began to circulate that he was quite a ladies' man. Indeed, several widows in town were cheered by his frequent visits—drawn to him by his sparkling, magnetic eyes and his luxuriant whiskers. He was blessed with such a sweet and gentle nature that his bedside manner made the patient overlook the size of his bill.

One lady in particular, who normally was the picture of health, found it necessary to call upon the good doctor with increasing frequency. His antidote for her problems included breathing in the evening air, and his kind consideration for his patient's well-being led him to accompany her on her nightly walks. The lady happened to be married and, when she disappeared from her home, it was said that she and the doctor had eloped by train to Modesto. When they returned the next day on separate trains, the rumors were proved wrong. The lady and her husband reconciled and all was well.

Not so with the good doctor's wife. She was tired of such shenanigans and filed for divorce. The husband of the doctor's patient died. The doctor felt honor bound to comfort the poor, widowed lady.

On July 15, 1893, the doctor and his patient were married. It was rumored that she had received a good settlement and he had some outstanding debts. Their honeymoon trip was to Dakota Territory. They left word with the county clerk that they wished their marriage to remain a secret for one month. By the time the creditors found out, all that was left for them to do was to hope for the couple's speedy return—if they returned at all.

On a cold December afternoon in the year 1889, a young man dressed in a blue flannel shirt, workman's overalls with the legs stuffed inside a pair of black boots, and a grey coat, was seen walking through the streets of downtown Fresno. He looked tired, cold, and hungry. He turned on Mariposa Street and entered the Fashion Clothing Store. One of the salesmen, R. W. Cole, asked if he could assist him.

The young man told him his story. His name was A. Sherman. He was twenty-seven years old and had left his home in England about two years before. He came to California, but the land of promise that had beckoned so many to its shores had not been kind to him. He was almost penniless and was desperate to find work.

Sherman seemed so sincere that Cole said he would see what he could do and asked him to return in an hour. As soon as Sherman left, Cole called his brother Clovis, who had a ranch on Big Dry Creek. When Clovis heard the story, he decided to come into town to meet this young man and see if he could help him.

When Sherman returned at the appointed hour, R. W. Cole had good news for him. When Clovis arrived, the men talked. Clovis Cole was convinced of the sincerity of the young man and offered him a job. Sherman was overjoyed. The two men left for the Cole Ranch. During the next month, Sherman worked hard for Clovis Cole and was a model employee.

On January 16, 1890, fortune smiled again. A letter from England brought Sherman the news of his uncle's death and of a bequest of $250,000 that his uncle left to him. Sherman still had to work to earn the money for a ticket home so he could accept his inheritance. It wasn't many days before Sherman was able to leave. When he did, his journey to England was made even pleasanter by the warm memories he carried with him of R. W. and Clovis Cole, who had shown him such kindness.

# A Test for Teachers

Mid-June of 1899 was fraught with tension for those who had applied for teaching positions in the Fresno School District. Submitting one's application was only the beginning. This was followed by an interview and a series of difficult examinations that took several days. Education was a serious business in the 1890s. It was important to the district that only those teachers who could satisfactorily pass the tests be hired to teach the young people of Fresno.

One of the days was taken up with the following subjects: composition, physiology, and spelling. The composition exam began with the following question—"what is a paraphrase? Give a quotation of not less than four or five lines of your favorite poem and then write a paraphrase of the quotation. What is scansion? Scan the quotation asked for above. What are the essential distinctions between poetry and prose? Illustrate. How may variation of expression be affected?"

After a number of questions regarding parts of speech, punctuation, and basic grammar rules, the applicant had to write a paragraph illustrating some object using the answers. Finally, an outline for a composition had to be written on one of the following topics: "Influences that worked on Tom Brown and what they made of him," "Shakespeare's Caesar and Brutus," or "Washington and Arnold."

The physiology section of the test required a full knowledge of the structure of the ear, bone structure, and the organs of the body. Other questions concerned antidotes for poisons, resuscitating a drowning victim, and stopping the flow of blood in a person who has been seriously cut.

The spelling section included a number of very tricky words including ellipses, chalcedony, moccasin, hypotenuse, presaged, counterfeit, and vengeance. By the end of this particular day, vengeance was probably uppermost in the minds of all those hoping to get through this ordeal and become bona fide teachers in the schools of Fresno.

# A Tradition of Academic Excellence

When Fresno High School was first planned, Thomas L. Heaton, who would be the first principal, and Professor William Carey Jones of the University of California directed the organization of the classes. There were to be two courses of study, scientific and literary. When the school opened in 1889, it had fifty students and three teachers.

In the late spring of 1892, members of the second class to complete the three-year course of study were required to have all their work scrutinized by examiners from the University of California. The result was that Fresno High School received accreditation in all the subjects that were offered.

This examination process occurred periodically. In 1899, Fresno High principal C. L. McLane received a letter stating that, once again, the school received accreditation in all its subjects. The fields of study that were offered had expanded. In addition to classes in English grammar and composition, United States history, mathematics, chemistry, Latin, and German, Fresno High students could also study Caesar, Virgil, Latin prosody, Greek history, Roman history, advanced Latin composition, solid geometry, plane trigonometry, and botany.

During the 1898-99 school year classes in Greek language were offered for the first time. It would not be until the second year a course of study in Greek was available that UC would grant accreditation in that subject.

The high school was just ten years old and was ranked among the finest college preparatory schools in California.

Today, one hundred and sixteen years after Fresno High was founded, the school offers students an International Baccalaureate Diploma Program that stresses academic excellence, the ideals of international understanding, and responsible citizenship. In so doing, Fresno High School is upholding the tradition envisioned by professors Heaton and Jones all those years ago.

# A Brilliant Ball at Armory Hall

On Thursday evening, the twenty-first of April 1892, the first social event of the post-Lenten season took place at the Armory Hall at the corner of Fresno and J (Fulton) streets. Hosted by the gentlemen of the Young Men's Institute, the festivities included a musical program, dancing, and, of course, a sumptuous buffet table.

As carriages pulled up to the door of the Armory, Fresno Street was transformed into an elegant setting. Beautiful young women in colorful evening dresses, elegant ladies, and handsome gentlemen in their finest evening attire descended from their carriages and slowly made their way inside. As the guests greeted one another, gentlemen of all ages were seeking out the ladies with whom they wished to dance, hoping to capture a space on their dance cards.

A short musical program featuring a duet on the pianoforte by Misses Lola Avila and Josephine Fahey, and vocal solos by Maude Lillian Berry and Mrs. William Glass ended with enthusiastic applause.

The ball began at 9:30 P.M. William Fahey and Mrs. Breslin, Henry Avila and Miss Lizzie Foin led the Grand March to music provided by Theodore Reitz, Mrs. J. W. Stouther, and Professor Smith. The second dance was a waltz. As the evening wore on couples performed the quadrille, the polka, the schottische, and the lancers, and ended with a medley.

Many of the young ladies had so many invitations to dance they had to divide their dances. The evening was made even more festive by Judge W. D. Crichton and Judge D. R. Prince, who had a friendly rivalry about who would have more dances. Reverend Father Garriga was seen standing against the wall watching the young people and enjoying their happiness.

The evening was a most memorable one and ushered in the social season that followed the period of fasting and reflection for many Valley residents.

# The Roots of a Symphony

Fresnans have always loved classical music. From the time the Barton Opera House opened in 1890, the finest artists of the music world have appeared in Fresno. As much as Fresnans enjoyed listening to visiting orchestras and musicians, they wanted a symphony orchestra they could call their own. Early efforts to establish an orchestra became almost a comedy of interruptions—finances, two world wars, and the Great Depression all played a role.

Sometime between 1908 and 1910, thirty-five traveling musicians and a number of local musicians combined their talents and presented a concert for an enthusiastic Fresno audience. Finances allowed only one performance. In 1916, Earl Towner, director of the Fresno High School Orchestra, brought together area musicians and formed the Fresno Symphony Orchestra. After one year of well-attended concerts, World War I intervened. The orchestra was put on hold until 1921 when it was once again able to present fine music to the Fresno community. In 1924, Towner left Fresno and the orchestra disbanded.

In 1930, the Fresno Philharmonic Orchestra was formed under the direction of pianist Daniel Popovich with Fresno State College's Samuel Hungerford as the concertmaster. The orchestra completed only three seasons of concerts. Meanwhile, Fresno State College had formed an orchestra under the direction of Arthur C. Berdahl. In 1934 Berdahl invited local musicians to join them. The old Fresno Symphony Orchestra was up and running again.

World War II put a strain on the orchestra as members were called to military duty. The orchestra did, however, perform a military "pops" concert on May 14, 1942. After the war years, the emphasis was on Fresno State's music department as Berdahl hired internationally known musicians as professors. These talented artists taught a whole new generation of Fresno musicians. It would not be until 1954 that a truly successful community-sponsored symphony orchestra would be formed in Fresno.

One of the most important women in Fresno musical circles in the early years of the twentieth century was Katharine Caldwell Riggs. Born in Wisconsin, she moved to California with her family when she was still a young girl. They settled in the Bay Area. Early in her life, Katharine's musical gifts became apparent and her parents saw to it that she received the finest training San Francisco could offer.

Katharine became a soprano soloist in the Catholic and Presbyterian churches and became the first soprano in the Clara Schumann Quartet, a highly respected professional group. In 1904, she studied in Boston with Arthur Foote and Stephen Sumner Townsend and, in 1908 and 1917, she traveled to London to study with William Shakespeare, a world-famous vocal coach.

Katharine met Don Pardee Riggs, who was prominent in musical circles in San Francisco and had made the arrangements for many of the musicians of the day to appear in Fresno. He was also a concert violinist and a voice teacher. They were married, moved to Fresno, and opened the Riggs Studios at Tuolumne and L streets.

In 1905, Katharine Caldwell Riggs became a leading player in the efforts to form the Fresno Musical Club. She served as the organization's first president from 1905 to 1906. Her husband also became a staunch supporter of this group's efforts. She continued to appear as soloist in the leading churches of Fresno and at benefit concerts such as the one held at the Barton Opera House in 1906 to benefit victims of the San Francisco earthquake.

Katharine Riggs' interests were not limited to the Fresno Musical Club. She also served as director of the Parlor Lecture Club Chorale and served as president of the society formed to support the Fresno Symphony Orchestra in the early 1920s. She continued to teach voice until she fractured her hip on June 23, 1942. She seemed to be recovering well, but, on the night of July 3, 1942, she died of an embolism. She is still remembered for her many contributions to the cultural life of the Central Valley community.

The Fresno Philharmonic Orchestra has been bringing classical music to Fresno audiences for more than fifty years. Here is its story.

Early in the 1950s, Haig Yaghjian, associate conductor of the Detroit Opera Association, came home to Fresno to assist with the family business. At church one morning he was introduced to the late Frank Moradian, who asked him what he did for a living. When he said he was a conductor, Moradian said, "You ought to start an orchestra." Moradian would become a life-long supporter of the orchestra. Yaghjian was drawn to Fresno's musical circles where he found people who were deeply committed to establishing a truly professional orchestra that would draw its financial support from the community. Yaghjian's enthusiasm was immediate—it was a case of the right person in the right place at the right time.

At lunch one day, Yaghjian, Clarence Heagy, instrumental music consultant for the Fresno county schools, and Stanley Keith, cellist and violinmaker, decided to invite twenty key people—all musicians—to a meeting. This small group began to recruit other musicians and to start rehearsals for a concert—an event that would give them some idea of whether or not Fresno was ready to support a symphony orchestra.

On the night of May 25, 1954, a large crowd filled the Fresno Memorial Auditorium to hear the premiere concert of the Fresno Philharmonic Orchestra. At concert's end, the enthusiastic crowd gave the musicians a prolonged standing ovation. It was clear that Fresnans wanted more.

During the summer months of 1954, the Fresno Philharmonic Association was organized with Lynn Stewart, a French horn player, as the first president. The Women's Symphony League also was formed.

On October 21, 1954, in the Roosevelt High School auditorium, conductor Haig Yaghjian lifted his baton and the members of the Fresno Philharmonic Orchestra began to play Richard Wagner's "Prelude" from Act 3 of *Lohengrin*.

The orchestra's first season had truly begun.

On April 30, 2004, the Fresno Philharmonic Orchestra celebrated fifty years of bringing beautiful music and fine musical artists to Fresno.

# The Ex-Mayor and Ex-Outlaw Meet Again

On a sunny September morning in 1932, two old acquaintances who were legendary figures in the history of the Central Valley met at the Pony Express Museum in Arcadia, California. Their meeting was not a casual one, but one with a purpose. Emmett Dalton, the reformed and pardoned member of the infamous Dalton Gang whose exploits kept the residents of Fresno County on edge in the 1890s, was invited to speak to a convention of the American Legion in Southern California.

By coincidence, the owner of the Pony Express Museum, Fresno's ex-Mayor W. Parker Lyon, who had served as a deputy sheriff in Fresno County during the 1890s, was also a featured speaker. The two men met ahead of time so that Dalton could present Lyon with a historic .45 caliber Colt revolver once owned by outlaw Bill Doolin. Lyon was quite pleased—the gun was immediately made part of the museum's Dalton Gang exhibit.

The two men had a lot to talk about. Lyon was a notorious teller of tales, and Dalton had his share of stories to impart. Lyon remembered that the Visalia jail had been dynamited. "Of course," Dalton said, "my brother Bob and I did that!" The two men decided they should share the stage at the Legionnaire's convention—what a rare opportunity for those in attendance!

Five years later, the historic ivory-handled, nickel-plated, hand engraved revolver was stolen from a glass case while the museum staff was in another part of the building. Lyon immediately called the police. He told them the history of the gun—how outlaw Bill Doolin it had taken it to Emmett Dalton for repairs just after he had broken out of jail. He never reclaimed it.

In an odd twist of fate, the gun was returned by mail a few days later. Lyon hoped the police wouldn't catch whoever committed the theft. After all, he said, "Maybe whoever took it has reformed—and I wouldn't want to prosecute a repenter."

On April 3, 4, and 5 of 1902, women delegates from all over California's Central Valley flocked to Fresno to attend the fifth annual meeting of the San Joaquin Valley Federation of Women's Clubs. Among those present were representatives of the Fowler Improvement Association, Sanger Shakespeare Club, Selma Wednesday Club, Oleander Club, West Park Thursday Club, Parlor Lecture Club, Query Club, Wednesday Club,

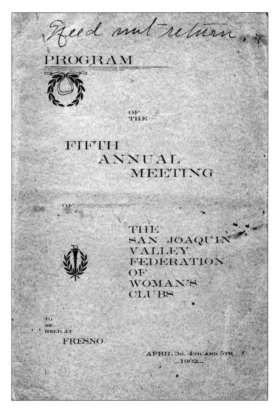

A program from the fifth annual meeting of the San Joaquin Valley Federation of Women's Clubs. This was a very serious event. One of the quotations in the program was from David Starr Jordan: "Wisdom is in knowing what to do next; virtue is in doing it." *Author's copy.*

Lemoore Women's Club, Bakersfield Woman's Club, Visalia Women's Club, and the Reedley Culture Club. The three-day event was held in Risley Hall and was presided over by federation president Miss Nellie Boyd.

The morning of April 3 was devoted to a meeting of the presidents of the organizations. Luncheon was open to all the members of the clubs and was very well attended. The afternoon session consisted of reports on the projects of all the clubs. Beautification of their cities, sponsorships of circulating community libraries, and improvement of their minds through the study of literature were the common thread—the goals that bound these groups together.

During the sessions on the second and third days, the ladies listened to a series of provocative speakers. Senator S. C. Smith of Bakersfield attacked the subject of "Village and Town Improvement." He spoke of the need to beautify all sections of our cities and called club women "…a force for the betterment of the world."

A letter was read from State Superintendent Kirk stating that he was in favor of allowing women to serve on school boards. A paper on this subject, given by Mrs. Roadhouse of Selma, followed. Other topics included "Civil Service Reform," "Influence of Fads on Character," and "The California Indians." Time was set aside for socializing and enjoying a variety of musical entertainments.

On the final day, Minna Eshelman Sherman spoke to the ladies about "The Women's Agricultural and Horticultural Union." She urged the women not only to continue their current projects, but also to join the newly formed union so that they could broaden their usefulness.

At the close of the three-day meeting, the delegates felt that much had been accomplished, but realized how much more must be done to attain their goals. These women, although they had not yet been granted the right to vote, were making a difference in their respective communities in the ways that were open to them at the time. They were a force to be reckoned with and, as such, are remembered in the tales of our Valley.

# The Reverend and Mrs. T. O. Ellis

One of the leading figures of the Kings River area near Centerville was the Reverend T. O. Ellis. Well educated, with strong religious convictions, the Reverend Ellis was a man who was dedicated to the calling he had received. Before coming to California in 1856, he served as a bishop of the Methodist Episcopal Church South in his home state of Missouri.

After the death of his first wife, he remarried. His new wife was always referred to as "Madame Ellis" and it is by this name that she will be remembered. When the couple left Missouri to travel west, they brought their nine children with them. One of the children died on the trip. They arrived in Visalia and made their home there for several years. In 1866, they moved to the Kings River area and settled three miles below Centerville.

The Reverend Ellis became a well-known circuit rider through all of Central California. His devotion to his ministry was legend. He spoke at camp meetings, organized missions, and healed the sick. In addition to being a theologian, the Reverend Ellis was a practicing physician and druggist. The people of the frontier communities needed a man with his skills. As busy as his life was, he found time to serve two terms as superintendent of schools for Fresno County.

The Reverend Ellis was the father of seventeen children—fourteen of whom lived to adulthood. Madame Ellis was very proud of her healthy brood and, in spite of her husband's often-meager income, managed to feed and clothe them in a way that she felt reflected their heritage of quality.

Historian Ernestine Winchell quoted Madame Ellis as saying, "A witty woman once said that her sympathies had always been with the Pilgrim mothers, for in addition to all their other trials, they had to put up with the Pilgrim fathers." A thought, perhaps, that just might reflect the attitudes of many of the pioneer women of our Valley.

# S. Adison Miller

On May 31, 1835, S. Adison Miller was born near Rochester, New York. His ancestors were from Scotland and England. When he was three years old, his family moved to Michigan City, Indiana. The romance of navigating on the Great Lakes captured his imagination, so he signed on as a cabin boy—eventually he captained his own ship.

In 1858, after making two voyages on the open sea, Miller decided to leave shipping and set off for California. Upon arrival in the Golden State, he headed for the gold fields and tried his luck at mining at a place called Little York. In 1860, he leased the Dutch Flat Hotel.

Four years later, in 1864, he left California and moved to Virginia City, Nevada, where he soon became an engineer in the silver mines of the Comstock Lode. He got into the hotel business again and, in 1869, took a wife—Sarah Dimond. By 1877, Virginia City's period of prosperity was beginning to fade.

Miller had heard about the colony farms that were developing around the new town of Fresno in California's Central Valley. He decided to become a land promoter and established the Nevada Colony on Frederick Roeding's lands northeast of Fresno. He did very well and, in 1879, invested his earnings in a new venture—he purchased *The Fresno Morning Republican* newspaper from Dr. Chester Rowell.

A man of many interests, Miller, in July of the same year, established Fresno's first telephone system—a twenty-line switchboard. Fifteen subscribers signed up immediately. All lines went through the *Republican* office where an operator, often Mrs. Miller, and a very vocal parrot, were always on duty.

In 1887, John W. Short and J. W. Shanklin bought the *Republican*. Miller turned his interests, once again, to real estate—a field he continued to pursue until his death in Fresno in 1898.

# Dr. Bradley Wayman Doyle

One of the early dentists of the pioneer city of Fresno was born on a plantation in Tennessee on December 10, 1853. He was the eighth of twelve children. The two-story home in which he was raised was set apart from the fields tended by slaves. It was the life lived by many before the Civil War. When the war broke out, the older boys joined the Confederate Army. Both parents died suddenly, just two months apart. An elderly relative, Aunt Nancy, and their devoted Nanny cared for the younger children. When Northern soldiers raided the plantation and burned the home, outbuildings, and fields, it was Nanny who hid the children and kept them safe. These early memories of Bradley Wayman Doyle would have an impact on his life.

When the Civil War ended, Bradley Doyle's brothers came home and began to rebuild the plantation. Doyle was sent to the Union Seminary at Newbern, where he completed his education. He then enrolled in a school in Peducah, Kentucky, and, in three years, completed a course in dentistry.

In 1875, he sold his interest in the plantation and came west to California with a group of friends. He settled in Kingsburg where he began to practice dentistry. He would drive his horse and buggy out country roads to take care of patients in their homes. If a tooth needed to be extracted, he would stay with the family and not only remove the tooth but also make the dentures before he left. He gained a reputation as a fine dental technician.

One night, at a meeting of the Centerville Literary Society, Doyle met a lovely young woman named Amanda Bacon. They were married October 6, 1878. They moved to Fresno and he opened his office in the Donahoo Building. The couple had four children— two boys and two girls—and had a long, happy life together.

Dr. Bradley Wayman Doyle was a man with a winning personality and a zest for life. He became active in a number of local organizations and made many friends. At the age of sixty-four, on July 16, 1918, he died in Fresno surrounded by his family. He was one of Fresno's first dentists and, as such, wrote his own page in the history of Fresno County.

# The Strange Disappearance of Phineas Loucks

In 1877, Phineas Loucks, his wife and young children arrived in Fresno County. Loucks was a native of New York who had settled in the Northwest. Now he was bringing his family to Squaw Valley.

Loucks was a beekeeper. By 1880, orchards began to proliferate in the Valley so he decided to move his family to Centerville so his honey bees could feed on the spring blossoms to their hearts' content. Seven years later Loucks homesteaded a parcel of land near Dinkey Creek. In this remote spot, he built a cabin for his family which now consisted of not only his wife, but also three boys and three girls—all under the age of ten. Just before the winter snows hit, he left his family in the remote cabin to fulfill the residency requirements of the homestead and returned to the Valley to take care of his much-loved bees.

As luck would have it, the winter of 1887-88 was a horrible one. A hunter who happened by saw a small portion of the cabin—the rest was buried in snow. He found no sign of life and reported this when he came to the next settlement. A search party left from Tollhouse to try to rescue the family, but could not find the cabin—it was completely covered with snow. When Phineas Loucks was told of this, he showed no concern. "I built the cabin well," he said. Spring arrived and, sure enough, his wife and family were intact—emaciated, but still breathing. In July, Mrs. Loucks, who had gone through this ordeal while pregnant, was ready to give birth. Dr. Rowell was sent for, but when he got there, the poor woman had died.

The following spring, Loucks took his children to the mountain cabin. A month later, Frank Dusy stopped by and found that Loucks had disappeared. Dusy took the children to Selma and found homes for them.

No trace of Phineas Loucks was ever found. His disappearance remains one of the stranger mysteries in the tales of our Valley.

# A Reformed Mr. Dalton Comes to Town

March 31, 1931, was a day during which the citizens of Fresno were treated to a little bit of historic irony. A very respectable-looking gentleman, a building contractor and real estate entrepreneur from Los Angeles, came to town to try to negotiate a land transaction. The property in question was in Wonder Valley and was owned by George Weston Pierson, proprietor of a dude ranch nearby. The property was Dalton Mountain and the man who hoped to buy the mountain was none other than Emmett Dalton, the only survivor of the famed Dalton Gang. It was on this mountain that his brother Grat hid out from the authorities after he escaped from the Visalia jail.

After serving for fourteen and a half years in the penitentiary, Emmett decided to live an honest life. In an interview for the *Fresno Republican* newspaper, he said that his brother Grat was framed for the train robbery near Tulare in 1890. It was that injustice, he said, that led to the formation of the Dalton Gang. When talking about the killing of his brothers in a shootout in Coffeyville, Kansas, during a botched bank robbery in 1892, Dalton said, "...it wasn't because we had changed from train robbery to bank robbery, it was simply fate that brought about the gang's destruction. There's a law of nature or God that intervenes. There is no such thing as a successful outlaw. The end of all violators of the law had been the same right through history. It is impossible for the few to pit their brains against the world for any length of time."

In discussing the possible purchase of Dalton Mountain, Dalton said that if the price was right, he would buy it. Then he told the reporter a most interesting fact. "I have made more in a single real estate deal, than out of all the robberies of the Dalton Gang."

A lesson learned the hard way, but learned, nonetheless, is certainly worth recording in the tales of our Valley.

A familiar sight at every Fresno gathering of a historic nature in the mid-twentieth century was a tall, angular gentleman who seemed to have stepped into the wrong century. His manners were courtly, his voice was wispy, but earnest, and, somehow, he seemed to be a little uncomfortable in his twentieth-century world. He was an intensely private man, a good man—a kind and gentle soul who walked quietly through life and was a good neighbor to those around him. He had one overriding passion—the history of Fresno. The man was George Healy Tondel.

Healy Tondel was born in Fresno in 1910. His father was in charge of the Bank of America's safe deposit box department in the historic Bank of Italy building on the northwest corner of Tulare and Fulton streets. Tondel graduated from Fresno High School and Fresno State College and did graduate work at the University of California at Berkeley and at UC Los Angeles in business and history. While attending Santa Barbara State College, Tondel developed his passion for history and for preserving historic buildings.

In 1941, Tondel served as the coordinator of the Millerton Courthouse Advisory Committee and was vice-chairman of the Fresno County Millerton Courthouse Advisory Committee from 1966 to 1974. He played an important role in the reconstruction of the historic Millerton Courthouse. He also was involved with efforts to preserve the Old Administration Building (on the grounds of Fresno City College), Kearney Mansion, and other historic buildings in Fresno. He spent hours in local libraries researching the history of Fresno. With a book or two tucked under his arm, he often walked up to friends and regaled them with his latest discovery.

Tondel would often appear at gatherings in his "Mayor of Millerton" outfit—a black cutaway coat, vest, top hat, walking stick, and gloves. The costume once belonged to the late congressman "Bud" Gearhart.

When Healy Tondel died on November 11, 1988, Fresno lost one of the people who cared most about its history. A legend of the Valley, indeed, was George Healy Tondel.

# The Roeding-Thorne Nuptials

June—that most memorable of months—is a time for graduations and weddings—two of the happiest occasions in the
lives of many. While we, in the twenty-first century, enjoy the
sunshine and traditions that are such a part of June, let us step
back in time to 1897 to the wedding of two respected members of
Fresno society.

It was decided by the bridal couple, George C. Roeding and
Elizabeth Evelyn Thorne, that their wedding would be a small one
with only their immediate families in attendance. The bride's aunt,
Mrs. Garrison, hosted the ceremony in her home on North J (Fulton) Street. Pink was the color scheme chosen by the bride and
was apparent in the flowers and decorations that filled Mrs.
Garrison's parlor and dining room.

As the music began, George Roeding and his brother Frederick,
the best man, walked into the parlor. Next came Olivia Thorne,
the bride's sister and maid of honor. The bride, wearing a beautiful
white silk dress, was escorted by her brother Thomas Thorne to
her place beside the groom. Under a wedding ball filled with roses,
the bride and groom said their vows before the Reverend William
Loomis of Saint James' Episcopal Church.

After the ceremony, the couple and their families retired to
the dining room where refreshments were served. Soon it was time
to leave. The couple hurried out the front door and down the steps
to the carriage that awaited them. They were well showered with
rice by the time the carriage pulled away. When they arrived at
the Southern Pacific Depot to depart on their honeymoon trip,
many of their friends were waiting to wish them well.

The bride's father, the late Andrew Jackson Thorne, was the
county treasurer for many years. Thorne Avenue is named for him.

On June 14, 1777, the Continental Congress enacted the Flag Resolution of 1777, which called for the creation of a national banner. It is thought that one of the signers of the Declaration of Independence, Francis Hopkins of New Jersey, designed the flag. George Washington noted, "The white stripes represent the purity and serenity of the nation…the red stripes represent the blood spilled by Americans who made the ultimate sacrifice for freedom. The white stars symbolize the purity, liberty and freedom within the nation. There is one for each state in the nation. The royal blue field stands for freedom and justice. The thirteen stripes remind us of the uniting forever of the separate colonies into one nation."

In 1885, B. J. Cigrand had his pupils in Fredonia, Wisconsin, observe June 14 as Flag Birthday, or Flag Day. The idea caught on. On April 25, 1893, the Colonial Dames of America adopted a resolution that asked the mayor of Philadelphia and all of Philadelphia's citizens to set aside June 14 as a day to honor the flag. On June 14, 1893, Independence Square became the setting for Flag Day exercises.

June 14 observances to honor the United States flag began to be held all over the country. Schools as well as local governments held special exercises that included speakers and patriotic music.

On May 30, 1916, President Woodrow Wilson issued a proclamation establishing June 14 as Flag Day. In 1949, the members of the United States Congress decided it was time to make this holiday official. On August 3, 1949, President Harry S. Truman signed an Act of Congress that designated June 14 of every year as National Flag Day—a day to honor our flag and to remember all that it symbolizes.

The visibly rough and tumble, Wild West flavor of the young community of Fresno began to change by the late 1880s as large brick buildings began to dot the streets of the downtown area. Beneath the surface, however, it was still the same. Even after the incorporation of the city in 1885, the saloon owners ran the town.

In 1894, the women of Fresno, who did not yet have the right to vote or to participate in government, decided there were other ways they could make positive changes in their city. Two of these women, Mrs. George Hoxie and Mrs. Lee Gundelfinger, founded a club whose purpose was to look at the needs of their community and find ways to make it a better place in which to live. Mrs. Thomas Hughes, whose husband's hotel on I (Broadway) Street was the finest hotel between San Francisco and Los Angeles, offered the ladies a meeting place in the hotel's parlor—so they named their group the Parlor Lecture Club. They drew up a constitution and by-laws. Membership was limited to 100. They set up departments—Literature, Music, Art, Philanthropy, Drama, Home, Science, and Education.

One of their first projects was to teach underprivileged young girls how to sew. A year later, the ladies planted trees on Belmont Avenue all the way out to Mountain View Cemetery. They later put up a fence to keep animals from wandering among the headstones.

In 1896, Parlor Lecture Club became part of the General Federation of Women's Clubs and, in 1900, joined the state federation. In 1909, their Southern-style clubhouse was completed on Van Ness Avenue—it would be an important part of the community until 1962 when, like so many downtown buildings, it was condemned and torn down.

Over the years the ladies of the Parlor Lecture Club have served their community in many important ways. They appeared before the members of the Board of Education and successfully urged them to establish kindergartens. They established a free clinic, the local chapter of the Red Cross, and, during World War I, began First Aid classes, staffed canteens, and used their clubhouse as a hospital for victims of the flu epidemic. They founded the Preventorium, which became the Nutritional Home, and gave their support to the Women's Emergency Home.

During World War II and the Korean War, Parlor Lecture Club members were busy sewing and mending for the war effort. They helped to restore the historic Einstein and Meux homes. Over the years, the members have started many projects that would later be taken over by public agencies established for that purpose. In every instance, the ladies saw a need in the community and stepped in to fill that need.

On May 6, 2004, the ladies of the Parlor Lecture Club hosted their 110th Annual Luncheon. It is not an overstatement to say that Fresno is a better city because of their labors. Happy Birthday, Parlor Lecture Club—thank you for all your years of service.

In the years just before and just after 1900—in those halcyon days before the First World War changed many societal patterns—life went on at a slower pace. The interactions between the bachelors and spinsters, the terms used to distinguish single young men and women of marriageable age, followed certain prescribed customs and about it all was an innocence that one might wish still existed today.

And so it was that on the evening of April 14, 1904, the Epworth League of the First Methodist Church hosted a basket social at the home of Mr. and Mrs. Charles Lindgren. Each young lady brought a basket containing food that she had prepared—enough for two people. She decorated her basket in as attractive a manner as possible.

When each young man arrived, he was given a slip of paper containing the first half of a well-known quotation. The young ladies received papers with the second half of the quotation. After all the young people were present they had to find their partner by matching up the quotations.

The couples then became lost in the windings of a large cobweb that had been carefully arranged. They each had to grab a string of the cobweb and follow it to the end where a treasure awaited. The couple that found a ring would be the first to marry. The finders of a penny would become wealthy, but those who found a thimble and a button would not find marital happiness. This all caused much merriment. A musical program followed.

Then the highlight of the evening arrived. Each basket was auctioned off. The highest bidder would then claim the lady who brought it as his dinner partner. The rest of the evening was spent in games and fun. A very good time was had by all.

# An Unfortunate Drink of Water

Walking outside to take a sip of water at a drinking fountain seems like a simple task, but for one Fresno boxer named Ernie Stout the drink of water cost him his freedom.

It seems that on the night of January 13, 1931, Ernie Stout, known in the boxing world as Red Hanlon, got into a fight outside of the ring with a fellow named George Maloney. The affair grew so heated that someone called the police. Detective Sergeant A. B. McCreary and Officer W. W. Kosmosky rushed to the scene and arrested Stout. They placed him in their police car and drove him to the police station. They left Stout in the lobby comfortably ensconced in a chair and went into their offices to fill out their reports. Thirty minutes passed, then another thirty minutes, and then another. The officers didn't return. Stout, who finally decided that the police had changed their minds and were really not interested in him or in the fight with Maloney, got up, walked out the front door of the police station, and went home.

A day or so later, Maloney signed a complaint against Stout. The charge was battery. The police could now pursue the case, but where was Stout? No one knew. A search for the boxer began.

Meanwhile, oblivious to the stir he had created, Stout was going about his life as though nothing was wrong. A couple of months passed and then on the evening of April 1, 1931, Stout decided to stop for a drink of water at a public fountain at the corner of China Alley and Tulare Street. As luck would have it, officers McCreary and Kosmosky were nearby and spotted the boxer as he was taking his drink. He saw the officers and called to them, "That was a good joke you played on me the night you took me to the station and let me sit there all that time. I thought you were playing a joke on me…so [I] left."

"We're glad to see you, too, Stout," McCreary answered. They were so happy to see him that they gave him a free ride to the jail where he was booked on a charge of battery. Poor Stout—he gave up his freedom for a drink of good old Fresno water.

Just over a hundred years ago, twenty-eight enthusiastic young men, all members of the YMCA, decided they were going to ride their bicycles all the way to Yosemite Valley. They left Fresno at 5:00 A.M. on June 15, 1904, a Wednesday morning, and pulled into Yosemite Valley at 6 p.m. on Saturday night.

The two wagons containing the cyclists' supplies left Fresno on Tuesday. Wednesday's journey was well underway when the riders caught up with the wagons. By dinnertime, all the bicyclists and their supplies had reached Coarsegold, where they ate a delicious dinner cooked by Walter Turner and bedded down for the night.

At three o'clock Thursday morning reveille sounded. The young men got up, ate breakfast, and were on the road by six o'clock. After a little while, the road became so steep the riders dismounted and walked their bikes on a trail that led into Fresno Flats, where the supply wagon awaited them. It was only 10:00 A.M., but they ate lunch and prepared for the next round of their journey. By evening they had reached the trail that led to the Sugar Pine Mill. They took the trail, toured the mill, and slept outside under the stars.

On Friday, another 3:00 A.M. wake-up call was heard. After breakfast they followed the trail to Fish Camp, arriving ahead of the supply wagon. After lunch, the bikes were loaded into the wagon and the young men walked the long trail to the Big Trees in order to observe everything without worrying about pedaling. After seeing the incredible giant redwoods, half of the group took the trail over Wawona Point and the other half took the longer, less precipitous trail around the point—both arriving at Wawona in time for dinner.

At 7:00 A.M. the next morning, the group took the steep stage road to Chinquapin. Then it was on to Glacier Point. They, like scores of people before and since, found the view magnificent— the majestic cliffs, the sight of water crashing down the falls—all spread out before them.

Nightfall found the party setting up camp on the floor of Yosemite Valley, where they stayed for about a week.

As tired and sore as they all were, they felt a sense of tremendous accomplishment. They had walked and/or ridden their bicycles all the way from the YMCA building in downtown Fresno to Yosemite. They had a week to rest up for the journey home. Somehow, that seemed easier—it was downhill most of the way.

# A Picnic at Clark's Bridge

On June 12, 1904, the members of the Printing and Newspaper Craft of Fresno gathered for a picnic at Clark's Bridge picnic grounds on the Kings River. Early in the morning about thirty newsmen, thirty invited guests, and the members of the Wienerwurst Band boarded the train in Fresno and headed south. The band played a number of selections along the way. When Kingsburg was reached, the party disembarked. This was the easy part of the journey.

Two large hay wagons, minus the hay, were waiting for the group, who readily climbed on board. It was a very hot day and the three-mile trip over a road filled with chuckholes was not a whole lot of fun. When the party reached Clark's Bridge they were more than ready for the goodies on the refreshment wagon that had been sent on ahead and was just waiting for their arrival.

The Wienerwurst Band members headed for the pavilion and set up their chairs. As soon as they began to play, the party heated up. George Clark broke into a buck and wing dance—others began to cake-walk. Colonel Eduardo Hamilton, the president of the day, called for order in a very loud voice. He then introduced Major W. S. Scott, who was scheduled to give an oration entitled "Grinding Out Copy in Santa Cruz." After giving a brief history of Fresno newspapers, he talked about his service at the National Guard encampment in Santa Cruz every year.

The talk was followed by several athletic events. Fred Jones, editor of the *Visalia Times-Delta*, took home honors as the athletic champion of the day.

While waiting for dinner, Dante Prince paid tribute to the Fresno newspapermen and printers.

The return trip was made more enjoyable by the band. While enduring a two-hour wait in Kingsburg for the train, the band began to play. So lively was their music that a good part of the town came down to the station to see what was going on and stayed to have a good time. The remaining refreshments were shared with the crowd—it was a memorable night for all concerned.

# The Call of the Klondike

The California Gold Rush of 1848 brought hordes of people to California. Some miners were drawn to the Pacific Northwest during the 1850s when there were gold strikes in the Fraser River and in the Cassiar region of British Columbia. In 1886, gold was discovered at Alaska's Forty-Mile Creek, but it wasn't until March and April of 1896 that tremendous numbers of men began to head north to the area that become known as the Klondike. Major gold strikes were being made in many of the rivers and tributaries of central Alaska and northwestern Canada—thousands of people left from Seattle and poured into the gold fields. Many fortunes were made, but many of the miners came home empty-handed. After 1900, large companies purchased many of the claims, and the individual miners began to leave. For them, the gold rush was over.

A number of young men from Fresno decided to try their luck in the gold fields of the Klondike. Arch Grant, Frank Neate, Frank Wyatt, and Ed Wolcott were among the group. Arch Grant was the first to return home, in 1899. He told a reporter for *The Fresno Morning Republican* that he didn't get rich, but he couldn't complain—he'd brought home a number of gold nuggets and had had a great adventure. When asked how he liked the Klondike he replied, "…the country is not half so bad as it has been represented to be. It's cold, of course, but…it is also golden—that is, if you can find the gold." He said it was a lot like gambling—every man who goes takes his chance.

Grant was of the opinion that, since most of the placer claims were taken up, bench claims would be the best way to make money. A bench claim is one that is situated on a mountainside rather than along a river.

He told the *Republican* that all his buddies were doing well in the Klondike and were determined not to come home until they had something to show for it. Gold fever had struck yet again in the tales of our Valley.

# The Secretary of Agriculture Pays a Visit

By 1899, Fresno County agriculture was blossoming on every front. The Valley had truly been transformed from a desert into a lush and fruitful oasis. However, the Valley was still often overlooked by the "powers that be," so when a group of prominent Fresno businessmen heard that Secretary of Agriculture James Wilson was going to be traveling by train from Los Angeles to San Francisco on August 2, 1899, they took matters into their own hands. When the train pulled into the station at 11:00 A.M., a delegation including R. B. Butler, Dr. Chester Rowell, T. C. White, and J. M. Collier, was on the platform. Collier, who headed the group, got on the train and told Mr. Wilson about the uniqueness of the Valley's agriculture. So impressed was Wilson that he immediately got off the train, met the other gentlemen, and asked to be shown all these wonderful agricultural achievements.

After a brief stop at the Hughes Hotel to arrange for lodgings, the group set out. Their first visit was to the icehouse and creamery where they tasted milk and butter. They drove through the vineyards of Butler Place and on to the Minnewawa Ranch where Minna Eshleman showed them her fine herds of cattle and took them through her dairy where the newest methods of sterilization were practiced. Secretary Wilson was impressed. Then it was on to Roeding Place where he saw Smyrna figs and discussed the Blastophaga wasp with George Roeding. Visits to the Eisen, Barton, and St. George vineyards and wineries were next on the agenda. After all of this, a private dinner was held at the Hughes Hotel.

The next morning, Dr. Rowell took Secretary Wilson through the post office and his *Fresno Morning Republican* newspaper plant. A drive through Chinatown delighted the secretary, who said he had never seen a Chinatown before.

When he left the following day, Secretary James Wilson told his new friends that he could hardly wait to share all he had seen with President William McKinley. It had been a most successful visit thanks to a group of men who valued their community and the hard work of its citizens. In the mind of at least one cabinet member in 1899, the word "Fresno" had great meaning.

# Let's Stop the Games Forever!

During the first four years of the twentieth century, when the reform administration of Mayor L. O. Stephens was trying so hard to shut down gambling in Fresno, the successes and failures of its efforts seemed to be a roller coaster ride. One week the games ended; the next week the games were up and running again. Police Chief J. D. Morgan had just about exhausted every avenue open to him.

Then the mayor had an idea. There was plenty of money in the city's coffers—why not use it to stop the games?

On May 31, 1904, the word went out to the whole Fresno community. The mayor was looking for men of good standing who would be willing to go into the gambling parlors, especially the fan-tan parlors of Chinatown that barred their doors to the police, and round up the gamblers and their paraphernalia and bring them to the police station. Police Chief Morgan would deputize these men before they made their arrests. If they were successful, these brave men would receive a reward of eighty dollars. The mayor felt that this was a good use of the city's money. Nothing else had worked; he was willing to give this a try.

The arrests would be made "of anyone playing [a] percentage card game or any game prohibited by law, having lottery tickets in his possession or maintaining or conducting a selling agency for lottery tickets or a lottery or gambling game of any kind."

A large number of Fresno's citizens had been clamoring for an end to the gambling. This new program would give them a chance to participate in ridding the city of it once and for all. It's one thing to talk about it; it's quite another to volunteer. It was an interesting experiment—only time would tell whether or not anyone would come forward and offer to help.

# Graduation Night in Easton

Friday, May 27, 1904, was an extremely busy day for the fifteen graduating seniors of Washington Union High School. So much had to be done, but they were up to the task. The old hall of the school, where the graduation exercises would be held in the evening, had to be decorated. The students first placed masses of greenery across the back of the stage. Baskets of floral arrangements were then placed in front of the footlights. The walls of the hall were next—when the students finished the walls had been transformed. Pennants in the school colors of violet and white were interspersed with the school's motto, "Culture before knowledge, character before culture," and the class motto, "For duty and nineteen four." All was now in readiness.

At the appointed hour, the fifteen students, with their parents and friends watching, filed into the hall and onto the stage. After an invocation by the Reverend John Habbick, Bessie Johnson read her essay on Lady Macbeth making a plea that her single bloody deed was prompted by wifely devotion. Haderup Jensen followed with his oration, "Should Russia Have Manchuria." Newton Johnson's oration on "High School Athletics" was followed by Mabel Bennett's essay on the "History of the Class." A number of musical selections were played and sung throughout the evening. After an address by the Reverend J. A. Blackledge and comments by Principal Osmer Abbott about why the community should be proud of these graduates, the diplomas were presented to each student by County Superintendent of Schools G. N. Freman.

Just before the students departed the stage, one of the graduates suddenly stood up and, with a great deal of feeling, gave a short speech and presented a set of Shakespeare's works to Principal Abbott as a token of the class's appreciation. It was only then that everyone arose to sing "America" and the new graduates marched out of the hall.

# Judge E. W. Risley

On December 15, 1918, Fresnans mourned the passing of one of their most prominent civic leaders. He was a man respected by all and was remembered not only for his accomplishments, but also for his colorful early life.

Judge E. W. Risley was born on March 1, 1853, in New Haven, Connecticut, a direct descendant of Richard Risley, a founder of Hartford, Connecticut, in 1635. He graduated from Knox College at the age of twenty-one. Along with his academic studies, he completed a course in the law.

In 1875, Risley set out for California hoping to find riches in the placers of the Golden State or in the silver mines of Nevada. News of mineral discoveries in Tombstone, Arizona, also beckoned. He decided to try his luck first in Arizona. Fortune smiled on him to some extent, but Risley found that his training in law was his true calling. He became the official court reporter for the entire territory of Arizona. He later served as a deputy United States marshal, as a deputy district attorney of Cochise County, where Tombstone is located, as a deputy United States district attorney, and as a member of the Tucson City Council.

In 1885, E. W. Risley moved to Fresno. Soon after his arrival, he was admitted to the Supreme Court of the State of California and to the United States Supreme Court. He served as deputy district attorney under Firman Church and W. D. Tupper and as city attorney during the tumultuous years of the early 1890s. He was appointed a superior court judge in 1895 and served in this office until 1900.

He served as a freeholder taking an active role in the drafting of the new city charter in 1900. The document was primarily the work of Risley and J. P. Strother. The new charter was written to put an end to the abuses that were such a part of city government at that time. Passage of the charter and the reforms that were implemented immediately following its adoption were a major achievement in the development of the pioneer village into a city ready to take its place among the major municipalities of California. Risley later served as police and fire commissioner for four years.

Judge Risley's wife, Eleanor, died in 1913. They had two children, Thomas and Marguerite.

On December 16, 1918, his lifelong friend Judge M. K. Harris conducted his funeral service. His friends and colleagues offered many tributes to Judge E. W. Risley—a man who had served his city well and who had led his life with honesty and dignity.

E. W. Risley served as a judge on the Superior Court for Fresno County. *Courtesy of Robert M. Wash.*

# Dr. Osmer Abbott

One of the most distinguished Fresno County educators in the early twentieth century was born in Indiana in 1864. He was a fine student and, from an early age, wanted to be a teacher. He graduated from Oberlin College in 1891 and received his Ph.D. degree from the University of Jena in Germany.

After spending two years teaching on the island of Maui, Dr. Osmer Abbott came to Fresno in 1899 to take the position of principal of Fresno High School—a job he held for one year. He left Fresno High to become the principal of Washington Union High School, serving in that position for eleven years.

In 1906, Dr. Abbott married Miss Sadie Main, a daughter of Mr. and Mrs. William Main of Fresno. Their union was blessed with six children.

Dr. Abbott was elected to the Fresno County Board of Education and served two terms. During this time, in 1910, Coalinga High School asked him to move to Coalinga and take over the administration of its school. Abbott moved his family to Coalinga and held the job of principal for six years. He became involved in community affairs and directed the organization of Coalinga's first public library.

In 1914, Abbott took on additional responsibilities, serving also as supervising principal of the Hanford schools. In 1916, he moved his family to that city. Dr. Osmer Abbott had been diagnosed with diabetes several years before. The disease gradually worsened and, in mid-November 1917, he was rushed to the Burnett Sanitarium in Fresno where he died on November 23.

Dr. Osmer Abbott was a man of refinement and was a gifted educator and administrator who made significant contributions to the development of many of our Valley schools. It is fitting that he be remembered as a legend of our Valley.

# James Riggs White

James Riggs White was born in Georgetown, Maine, on December 10, 1827. After completing his education, he learned the trade of carpentry. In 1848, news of the California Gold Rush reached Maine and ignited a spark in our young man which would not be extinguished. Gold fever had seduced another victim. In December of that year, White and thirty of his friends headed for California. They sailed down the East coast in a chartered boat that took them all the way around Cape Horn. They reached Yerba Buena (San Francisco) on May 18, 1849.

White headed for the gold fields and tried his hand at placer mining on the Tuolumne River. He left for a short time to run a ferry business on the river, but returned to mining. He was one of the earliest miners to prospect in the southern mines in what are today Madera and Fresno counties. There he met Major James Savage and the two men became friends.

White moved to Stockton and worked in the livestock business, then returned to Dry Diggings, later called Columbia (in Tuolumne County), to mine some more. He stayed for sixteen years and served as a deputy sheriff. Restlessness overcame him again, so he crossed the Valley and spent a year operating the Gilroy stage line. After a brief try at stock raising in Tulare County, he returned to the west side of the Valley and began a settlement on the south branch of the San Joaquin River. Here he built a store, a hotel, a warehouse, and a bridge over the river. The settlement became known as White's Bridge. In 1885, James R. White moved to Fresno where he became a director in the Fresno Loan and Savings Bank and was president of the first street railway company.

On May 6, 1907, James R. White passed away in Fresno's Burnett Sanitarium. During his lifetime he had been a participant in the most colorful period of our Valley's history. He had crossed our pristine Valley just four years after John C. Fremont's expedition, had been part of the Gold Rush, had witnessed steamboat travel on the San Joaquin River, and had been part of the economic boom period of Fresno's growth. His legacy lives on in the highway that bears his name—White's Bridge Road.

# July 4, 1917

The Fourth of July in 1917 found the nation at war—World War I was being fought on the battlefields of Europe. Americans had sent their sons to the front. They were sacrificing in every way they could for the war effort—it was hard to think about planning a celebration of any kind. Many were finding their feelings of patriotism waning.

President Woodrow Wilson told Americans that now more than ever the Fourth of July needed to be celebrated and urged every community to plan a special celebration. Mayor W. F. Toomey decided that Fresnans should plan a celebration of our national holiday unlike any in the city's history.

T. J. Hammond, chairman of the July 4 committee, made a list of duties for every citizen. Every house should display a flag. Every person should either view or walk in the parade, attend the literary exercises and Congress of Nations pageant in Courthouse Park, join in the dancing in the evening, and have a good word for everyone. Fresnans heard him and responded to his call.

At dawn on that special day, a salute of guns and the firing of dynamite charges made sure that everyone was awake and ready for the parade. By 9:00 A.M., the streets were filled with spectators who viewed one of the greatest parades they had ever seen. At the parade's end, five thousand people walked to Courthouse Park and filled the area in front of the bandstand and the rest of the park.

"The Star Spangled Banner" was sung. Mayor Toomey introduced Judge Lewis F. Byington, who gave a speech about our nation's fight for liberty. By the time his oration ended, thousands more had come to the park. The crowd now spilled into the streets.

Promptly at 2:30 P.M., the Congress of Nations pageant began. The color guards made their way to the stage of the bandstand. The American flag was raised and, one by one, ladies wearing the costumes of the friendly countries of Europe and Asia walked onto the stage, each carrying the flag of the country she represented. With each woman was a speaker who made brief comments about that country and its role in the war in Europe. As the presentation ended, the flag was lowered while "The Star Spangled Banner" was again sung. The message of the pageant was love of our fellow man. At the end of each speech, the crowd broke into applause.

For those in attendance that day, it was a moving experience—it brought home the sobering realization of the meaning of what was happening in Europe and what each of these countries was suffering. It was a Fourth of July unlike any other in the tales of our Valley.

Eighteen of Dr. Walter Sherman and Miss Minna Eshleman's closest friends and family left Fresno, Sacramento, and Berkeley, and traveled to San Francisco to attend their wedding. Dr. Chester Rowell was part of the Fresno contingent making the trip.

At twelve noon on Wednesday, September 20, 1899, the parlors of the Hotel Baltimore in downtown San Francisco were all in readiness. Palms, smilax, and La France roses gave softness to the décor of the rooms.

After the guests were seated, the Reverend Dr. Warren Sherman, twin brother of the bridegroom and the minister who was going to perform the ceremony, took his place under an arch. The parents of the groom and the groom's sister came in next, followed by the bride's mother. They formed a semicircle in front of the Rev. Sherman. Dr. I. S. Eshleman, with his daughter Minna on his arm, walked in and stood next to the groom. The bride was wearing a gray traveling costume.

The ceremony had a charming air about it due, in part, to the fact that it was performed by the groom's twin brother. After the couple was pronounced husband and wife, the entire party sat down to an elegant wedding breakfast.

After the last toast had been given and all the good wishes had been expressed, everyone went outside to wave the couple on their way. Just as the bride and groom stepped into their carriage, a regiment of volunteers made their way down the street playing the song "Union Forever." On this appropriate note, the couple left for a honeymoon at the Hotel Del Monte near Monterey.

A week later, a huge reception was held at the Fresno home of Dr. and Mrs. I. S. Eshleman so that all the couple's many friends could celebrate with them. It was a most happy time in the tales of our Valley.

On February 28, 1923, the residents of O'Neals, a small community in the foothills of Madera County, went into mourning. News of the death of the man for whom their town was named spread quickly. Stories of his fascinating life were told and retold by all who knew him.

Charles O'Neal was born in Vermillion County, Illinois, on February 11, 1830. When he was six, his family moved to Texas. At age fifteen, he enlisted in the United States Army to serve in the Mexican War. After a year with the Ninth Cavalry, he was mustered out and returned home to complete his education.

In 1856, he joined a wagon train headed for California. When the train split into two groups, O'Neal headed the group that took a southern route. He left the wagon train at El Paso and crossed the Mexican border. He served under Gandier, an American soldier of fortune, for three months and left Mexico with a price on his head. A sergeant who wanted to collect the reward arrested him and turned him over to his colonel. The furious colonel demoted the sergeant and freed O'Neal stating, "I am not in the business of capturing …men to turn over to Mexico to be tortured." O'Neal crossed the Colorado River and walked to Los Angeles, then moved to Watsonville, where he married Miss Bettie Douglas.

In 1876, the couple moved to Fresno County, where O'Neal worked as a superintendent on the Hildreth Ranch. A few years later, he purchased the Captain Russell Perry Mace Ranch and, over the years, increased his holdings to 1,100 acres. He bought Mace's store, built a small hotel, served as the postmaster, gave the small community his name and contributed the land for the town's first school. In addition to his livestock interests, O'Neal was also a miner. He bought and sold several gold mines, including the well-known Zebra mine.

Charles O'Neal was a big-hearted man who loved the outdoors. On March 2, 1923, O'Neal was buried in the free cemetery he established for the residents of the area on his land. At the celebration of his ninety-third birthday, just a short time before his death, he told his friends, "I have had lots of trouble, but have had lots of fun." Not a bad summation of a most interesting life.

At a gathering at Saint James' Episcopal Cathedral, early in 1930, three women who had served the Fresno community in a host of ways were honored. These women had a number of shared experiences, but, on this day, their common thread was that they were Fresno pioneers and were all charter members of their respective churches.

As the women talked about their lives in the earliest days of Fresno, they remembered how everyone helped each other when help was needed—in the young town there was no other help available. They remembered how everyone got dressed in their best clothes and set out in groups to walk to the church sociable, gathering more people along the way. They remembered chats over the back fence with their neighbors and the fragrant smell of molasses cookies baking in the oven.

Mrs. E. G. McCardle, the oldest living charter member of Saint Paul's Methodist Church South, reflected on how neighborly everyone was in the days before Fresno had any church buildings. Her church was the first to erect a structure. Everyone helped and then helped use the building. She said that when the Methodists had a sociable there were usually as many Baptists and Catholics in the gathering as there were Methodists.

Mrs. H. C. Tupper, the only living charter member of Saint James' Episcopal Church (in the days before it became a cathedral), remembered that when the church applied for a permit to hold services in the Hawthorne School, Mr. McCardle, superintendent of schools, signed the permit. The first nine communicants were all women. They had trouble deciding on a name for the church until they all realized that most of them had a James in their family. Then, the decision was easy.

The third honoree, Mrs. John Hoxie, was Fresno's first schoolteacher. She was a charter member of Saint John's Cathedral.

For all those present, it was a day to reflect on the past and to honor three women who played a role in the growth of their city from a tiny railroad stop into a major California city. It was a day to remember in the tales of our Valley.

# Life in Washington Colony in 1874

In the pages of the March 26, 1926, edition of *The Fresno Morning Republican*, a story appears that is told by one of Easton's earliest pioneers, Richard T. Skewes. It gives the reader a marvelous insight into what life was like in rural Fresno County in 1874.

Skewes grew up in the eastern United States. His career in the mining industry took him to Mexico, to New Jersey, and, finally, to Grass Valley. One day an agent from the Fresno area arrived in Grass Valley. He was a promoter of the Washington Colony and was selling ten-acre lots. He told Skewes that if he bought ten-acres of this fertile land, he could grow Egyptian corn—enough to support his family.

Skewes paid the man $400 for ten acres of Washington Colony land and moved his family to Fresno. The year was 1874. When they arrived and visited their land, all they could see was hot sand in every direction. The only sign of vegetation was a few oak trees near Riverdale. Skewes built a house on his land and began to farm. He remembered that every morning when he stepped outside his back door there were large herds of antelopes eating the sagebrush. He said that the early settlers called them "California Lions."

Visits to Fresno were an interesting part of life. The town was small in 1874. Skewes asked a clerk one day if he thought Fresno would ever be a city. The clerk said, "I have my doubts."

In the early 1880s, the first death occurred in the district. Since there was no cemetery, Skewes dug a grave on the Cornell Ranch on Cherry Avenue, but soon after burial found out that no one could be buried there. The problem was solved with the creation of a cemetery committee. John Smith donated land to the community for the Washington Colony Cemetery in 1893.

Skewes' vivid descriptions of the early colony settlements gives us a bird's eye view of life lived by those who first farmed our Valley. It wasn't an easy business, but with perseverance came success and a blossoming agricultural paradise to be enjoyed by later generations.

# The River of Mercy

In the summer of 1806, Ensign Gabriel Moraga, accompanied by Father Pedro Munoz and twenty-five soldiers, once again entered the San Joaquin Valley. The year before, on his expedition to search out mission sites in the interior valley, Moraga had named the Kings and San Joaquin rivers.

Moraga's party left Mission San Juan Bautista and came across the Coast Range Mountains following the ancient Indian trail that had provided trading opportunities for the coastal and Valley tribes. They followed San Luis Creek, crossed the San Joaquin River north of present-day Firebaugh, and headed east to present-day Chowchilla. It was on this trip that they were greeted by swarms of yellow butterflies (*mariposas*). Moraga named the area Mariposa. The party turned north following much the same route of today's Highway 99.

By the time the party had "crossed and named Mariposa Creek and Bear (*Oso*) Creek," they were tired and thirsty from their long journey across the hot plains of the Valley. They came upon a river that mercifully provided cool water to quench their terrible thirst. In gratitude, Moraga named the river *El Rio de la Nuestra Senora de Merced* (The River of our Lady of Mercy). Merced would remain the name of the river and would later be given to the county through which it flowed and to the city that would become the seat of that county's government.

Moraga felt the Merced River provided a good potential site for a mission. The party continued north and then turned south revisiting the San Joaquin and Kings rivers and camping on the Kaweah River. In 1810, on another expedition into the Valley, Moraga decided that the Merced River site was not workable for a mission. It would be quite a few years before the white man created settlements along the "River of Mercy."

# Merced County Is Created

In 1850, when California became a state, a number of counties were created. Mariposa County was the largest, encompassing most of the Central Valley. On April 19, 1855, Merced County was created out of the northwest section of Mariposa County. On the second Monday in May an election was held to choose county officers and to determine a location for the county seat.

The first county seat was a site on the Turner and Osborne Ranch seven miles east of present-day Merced. Although an unfinished twenty-five-by-twelve-foot building was designated as the courthouse, it was not used. Instead, a grove of oak trees beside Mariposa Creek was the setting for trials. The Grand Jury met under one tree, the jury sat under another, and any onlookers had to find a place for themselves under any of the other trees. When the jury went into deliberation, they did so in the dry creek bed. When the wind came up, papers were carried off, with people in hot pursuit. The situation was primitive to say the least.

Merced County's early settlements were in two areas. The first was along the Merced River. Snelling, Forlorn Hope (now Hopeton), and Hill's Ferry, the hub of steam navigation between the Merced and Stockton rivers, were in this area. The second was along the creeks and on the Valley floor. On the west side of the county were Mexican land grants. On the east side cattle, sheep, and grain ranches predominated.

During the summer of 1855, a petition was filed for another county seat election. This time the Snelling Ranch won. In 1857 a courthouse was erected where business could be conducted with a little more dignity. This building served the county until December 1872, when another election was held and the county seat was moved permanently to the not quite one-year-old town of Merced.

One of the foremost pioneers of Merced County was born on October 22, 1822, in Rockingham, North Carolina. When he was twenty-four, he joined the First Mississippi Rifle Regiment commanded by Jefferson Davis. During the war between the United States and Mexico, he saw action at the battles of Monterrey and Buena Vista, where he was wounded. At the end of the war, he was honorably discharged and, in 1849, the subject of our story, Robert Johnson Steele, came to California.

The Gold Rush was well underway—Steele headed for the mines first in El Dorado County and then in Tuolumne County, finding success in both areas. With several thousand dollars in his pocket, he returned home to visit his parents. In 1853, he headed back to California and began to mine a claim on Pierson's Hill. Later, he mined in Columbia. Once again, he was successful and used his resources to enter the field of journalism, publishing several newspapers in gold mining towns during the 1850s and early 1860s—the *Columbia Gazette*, the *Placer Courier*, and the *Democratic Signal* in Auburn.

In 1861, he married Rowena Granice, a divorcee with two young sons. In June 1862, the family moved to Snelling in Merced County. Steele and his wife started a newspaper there, the *Merced Banner*, the first newspaper in Merced County. A few years later, the *Banner* shut down. The *Democrat*, edited and published by William Pierce, alias William Hall, began publication. It only lasted for three weeks because Pierce was arrested, charged with treason, and sent to Alcatraz.

In 1869, Steele began the *San Joaquin Valley Argus* in Snelling. In 1873, he moved his newspaper to Merced.

With Steele's death in January 1890, the life of one of the Valley's pioneer journalists and publishers was brought to a close.

George Steele,
Robert Johnson
Steele, Rowena
Granice Steele,
and Lee R.
Steele.
*Courtesy of
Merced County
Historical Society
Archives.*

## Rowena Granice Steele

The lady whose story we will tell today was a survivor in the truest sense. She looked adversity square in the face and, instead of giving up, went on to achieve things she might not have accomplished otherwise.

Rowena Granice Steele was born in Goshen, New York, in 1824. Six years later, her family moved to New York City. It was there that Granice received her education. She married Tom McClaughley—they had two sons. When gold was discovered in California, McClaughley, like so many others, left his family and headed west to seek his fortune. In order to support herself and her boys, Rowena got a job as an actress in P. T. Barnum's America Museum. She found her calling and gained fame not only for her performances, but also for her dramatic readings.

In 1856, Granice left her boys in New York and headed for San Francisco so she could join her husband. When she arrived, she found that he was living with another woman. She divorced McClaughley.

She sent for her sons and, determined to support them, appeared on stage in San Francisco and Sacramento to earn a living. She started writing stories—going door to door in the gold country selling her work. She also gave entertainments at gatherings throughout the state. In 1860, Granice published *Victims of Fate*, the first novel published by a woman in California.

A second marriage also ended in divorce. Her luck changed in 1861. She met Robert Johnson Steele in Placer County. They married soon after—her boys now had a father and one who would be a mentor for them. The family moved to Snelling where they began the first newspaper in Merced County, the *Merced Banner*.

Granice Steele became a proponent of women's suffrage and temperance—two of the popular causes at the end of the nineteenth and beginning of the twentieth centuries.

A woman of strong opinions, great strength of character, and an indomitable spirit—Rowena Granice Steele most certainly is a legend of our Valley.

# From the Argus to the Sun-Star

The first newspaper in Merced County was the *Merced Banner*, which began publishing in July 1862 at Snelling, the county seat. Robert J. Steele, a Southerner, and his wife, Rowena, were the editors. It was the time of the Civil War. On February 1, 1864, a unit of the United States cavalry (Union soldiers) rode into Snelling and entered the office of the *Banner*. They broke up the press, scattered the type, and destroyed the tables and stands— they wreaked total havoc on the newspaper. Two weeks later, Steele managed to put out a newspaper half the size of the original editions. By June the *Banner* was no more. Two other newspapers followed, the *Merced Democrat* and the *Democratic Record*, but neither lasted very long.

On May 13, 1865, the *Merced Herald* started publishing. It flourished for a while and then the owners began having a series of problems and, by the end of 1867, it folded. On August 22, 1868, it was brought back to life by Robert J. Steele. After a year, Steele ceased publication and founded a new newspaper, the *San Joaquin Valley Argus*. It was very successful—at the time it was the only newspaper in Merced County. In its pages, Steele fought hard to keep the county seat in Snelling after the railroad had established the new town of Merced.

Even though he lost that fight, on April 15, 1873, Steele moved his family to the new county seat of Merced. He moved the *Argus* with him. Steele died in January 1890. In that year, his widow merged the *Argus* with the *Merced Journal*—the newspaper was now called the *Merced County Sun*. In 1925, another merger took place. The newspaper thus created was the *Merced Sun-Star*, still the major newspaper in Merced County.

From its beginnings in Snelling, in 1869, to its latest edition today, the *Merced Sun-Star* has been in business for one hundred thirty-six years, making it one of the oldest newspapers in California.

In the spring of 1851, three gentlemen, Dr. David Wallace Lewis, John Montgomery, and Colonel Samuel Scott, chose a site on the north bank of the Merced River, just six miles from the head of the Merced Valley. There they built a large hotel and opened a house of entertainment. Before the wooden structure was finished, the business operated out of a brush tent.

Montgomery and Scott, both from Kentucky, arrived in the area in 1849. They took up cattle ranching, became very wealthy, and were known as the "Cattle Kings of Merced."

In the fall of 1851, the William Snelling family, from whom the community would take its name, arrived and began farming and ranching. They made enough money to buy the hotel and a considerable amount of property.

In 1853, when a post office was established, it was named Snelling's Ranch. William Snelling was the postmaster. During the first year he earned $87.20. Three years later, in 1856, the town of Snelling was laid out and it became the county seat. A courthouse was built—also a jail, homes, and stores. The town began to grow.

A flood hit the town in the winter of 1861-62, destroying the hotel and several buildings. In September 1862 disaster struck again. A fire broke out that destroyed an entire block of business buildings. The citizens rebuilt their stores and the community began, once again, to grow. With the removal of the county seat to Merced in 1872, the population began to shift toward the new city.

Today, Snelling is a peaceful community of people who care about their history. Merced County's first courthouse is still standing, is carefully maintained, and is used today for community meetings.

Anderson Hotel in
Snelling in 1900.
Courtesy of Merced
County Historical
Society Archives.

# *Crackaloo*

Now one wouldn't think that a two-bit coin and a crack in a wood floor could cause much trouble, but on one winter's day in the Merced County town of Snelling in the year 1857, those two innocent objects started a vendetta that ended in the deaths of four people.

The Snelling Hotel boasted a wood floor. The wood floor had a nice sized crack in it—making it a perfect target for a game of crackaloo. The object of the game was for men to place a bet and roll quarters toward the crack in the floor.

On the winter morning in question William Edwards, a tough character, and a fellow named West began to fight over their bet and the outcome of the game. William Snelling, West's brother-in-law, took West's side in the argument. This infuriated Edwards, who turned his hostility on Snelling. Guns were drawn several times, but cooler heads prevailed.

A few days later, on December 5, Edwards entered the hotel dining room and saw Snelling sitting there. Snelling got up and followed Edwards into the bar. Edwards shouted at Snelling, drew his pistol, and shot him—the bullet pierced both lungs. Although mortally wounded, Snelling fired at Edwards who ran outside where Sheriff George Turner took Edwards' gun. Even without the gun, Edwards made good his escape—he fled to Nevada.

Snelling's friends began to hunt down Edwards. Charles Bludworth, who was married to Snelling's granddaughter, was nicknamed "Bloodthirsty Charlie" for the role he had played in the manhunt for Joaquin Murrieta. He was Merced County's first sheriff. Three friends of Edwards—William Stevens, E. G. Barclay, and James Wilcox—meanwhile threatened to kill Bludworth.

Our story will continue…

A simple game of crackaloo led to the killing of William Snelling by William Edwards. As a result, sides were taken—Sheriff Charles Bludworth, Snelling's grandson-in-law, against Edwards' friends, William Stevens, E. G. Barclay, and James Wilcox. At high noon on January 23, 1858, Stevens, Barclay, and Wilcox rode into Snelling. They tethered their horses in front of the courthouse, all the while loudly proclaiming their threats to kill Bludworth, and walked inside to visit the sheriff. Two of them carried double-barreled shotguns. Bludworth, hearing the news, gathered his friends, a fellow named White, and Dr. Jeff Goodin, and headed for the courthouse. No sooner did they step inside the sheriff's office than a gun battle broke out. The sheriff ducked for cover while the six men decided to shoot it out right then and there. Bludworth killed Stevens. White and Goodin shot Barclay and Wilcox. Wilcox shot Goodin. Goodin stood over the mortally wounded Barclay, getting ready to finish him off. Barclay, gathering his last ounce of strength, killed Goodin. It only took three minutes and forty-five shots to kill three men.

The three who were left standing were taken before the justice of the peace, who ruled they had acted in self-defense. They were released. And what of Edwards, the man who started it all? He high-tailed it for Nevada and hooked up with a gambler named Lucky Bill Thorrington. The two were lynched by a group of vigilantes five months later.

A letter from Clarissa Snelling to Elizabeth Goodin, the widow of Dr. Goodin, written on January 30, 1858, is filled with sadness. It fell to Clarissa to inform Elizabeth of her husband's death. In so doing, she shared the doctor's kindness when her own husband was killed seven weeks before. "The Dr [doctor] stood over him until he died. He died with his arms around the Dr neck for he loved him as a brother. He had bin [been] a brother to me since Mr. Snelling's death. You have lost a good husband. I [lost] a good friend an [and] society one of its brightest objects." She sent Elizabeth a lock of Dr. Goodin's hair hoping it would bring her comfort. With the letter, a sad chapter closed in the tales of our Valley.

# Hopeton and Plainsburg

In 1854, a post office was established in a small community on the Merced River. It was named for a nearby mine—Forlorn Hope. It had a school, two churches, a few businesses, and several homes. In 1866, the community was renamed Hopeton. As in many small villages, homes and ranch houses were called upon to act as hotels when the need arose. The community was surrounded by rich agricultural land—farming drew people to the area.

Another small settlement developed on Mariposa Creek in southeastern Merced County. It was called Welch's Store. Later it became known as Plainsburg. The village had numerous houses, a saloon, a blacksmith shop, a store, and a hotel. A half mile east of the town was a general store run by Mr. Albeck, a pioneer merchant of note. He had a large inventory of merchandise and enjoyed a lively business.

Plainsburg was surrounded by farmland and the projections for the town were that it would become a major city. Unfortunately, in 1872, when the railroad came through Merced County, the route was several miles from Plainsburg. Because of this and the new towns created next to the railroad, Plainsburg did not develop the way that had been envisioned. The railroad built a station that they called Plainsburg expecting Plainsburgers to move their town next to the station. When they did not, the name of the station was changed to Athlone. Today, all that remains of that name in the area is the Athlone Road.

Today, greater downtown Plainsburg consists of a two-story Plainsburg Grocery. It is at the corner of Le Grand and Plainsburg roads. The major crop in the area is tomatoes.

Both these communities, Hopeton and Plainsburg, have deep roots in the pioneer past and played a role in the history of Merced County.

A group of people standing in front of the Hopeton Saloon about 1870. *Courtesy of Merced County Historical Society Archives.*

Men harvesting wheat in Plainsburg in 1892. They are using an E. L. Morley Harvester. *Courtesy of Merced County Historical Society Archives.*

# The Founding of Merced

Beginning in 1869, much of the conversation in Merced County centered on talk of a railroad line. What direction would it take? Who was going to build it? It soon became clear that the Central Pacific Railroad was the company and the line's name was, in popular parlance, the San Joaquin Valley Railroad.

On July 29, 1871, Snelling's newspaper, *San Joaquin Valley Argus*, reported that the "construction train of the San Joaquin Valley Railroad passed over the Tuolumne River Bridge at Modesto and are now extending their works south toward the Merced River…it is believed that upon Bear Creek will be built the large town of the valley." There was a great deal of excitement over the prospect of the new town. Exactly where would it be located? How soon would the town site be laid out so lots could be purchased?

In September the *Argus* reported that the railroad was boring an artesian well at the new town site on Bear Creek. The November *Argus* gave the name of the town for the first time. It would be called Merced City.

The winter of 1871-72 was a wet one. When the railroad did arrive, in November, it was greeted with a flood. Heavy rains caused Bear Creek to overflow. The railroad still managed to get lumber to the new town site so that a depot and a hotel could be built. Scheduled rail service would begin on January 25, 1872.

On January 20 it was reported that the new town was getting some business. A saloon and eatery were open and temporary buildings for the depot and hotel were well underway. Just a week later, two livery stables were being built. More saloons and eating establishments were opening.

On February 3, excitement was really in the air—the sale of lots was to take place. A butcher shop was about to open in anticipation of providing food for new residents.

On February 8, the sale of lots began. Lots varied in size from 25 by 150 feet to 50 by 150 feet. The prices ranged from $125 to $500 per lot. John C. Smith made the first purchase for $575. Silas I. Simon made the second for $495. They each purchased half of a 50 by 150 foot parcel. They were followed by many others. The Con-

Merced's Sixteenth Street in 1890. *Courtesy of Merced County Historical Society Archives.*

tract and Finance Company, a subsidiary of the railroad, plotted the town. They made N Street the widest street in town in anticipation of a future county courthouse at its end. The lots on N Street were priced higher, leading future merchants to buy parcels on L Street instead. This resulted in a change in the railroad's plans for the design of the future commercial district.

The new town of Merced was up and running. People began to leave Snelling for the new town. The railroad construction crews headed south. The Iron Horse marched on.

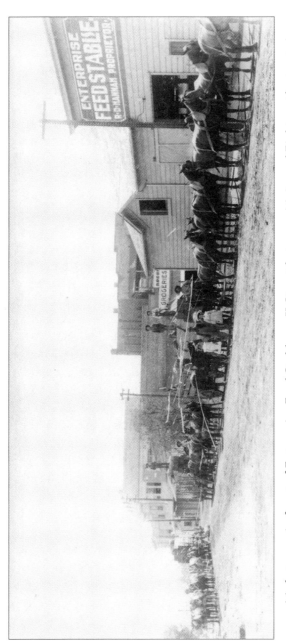

Mule teams in front of Enterprise Feed Stable on K Street between Main and Eighteenth streets in 1890. *Courtesy of Merced County Historical Society Archives.*

# Snelling or Merced—The Great Debate

In the summer of 1872, just a few months after the new town of Merced was founded, a controversy began that was played out in the pages of two newspapers—the Snelling *San Joaquin Valley Argus* and *The Merced Tribune*. The editors of these publications, Robert J. Steele and Edward Madden, respectively, held opposing viewpoints on the matter of the possible removal of the county seat from Snelling to Merced. Steele advocated keeping the county seat at Snelling; Madden enthusiastically supported moving the county seat to the new town of Merced. It proved to be a heated debate.

As was its wont, the Central Pacific Railroad, in laying out the town of Merced, provided four blocks for a courthouse park. Obviously, it wished to see the county seat moved to Merced and would use whatever influence it needed to make it happen.

Robert Steele argued that moving the county seat from Snelling would incur major costs for the taxpayers. The construction of a new courthouse would be expensive. While such a building was being built, office space would have to be rented, adding another unnecessary cost. As a resident of Merced, Edward Madden, of course, was strongly in favor of bringing the county seat to the new town. Such a move would enhance the future of Merced.

The Merced County Board of Supervisors called a special election for December 12, 1872, for the purpose of voting on the issue of the county seat. With this announcement, Steele's editorial thundering increased in intensity. He argued that the removal would only increase the wealth of the railroad and land speculators. Every argument he could conjure up was brought to bear against removal. On November 23, a group of businessmen filed a bond with the county clerk to provide free office space for the county if the seat of government came to Merced.

On December 12, the election was held. Of the 983 votes cast, "Merced received 566, Livingston 236, and Snelling 181. The Board of Supervisors ordered that on and after December 30, 1872, Merced would be the county seat." The debate was over. Now it was time to move on and make plans for a proper courthouse.

January 1873 was another milestone in the development of the town of Merced. It was now the seat of government for Merced County. The old courthouse at Snelling was the scene of much activity as boxes of documents were packed and moved to the new county seat. The first county offices were on the second floor of the Olcese and Garibaldi Building at Sixteenth and L streets. Court was held in the Washington Hall on Seventeenth Street.

Almost a year later, on December 22, 1873, the California State Legislature authorized the Merced County Board of Supervisors "to issue not to exceed $75,000 in bonds bearing interest at 10 percent per year and payable in 20 years." These funds were earmarked for a courthouse and jail to be located in Courthouse Park at N and Twenty-first streets.

A few days later, the board invited bids for plans. Eight architects responded. On February 13, 1874, the board selected Albert A. Bennett's design. On April 2, A. W. Burrell, who came in with the lowest bid, $55,970, was awarded the construction contract.

On July 8, 1874, after a parade and ceremony, the Masonic Grand Lodge of California laid the cornerstone for the new courthouse. Beneath the cornerstone a casket was placed containing important Merced County documents, copies of newspapers, a complete set of United State coins, and a pint each of wheat and barley.

Just ten months later, on May 5, 1875, the new courthouse was inspected and the reports of the architect and contractor were read. Board Chairman J. K. Mears accepted the building on behalf of the people. The new Merced County Courthouse was duly dedicated. The grand Italianate structure was open for business. Bart Ahren was hired as a janitor to "take charge of the new Court House, wind mill and tank, coal bin, fuel, etc." at a salary of seventy-five dollars a month. The old Snelling Courthouse was put up for sale. A new era had begun.

Merced County Courthouse in 1879. Note the tank house and windmill on the right. Restored and listed in the National Register of Historic Places, this building is now home to the Merced Courthouse Museum. *Courtesy of Merced County Historical Society Archives.*

The county clerk's office in the Merced County Courthouse, c. 1912. Seated, left to right, Catherine Aiken, County Clerk Thornton, Deputy Clerk Lester White. *Courtesy of Merced County Historical Society Archives.*

# The State Architect

Albert A. Bennett was born on July 26, 1825, in Schoharie County, New York. When he was sixteen, he apprenticed as a carpenter and joiner under his brother William. Two years later, he began to study architecture with his brother-in-law Orson Phelps. After a stint in Montgomery, Alabama, where he helped to design the Alabama State Capitol, he and thirteen friends went to New Orleans where they boarded the steamer *Galveston*. When one of the ship's piston rods broke, the captain had to depend on the sails to take his passengers to British Honduras. From there the group chartered an English ship, *Thetus*, to bring them as far as Chagres where they hired small boats to get as far as Gorgonia where they set off on foot for Panama. After a two-month stay, they boarded another ship, the *Alexander Von Humboldt*, and arrived in San Francisco on August 30, 1849, 102 days after they had sailed from New Orleans.

In 1850, Bennett moved to Sacramento and practiced architecture there until 1876 when he became the State Architect, a post he held until 1883. During this time, he worked on the State Capitol and designed eight courthouses for the county seats of Yolo, Stanislaus, Merced, Tulare, Kern, Sonoma, Humboldt, and Fresno counties. Of all of these courthouse buildings, the Merced County Courthouse is the only one that is still standing. Bennett's Fresno County Courthouse was the focus of a huge public debate when, in 1966, the Board of Supervisors voted to demolish it.

In 1883, Bennett returned to San Francisco and opened a private practice. While on his way to Europe in 1890, he became ill. He died in Philadelphia in December 1890.

# The Merced County Courthouse

Architect Albert A. Bennett's 1875 design for the Merced County Courthouse is a stunning example of Italianate architecture. The exterior of the three-story building features Corinthian columns, ornamental urns, and hooded window frames, and is capped by a cupola. The architect designed the building with certain symbolic features. The jail was placed on the ground floor to signify that the prisoners were grounded to the earth. As one ascends the outside front stairway to the first floor, one passes between two light posts—this is the beginning of enlightenment.

The first floor contained the offices of middle management. The second floor was more elaborate and contained the offices of the board of supervisors, the judges, and the court. The cupola, which housed no one, symbolized the heavens.

Atop the cupola is a statue of Minerva, the Goddess of Wisdom. Three sides of the roof are graced by hand carved statues of the Roman Goddess Justica. These are unusual because Bennett insisted that they not wear blindfolds. He did not believe that justice was blind. It is also notable that the side of the building that is not overlooked by Justica is the side that faces Snelling—the former county seat whose citizens opposed the move of county government to the new town of Merced.

Of the eight courthouses Bennett designed, the Merced Courthouse is the only one still standing. It was threatened with demolition, but due to the efforts of a number of concerned citizens, it was saved. After a $1 million restoration project, it is now the Merced County Courthouse Museum and is listed in the National Register of Historic Places.

# The Merced County Courthouse Museum

As the traveler drives up to the front of the Merced County Courthouse, her thoughts are on another, identical courthouse in her hometown of Fresno that thoughtless county leaders demolished in 1966. Looking at the pristine Italianate building that, after a massive restoration and refurbishing project using nearly $1 million in federal, state, and county monies, is listed in the National Register of Historic Places, her eyes follow the lines of the building as they move upward toward the dome. Her eyes fill with tears remembering. Then she walks toward the building, climbs the stairs to the first floor, walks through the front door, and enters the Merced County Courthouse Museum.

Zoe Bishop, docent coordinator for the museum and for the Merced County Historical Society, welcomes the traveler and the museum tour begins. They are standing in a long hallway that stretches to the back of the building. On either side of the hall are offices that now house exhibits. The former treasurer's office still contains its two large safes. The built-in grill and counter are original and were in use until 1975.

Other rooms showcase California Pottery Company crocks that were made at the Merced plant, items from the White House Department Store, a complete blacksmith's shop, and a huge Chinese temple altar from the 1870s that was once located in a building in Merced's Chinatown. The huge room at the end of the hall contains many fascinating treasures, but its centerpiece is "Old Betsy," Merced's first fire engine. An 1853 hand pumper made by William Jeffers & Co. of Pautucket, Rhode Island, it took twelve to sixteen men to pull it and to operate the hand pumps. It was retired in 1906, but is kept in operating condition.

A beautiful staircase with walnut banisters takes the traveler and her guide to the second floor. One room contains schoolroom items. The former board of supervisors' office, which was turned into a display room of early household objects, still has its original furniture from Breuners.

At the end of the hall, the *piece de resistance* awaits. On entering this magnificent former superior courtroom, Zoe said, "This is the miracle room." Before restoration, the room had been stripped of its furnishings and much of its paneling. It was filled with modular office furniture. A huge outreach to the community and a lot of hard work on the part of Merced County Historical Society staff and volunteers resulted in the return of all the original furnishings including the magnificent carved walnut bar that separates the visitors' gallery from the court. It was found at the city dump. Now the room has been returned to its former elegance. One interesting feature is the marble washbasin in the corner near the judge's bench. Here, the judge could wash his hands before each case. Looking upward, the traveler sees gaslight diffused through beautiful glass panels set into the ceiling. It is a room that commands awe and respect.

The tour ends. The traveler departs thinking of the caring people of Merced who fought to keep their historic courthouse. It is now the home of the Merced County Historical Society and a fine museum that shares with its visitors the story of Merced County. For all those who love our great Central Valley, it is well worth a visit.

# El Capitan Hotel

As soon as the Central Pacific Railroad reached Merced in 1872, it was imperative for the owners of the railroad to provide lodgings for their passengers. A temporary structure was erected for this purpose. Meanwhile, a new, elegant hotel was being built next to the railroad at Sixteenth and N streets.

The new hotel, the El Capitan, opened in June 1872. It was a huge structure that dominated the skyline of the small village of Merced. The El Capitan had a ground floor and three upper stories and served as a passenger depot and stage station as well as a hostelry. It was presided over by H. A. Bloss, whose fame as a hotel-keeper was known throughout the country.

The ground floor consisted of elegantly appointed parlors. According to Colleen Stanley Bare, in her book *Pioneer Genius Charles Henry Huffman*, "a large billiard room, bathrooms, shaving and hair-dressing saloon, private clubrooms, bar room, oyster rooms …reading rooms…dancing hall, and a capacious dining room…[were the elegantly appointed parlors on the first floor]." Also on the ground floor were the town's post office, a telegraph office, and express office.

The rooms on the first, second, and third floors were "splendidly furnished, well-lighted and comfortably ventilated parlors, bedrooms, [and] suites of rooms." For guests arriving in Merced, every luxury possible was available at the El Capitan Hotel.

In 1900, the hotel was torn down by the Southern Pacific Railroad. In 1912, a new four-story hotel was built on the northwest corner of Main and M streets. It was called the El Capitan and was erected at a cost of $80,000. It had ninety rooms and forty baths and was the first building in Merced to have an elevator. In 1925, an annex was added. Today the building is no longer standing. It, like its namesake, is just a memory in the history of Merced.

This photo of the El Capitan Hotel in the 1870s shows that it was situated, quite literally, next to the railroad. It also is evident that, for the time, this was a very elegant place to stay. *Courtesy of Merced County Historical Society Archives.*

For most of the soldiers who fought in the Civil War, the memories of their experiences cast a shadow over their lives. That, however, was not the case for Dennis McCarty of Fresno—originally from County Cork, Ireland, where he was born on December 29, 1844.

McCarty's family immigrated to the United States and settled in Kansas. When McCarty was seventeen, he enlisted in the Ninth Kansas Cavalry. It was September 1861. McCarty told the enlisting officer that his birthday was January 3, 1845, so that he would qualify as an eighteen-year-old. He would later joke that he got two birthdays out of the war.

Looking back on his war experiences, he told a reporter for *The Fresno Morning Republican* that he "had a good time in the war." Yes, his feet were frozen a few times and, yes, he spent two winters marching without the opportunity to go into winter quarters, and he did see combat in two or three major battles, but, by and large, his memories were good ones.

McCarty's sense of humor probably played a role in his ability to cope. His company was sent out on picket duty on an island. They were there longer than planned and their food supplies ran out. He and two other soldiers began to forage for something to eat. They saw a fat dog, shot it, and dressed it. They took the meat back to their camp and told their comrades that it was mutton. The meat was cooked and everyone ate it with gusto. When McCarty finally told the others what they had eaten, they refused to believe him. It was too good, they said.

After the Civil War ended, McCarty headed west. After a short stay in San Francisco, he settled in Visalia and moved to Fresno in 1901.

McCarty's stories of the war were often about food. He remembered stealing hot biscuits from a Southern housewife that he ate with stolen honey, but his favorite food of the war, he said, was "a piece of hardtack and a big hunk of raw bacon. It's better than any cake I ever ate."

# William Thomas Riggs

E arly in March 1912, death brought to a close the life of a man who had been a pioneer in a number of communities as he made his way west to Fresno. William Thomas Riggs was born on July 5, 1832, in Harrodsburg, Kentucky. When he was still a child, his family moved to Clay County, Missouri. His only education was two terms in a log cabin schoolhouse twelve miles from his home. In 1847, Riggs' brother-in-law Holmes Hakes, took him to Rock Island, Illinois, and taught him all he knew about the watch repairing and jewelry business. At age seventeen, he headed for the gold fields of California with a party led by Captain Jacks and Andrew Wolf. They arrived at Hangtown in 1849 and mined for three years. Riggs returned to Rock Island with $16,000, entered the jewelry business, and married Fannie Cossom.

Riggs, Hakes, and five other men organized and built the Rock Island and Coal Valley Railroad and also entered the coal mining business. The railroad was later extended to Chicago and Council Bluffs. During the Civil War, Rock Island became the headquarters of the Army of the Mississippi. Riggs' jewelry business thrived. He became involved in a number of other ventures including the Camden Flour Mills and the Rock Island Gas Works.

In 1869, Riggs moved his family to the frontier town of Sioux City and then to Chicago. After suffering major losses in the great fire, he moved his family to Fresno in February 1881. He and his son, Roderick G. Riggs, began a business, Riggs and Son, which would become the largest retail grocery business in the Valley. Twice the business was hit with massive fires. Riggs would move and start again each time. Finally, after losing everything in the Fisk Building fire of 1889, he gave up. Riggs' later years were spent selling magazines to eke out a living.

His March 12, 1912, obituary notice in *The Fresno Morning Republican* was worthy of two columns. In it, the reporter remembered his enterprising spirit that played an important role in building the young city of Fresno. His kindness, gentleness, and good nature toward all who knew him would be his monument. Such nobility of spirit will be remembered in the tales of our Valley.

Memories of the Civil War abound in the tales of members of the Atlanta Post of the Grand Army of the Republic. For these former Union soldiers, the war was never far away—it continued to haunt their dreams as well as their quiet moments. For one Valley resident, J. H. Treanor of Fresno, service began on an August day in 1861 when, although he was only sixteen, he told the enlisting officer he was eighteen so he could join the Union Army in Galena, Illinois. On the eve of his first battle at Fort Henry, he was filled with a deep longing for his mother. He was scared to death, but had to appear to be brave in front of the other soldiers. He survived the battle, but still longed for home.

His unit was continually on the march. It was at Cairo that another kind of war ensued. Cooties attacked his clothes and his person. It was so bad that he threw off his clothes and tossed them into a mud puddle. He went to headquarters and asked for another uniform. When asked where his clothes were, he told the soldier, who then ordered him to retrieve them and put them back on. According to Treanor, "We used to wash our clothes and hang them on the tents and the cooties moved around in them so much that they dried just the same as though there had been a wind."

The lack of clothing for many of the soldiers made the Battle of Shiloh on April 6 and 7, 1862, even more of a nightmare. Treanor said that many of the soldiers were forced to fight in their underwear. He saw Confederate General A. S. Johnston mortally wounded during the battle. One of the soldiers asked for the general's clothes, but was told that he could not have them. Lack of proper, warm clothing brought on severe rheumatism. Treanor was sent to a hospital and soon after was sent home.

Treanor decided to come to California in 1867. He traveled by ship, in steerage with 1,400 Chinese. He arrived in San Francisco—a city that he didn't like. He came to Fresno and became an active member of the Atlanta Post 92 of the Grand Army of the Republic. He held the position of chaplain for many years. Like other G.A.R. members, his memories of the war remained uppermost in his mind and now have been duly recorded in the tales of our Valley.

# The Watchmaker

The story of a Fresno watchmaker named Albert Riley begins in Coventry, England. In order to learn his vocation, he became an apprentice to a stern jeweler named William Taylor. The year was 1864. Riley was only fourteen, but the terms of his seven-year indenture made him a virtual slave. The document said, "The apprentice his master shall faithfully serve, his secrets keep, his lawful commands everywhere gladly do; he shall do no damage to his said master, nor see it done by others, but to his power shall tell or forthwith give warning; he shall not waste the goods of his master nor lend them unlawfully to any; he shall not contract matrimony, shall not play cards, dice or any other unlawful games, shall not haunt taverns or playhouses, or absent himself from his master's service day or night, unlawfully." It was the twenty-eighth year of Queen Victoria's reign.

During the seven years and three months of his apprenticeship, Riley received four shillings and three pence per week ($1.06). When he completed his service, in 1871, he won his freedom by taking the Oath of a Freeman in Coventry. A few years later he left for the United States and found a job with the Elgin Company. Six years passed and he decided to head west. He arrived in Fresno in 1884 and immediately went to work for H. C. Warner.

In 1884, watches were made by hand and the skilled craftsmanship that Riley brought to the Warner Company was an important component in building the store's reputation for quality.

Albert Riley also took part in civic affairs and served as the exalted ruler of the local Elks Lodge. He had watched the city grow from a tiny village to a bustling city. He was honored in the pages of *The Fresno Morning Republican* on January 6, 1924, as he celebrated sixty years as a watchmaker. He told the reporter that he still considered his workbench at the Warner Company his favorite place to be. He was a man who had found his true calling in life. It had been a long journey, but a fulfilling one.

# Lyon—Fresno's Hot Tamale Champion

At summer's end it seems only fitting to dip one's pen into the well of local history for the summer of 1904. A lot was happening—events were being planned for the Fourth of July, Fresnans were making travel plans, and ways were explored to keep oneself cool. And, of course, that P. T. Barnum of Fresno…that most outrageous businessman of Broadway…that most eloquent writer of advertising copy was at it again. W. Parker Lyon's summer ad was something to behold. The title said simply, "Chew This."

"A Toothless Monkey, exalted upon a box of Tuti-Fruti-Ti and calmly chewing his own tail, is a tolerable pleasing spectacle of misdirected reform.

"A Shovel Bill Hog inserting his nose under a running truck with the idea of lifting it over his head is a high type of hopeless endeavor.

"An Enraged Hen pecking at a sunbeam in a pan of water is an instructive example of unrequited zeal.

"Other Furniture Dealers trying to undersell W. Parker Lyon, when he is the acknowledged Champion of Low Prices reminds one of a compound cathartic impossibility, things that are dreamed, but not actual occurrences. I am the leader, the people all admit and this is why I am enjoying such a wide scope of notoriety and success."

The ad was signed, "W. Parker Lyon, Hot Tamale Champion of Champions and a future President of the United States. Dispenser of the best 75 cent chair on the earth."

The heat of a Fresno summer made most folks want to just sit in the shade and pray for a cooling breeze. For the irrepressible Mr. Lyon, it only seemed to make him wax more eloquently than usual.

# A Gathering of Pioneers

On the evening of June 24, 1904, the parlor of the Hughes Hotel became the gathering place for sixty gentlemen who had come to Fresno before 1885 and who had all played a role in the earliest years of Fresno County and the fledgling village of Fresno Station. So warm were the welcomes on every hand, so energetic were the memories each person evoked that the cocktail hour lasted well past the time set. Someone looked at his watch and announced that the dinner hour was at hand. They all adjourned to the Hughes' banquet room for what would prove to be a memorable occasion.

Dr. Chester Rowell was the toastmaster for the evening. He began by introducing John Byrd, who came to Fresno County in 1858, and called upon him to speak. Byrd, being a modest man, said he only wanted to listen. When Rowell introduced A. M. Clark, who arrived in California in 1867, it was a different story. Clark was delighted to share his mining experiences in the streams of the Sierra before coming to Fresno County. Thomas Brown stood up and regaled the group with the story of his arrival. The year was 1868. He came driving a band of cattle and found work on the Easterby Rancho. He built a one-room shack out of 300 shakes for his shelter. Leo Gundelfinger remembered that by 1876, so many people were moving to Fresno it felt crowded so the pioneers were beginning to move into "unsettled areas."

One after another the gentlemen got up to speak—each one sharing important memories. Then A. M. Drew rose to talk about "The Pioneers Who Have Fallen by the Way." He paid tribute to those who had died—Moses Church, Dr. Lewis Leach, Henry Clay Daulton, and numerous others—men who had truly built Fresno County.

The evening ended with remarks by Mayor L. O. Stephens, who told the group, "If you and I do the work here we ought to do our children and grandchildren will find much to be thankful for when they grow up and make [Fresno] their home."

Henry Clay Daulton, early cattleman and member of the board of supervisors. *Courtesy of Robert M. Wash.*

Dr. Lewis Leach, first Fresno County Physician, began the Fresno County Hospital at Millerton. *Courtesy of Robert M. Wash.*

Dr. Chester Rowell, founder of *The Fresno Morning Republican,* mayor of Fresno, and state senator. *Courtesy of Robert M. Wash.*

On the night of June 24, 1904, when the pioneers of Fresno County assembled to break bread together and to share memories, Dr. Chester Rowell acted as toastmaster. During his opening remarks after dinner, he told some remarkable personal stories about his early days in Fresno.

Shortly after he came to Fresno in 1874, Dr. Rowell was invited to dinner at the Kutner-Goldstein home. As conversation proceeded around the table, Rowell turned to Dr. Graves of Centerville and told him about his vision for the development of agriculture in the Valley. Graves' reply was an emphatic, "It's only good for sheep!" Rowell told the group that he still took great delight in reminding Graves of his comment.

This story reminded Rowell of another gentleman who was unable to see the vision he had for the county. Jonathan Rea, who lived in the mountains, tried in vain to convince Gustav Eisen that he should not come to the Fresno area. "Thank goodness," Rowell said, "that Eisen did not heed his advice." Eisen's contributions to Valley agriculture laid the foundation for all that followed. "Those people," Rowell continued, "did not realize that nature makes no place for nothing. Neither does nature make any place so perfect that man has nothing left to do but live in it."

Dr. Rowell ended his remarks by paying tribute to the memory of Dr. Lewis Leach, the pioneer doctor of Fresno County. He also told a story. It seems that one of Leach's patients died. A friend volunteered to sit up all night with the body. After a couple of hours the friend got thirsty and decided to leave for a bit to find something to quench his thirst. The drink was so refreshing that he had several more. While he was gone, a cat wandered into the room where the body was laid out and ate the nose off the corpse. When the man returned, he took one look at his dead friend and exclaimed, "Hic...Tom you was a pretty good looking chap two hours ago, but now I don't think they'll let you into Hell!"

# The Missing Wine and the Tall, White Hat

At the gathering of pioneers at the Hughes Hotel on the evening of June 24, 1904, not only were memories shared and tributes given, but a great deal of fun was had. Laughter filled the banquet hall that night.

Dr. Chester Rowell, who served as toastmaster, was at his best. He decided to have a little fun at the expense of A. M. Clark, who had come to the county in 1867. It seems there were a couple of questions on everyone's mind that needed answers.

Rowell recognized John C. Nourse who rose to ask Mr. Clark if he remembered the wedding of Judge Hart. On that festive day, the judge put a great deal of wine in a cellar and told the assembled guests that this wine would be served at his silver wedding anniversary. Clark was given the key to the cellar—he became responsible for the wine. On the day of the silver anniversary, the bottles were brought up from the cellar and made ready to be opened. To the surprise of the people uncorking the bottles, they were filled with water, not wine. "How could that happen?" Nourse wanted to know. Clark remained silent.

Rowell retook the floor. He said that in the earliest days of the county there was only one registered Republican. He lived in the mountains and, on election days, he would come down, cast his vote for the Republican ticket, and return home. One day this man was sent a tall, white hat. The man gave it to Mr. Clark and told him to keep it until the day a Republican was elected to an office in Fresno County. When that day came, the man wanted Mr. Clark, who was at that time a county official, to give the Republican officer holder the hat.

Many years later, when that day finally arrived, someone asked about the hat. It was nowhere to be found. "Where," Dr. Rowell asked Clark, "did the hat go?" Mr. Clark smiled to himself and remained silent. By this time, the room filled with laughter. Wherever the hat had gone would never be known—it would remain forever a minor mystery in the tales of our Valley.

# First Chinese Baptist Church–Mission Years

The First Chinese Baptist Church began, in 1884, as a mission in a two-story building at 805 E Street. Established by Frances Potter, wife of the minister of the First Baptist Church, the land and building were purchased with funds raised by the Chinese community, Mrs. Potter, and the American Baptist Home Missionary Society. After Mrs. Potter's sudden death at age forty-six, her missionary work among the Chinese in Fresno was carried on by others until 1888, when Sarah Stein, who had worked as a missionary of the Southern Baptist Convention in Canton, arrived in Fresno to assume the missionary duties here. By 1895, Miss Stein had enrolled one hundred and thirty-five pupils in the church school. For the next twenty-five years, Miss Stein's commitment bore fruit as the number of people attending the programs of the mission grew.

The arrival of missionaries Amy Purcell and Ruth Nelson, in 1918, launched another period of continued growth. Miss Purcell won the trust of the Chinese people by going into their homes, helping the sick, teaching the women domestic arts, and teaching English.

In 1939, the Chinese Baptist Christian Center was established with Mr. Edward Tong serving as minister. The mission had been moved to 1053 E Street in 1915. Now, with its new name, it moved again to 610 Tulare Street—at the corner of Waterman. Next to the old structure, a new chapel was built.

Mr. Tong left in 1943 to become the director of the Chung Mei home in El Cerrito.

In 1945, under the leadership of the pastor of the Chinese Baptist Christian Center, Dr. John Hestenes, the mission was organized as the First Chinese Baptist Church. The church and the Chinese Center, from that point on, worked together.

Our story will continue…

# First Chinese Baptist Church-

In our previous story, we learned about the beginning of the Chinese Baptist mission in 1884 and how it grew into the First Chinese Baptist Church.

In 1954, the Reverend Edward Tong was called again as minister of the church. Under his leadership, the programs for young people grew to such an extent that for several years, one church service was turned over to the youth. A number of years before, the church had organized Boy Scout Troop 10. In 1958, Reverend Tong organized Boy Scout Troop 33. Three doctors, an optometrist and an architect, who had all been in Troop 10 as young boys, took on the leadership of the new troop. Due to their commitment, five Eagle Scouts completed their badges. This was a proud moment for Fresno's Chinese community.

In 1959, the church became self-supporting and, in 1960, was incorporated. Plans were underway for a new sanctuary. On March 25, 1962, a new church on Waterman Street, designed by architect Allen Lew, was dedicated. In September of that year, the congregation invited the Fresno community to their first "Food and Fun Festival"—an event that still is held.

In 1991, with so many members no longer living in West Fresno, the congregation decided to move north. A parcel of land was purchased at Mesa and Angus streets. Architect Jim Leong, Allen Lew's son-in-law, was hired to design a new church building. The old property was sold and, for two years, the congregation held their services at San Joaquin Gardens.

In November 1995 the first services were held in the new church building. Many of the components from the historic church were incorporated into the new structure. The cross, communion table, and stained glass Resurrection Memorial Window behind the baptistry blend beautifully into their new setting. Ten new stained glass windows, five on each side of the church, each portray one of the "I Am's" of the Gospels. Two large centennial banners, designed by the late Donna Kaye Leong and made by the women of the church, also hang in the sanctuary.

On Saturday, October 2, 2004, the members of the First Chinese Baptist Church celebrated their 120th birthday. With a long history of service to their church, the members are aware of the unique role they have played in the history of the Fresno community.

# Josiah Royce Hall

On the morning of October 15, 2002, smoke began to pour out of the upper part of historic Royce Hall on the Fresno High School campus. Fire trucks raced to the scene—within minutes firemen were pouring water on the blaze, ultimately putting out the fire.

When the smoke had cleared and the damage could be assessed, the task facing the school was staggering. Two classrooms on the third floor were lost. Water had run through the building down to the basement—not only doing extensive water damage, but bringing with it lead-filled paint that attached itself to everything. Since there was asbestos under the floor tiles, the state brought in HAZMAT, the hazardous material team. The south side of the building was hit particularly hard.

What were they going to do? It was imperative to save the building. After all, Royce Hall is the only tangible symbol left of the historic campus and its importance as a symbol to the entire neighborhood cannot be overstated. Luckily, a major modernization of the whole campus had already been planned. Money was available for that project and, out of those monies, funds were available to restore Royce Hall.

The firm of Temple-Andersen-Moore Architects was hired to be the consultants for the project. According to Martin Temple, himself a graduate of the school, they did a "restoration with a little bit of artistic interpretation."

Principal Robert Reyes said that the completion of the project has brought a renewal of school spirit. "When you almost lose something, you realize how precious it is. The 1922 plans for the building showed medallions and sconces on the walls [of the main hall] that were never put up," Mr. Reyes said. Jack Fowler and the FHS Alumni Association members took on that project. Royce Hall is now painted in shades of lavender with highlights of gold. It is stunning!

Out of the ashes of a devastating fire came a new beginning for this historic building. It is once again the centerpiece of Fresno High School and the neighborhood that surrounds it. For all the generations of students who have learned within its walls, it will forever be a reminder of the great traditions of their school and of the treasured memories of their years at Fresno High.

# Gustav Eisen's Dates

Gustav Eisen, a horticulturist by education and profession, arrived in Fresno in 1873 and partnered with his brother, Francis, on a whole host of agricultural projects. Several years later, Eisen left Fresno. From time to time, he would write letters to the editor of *The Fresno Morning Republican* either to share a memory with its readers or to provide a correction to an item appearing in its pages. His letters still manage to fascinate and to inform.

In a letter written from Rome on August 6, 1912, Gustav Eisen wishes to correct some information given about date trees that he planted in the Eisen Vineyard—in so doing he educates the reader about date production.

Eisen purchased the finest dates he could find in San Francisco, brought them to Fresno, and set out the seeds from this fruit in 1874. In 1875 and 1876, he received a different variety of dates from Mrs. Cubillas of Hermosillo, Mexico. The seeds from these dates were carefully planted in beds near the others. In 1877, sixty date palm trees were beginning to grow. Eisen took these trees and replanted them near his house although the soil in this location was not the best for date production. It seems that every other available spot was either taken up with vineyards or was open to attack by sheep, horses, or rabbits.

As the trees grew and produced fruit, Eisen was amazed to discover that the seeds of the Mexican dates bore a fruit that was superior to any of the Turkish or Arabian dates on the other trees. In quality and size, he found them equal to the best yellow dates from Tunis. Their only shortcoming was that they ripened later in the season and, therefore, were not as suitable for production in the San Joaquin Valley.

Gustav Eisen signed off his letter with the words, "with salutations to Fresno," and now his memories of planting the first date palms in the Central Valley have been duly recorded in the tales of our Valley.

Late in the evening of April 8, 1927, one of Fresno's businessmen passed away quietly in his home. He could not truly qualify as a pioneer because he arrived in Fresno in 1889, after the incorporation of the city, but he had played an active role in the business and religious life of the community and he remembered the young city of Fresno.

Albert Downing Olney and his family left their home in Peoria, Illinois, and arrived in Fresno on April 15, 1889. In an interview he granted to *The Fresno Morning Republican* a year before his death, he remembered what Fresno looked like. The Hughes Hotel had just been completed, but none of the streets were paved. "When it rained…the streets were inches deep in mud. At the crossings of the principal streets downtown, planks were put across the gutters so that a person could walk without sinking to his shoe tops."

Olney remembered the horse car lines. One of the lines extended to Belmont Avenue, which was way out in the country. He also shared his memory of a spectacular fire that wiped out most of the buildings on Mariposa Street between Fulton Street and Broadway.

Shortly after his arrival in Fresno, he bought out the interest of John Jonsen in the firm of Kirk & Jonsen. The firm, which dealt in the retail shoe business, was then known as Kirk & Olney. After Kirk was elected school superintendent in 1890, he sold his interest to Jonsen. The firm was thereafter called Olney & Jonsen and remained so until Olney's retirement just a month before he died.

Olney also was an active member of the First Presbyterian Church, serving as an officer for many years.

A. D. Olney was survived by two sons, Walter and Albert C., who was principal of Fresno High School. His daughter Ruby was the society editor for *The Fresno Morning Republican*. His other daughter, Bernice, taught at Fresno High for many years and will still be remembered by the alumni of that school.

# A Flood on a Spring Night

In February 1927, pioneer Abram Henry Hensley shared a number of memories with a reporter for *The Fresno Morning Republican*. Hensley arrived in California in 1853 after a grueling trip across the plains from Missouri.

By the time the Civil War broke out, Hensley had left the northern gold fields and found his way to Millerton. Hensley had witnessed gunfights on the Fresno and San Joaquin rivers—it was a wild time when men took justice into their own hands.

Two experiences during the early 1860s stood out in his mind. He happened to be at Fort Miller when an express rider appeared, riding as fast as possible—he was bringing word of General Robert E. Lee's surrender at Appomattox. He was also at the fort the day another rider brought the news of President Abraham Lincoln's death.

Hensley put his money into the sheep business. He built a home for his growing family on an island in the San Joaquin River. A second home was built on a higher part of the island. On a spring night in 1867, the family was sleeping in the home on lower ground. They were awakened by water lapping across the floor. The water was rising fast so they all went to the other house on higher ground. The river was flooding dangerously. They realized they couldn't swim to shore—the night was moonless and the flooding river was filled with logs. Seeing no alternative, they began to knock down the wood partitions inside the house. From these they made a raft. With the howling wind and roaring river making their hoped-for escape rather frightening, they launched their raft, got on board, and made it to shore.

While they stood on the river's bank, they realized they had forgotten to turn off their lantern—it was still lighting their house. Suddenly the lamp began to sway back and forth. They watched as their home, rather like some phantom ship, began to move down the river.

One of the most memorable figures of the early twentieth century temperance movement was a woman who was born in Garrard County, Kentucky, on November 25, 1846. Ill health, her mother's unstable temperament, her adored father's frequent absences from home, and the uncertain finances of her family marked her childhood years. All these combined to create an unstable situation for a child.

The family moved to Belton, Missouri, and it was there, in 1865, that she met Dr. Charles Gloyd. They were married on November 21, 1867. It was an unfortunate marriage. Dr. Gloyd was an alcoholic. The couple separated shortly before the birth of their daughter, Charlien. He died a few months later.

Our young woman completed her education and obtained a teaching certificate, but was unable to make enough money to support her child. She met Dr. David A. Nation, an attorney, minister, and newspaper editor. They were married on December 27, 1877. Our young woman, Carry A. Nation, had now acquired the name that would go down in history. They settled in Houston, Texas, and remained there until 1889 when Dr. Nation was called to serve a church in Medicine Lodge, Kansas.

The voters of Kansas had passed a constitutional amendment in 1880 that outlawed the manufacture and sale of alcoholic beverages. However, the saloonkeepers violated the law by openly selling alcohol. Carry A. Nation helped found the Woman's Temperance Union and served as a jail evangelist. She asked God to help her save Kansas. She believed that God was calling her to carry a nation to prohibition. On June 1, 1890, with a hatchet in hand, she walked into a bar and began smashing liquor bottles and bar fixtures. For the next ten years, she would go into bars alone or with a band of hymn-singing women. As prayers were said and songs were sung, she would get busy with her little hatchet and do what she considered to be God's work. She was arrested more than thirty times.

A large woman—she was almost six feet tall—with a resounding voice, she was a formidable figure. She lived the last few years of her life at Hatchet House, a home for abused women that she established in Eureka Springs, Arkansas. After becoming ill, she moved to Leavenworth, Kansas, to the home of her sister-in-law. She died on June 9, 1911. A few years before her death she came to Fresno and provided fine entertainment for the local folks. This story will follow.

# The Woman with the Hatchet Comes to Town

The quiet of a warm spring Fresno night was broken by the sounds of a train pulling into the Santa Fe station. It was midnight and the platform was deserted except for a couple of men hoping to earn a little money carrying suitcases. A few passengers stepped off the train. One of them was a very tall, very formidable looking woman dressed entirely in black save for a large piece of white lace at her throat. She looked around and seeing policeman Frank Nelson asked him where she might find a hotel without a bar. He directed her to the California Hotel. She went there immediately and on the hotel register wrote the following words: "Carry A. Nation, I am living Home Defender, Topeka, Kansas." The woman with the hatchet had arrived in Fresno. She was going to speak that night in Armory Hall.

The residents of Fresno were well aware of Mrs. Nation's reputation for smashing saloons and their liquor with her little hatchet. Fresno, since its very inception, had been a saloon town. Now the forces of temperance and reform were working to change that. A reform administration was running the city. Carry Nation had arrived on fertile ground to espouse her message against alcohol.

Not everyone in Fresno was rejoicing in her visit. The saloon-keepers were more than a little worried about their property. The local churches, although their congregations would probably attend her speech in Armory Hall, would not allow her on their premises. They literally barred their doors. It was first thought that Carry Nation would speak at the Adventist Church; indeed, the Prohibition Alliance was said to have rented the building for ten dollars. But the minister said no. The Christian Church found they had another commitment for their sanctuary that night. So the Armory Hall was going to be the setting for Carry's talk.

It was going to be a memorable night in Fresno, that's for sure.

# Carry Nation at Armory Hall

On the evening of March 31, 1903, Armory Hall was filled to capacity. All of the few chairs were taken and every other possible spot where one could stand was occupied. It was a very warm night and, for some reason, the janitor, who had been hired at the top rate of twenty-five dollars for the evening, decided not to open the windows. It was definitely going to be a hot time in Fresno this night.

The free program opened with a song or two by the Alliance Glee Club accompanied on the piano by Mrs. W. W. Wharton. A prayer by the Reverend C. C. French brought the rather boisterous crowd into line. The hall was silent. The Reverend J. W. Webb strode to the podium to address the crowd with "My Personal Experience in Saloon Smashing." The crowd wasn't very interested—they were eagerly awaiting the principal speaker. Webb's talk was mercifully short.

Then, accompanied by Judge J. B. Campbell, Carry Nation walked on to the stage. Her formidable appearance—she was almost six feet tall—caused a hush to fall over the crowd. She began to lecture the assembled multitude in a voice that filled every corner of the hall. "I understand the large churches wouldn't have me there," said she, "and we had to come here…they think I will chop up the Bible, I suppose…[and] the saloons. They ought to be smashed. They're smashing communities, smashing homes, smashing lives, smashing souls into hell."

"Oh," she cried, "God will curse [the] men behind [the saloons]."

As she warmed up to her topic, the rapidity with which she spoke increased. "I am not a temperance worker…I'm a prohibitionist. God formed the Prohibitionist party." She told the audience that she had used her hatchet to destroy as many saloons as she could. Their hatchet was the vote and she urged them to use their vote wisely. "God put a jaw-bone in the hands of Samson and it raised an agitation," she said. "God put a hatchet in the hands of Carry Nation and it waked you all up."

When Carry Nation finished speaking, the sweltering members of the audience generously opened their wallets and filled the collection plate. They also purchased little platinum hatchets to wear as pins.

Yes, indeed, it was a hot time in Fresno when Carry Nation came to town.

# *Thanksgiving 1894*

In the fall of 1894, Fresnans were just beginning to come out of the serious financial troubles brought about by the economic depression of the late 1880s. Pocketbooks were still feeling the pinch of bad times and, for many in the community who had lost their jobs, Thanksgiving was not going to be the joyous holiday that it usually was.

F. F. Letcher, chairman of the board of supervisors, took matters into his own hands. Because of his position, he knew firsthand the needs of families in Fresno. He asked the nonsectarian ladies' group dedicated to good works, the King's Daughters, if they would organize donations for the needy families of the community. Mrs. Lucius Baker, president of the King's Daughters, readily accepted the task. She and the other ladies of the organization began to solicit donations of food and clothing. Chairman Letcher personally visited many downtown businesses and obtained donations of larger items like bedding and mattresses. He also began a clothing drive—asking Fresnans to bring clothing to his home for distribution to the families who needed it.

In the windows of the butcher shops, turkeys were advertised at twelve to fifteen cents a pound. Frozen oysters were available for stuffing and cranberries were priced at fifteen cents a quart. For the affluent in town, their Thanksgiving tables would be filled with traditional fare.

The First Baptist Church planned a service of song and praise on Thanksgiving morning. Saint James' Episcopal Church was also planning a service at the same time.

When asked by a reporter for *The Fresno Morning Republican* if he was thankful on this day of Thanksgiving, chairman Letcher said, "I am as happy as a clam." So, too, were the many families in Fresno who, because of Letcher and the others who responded to his call, had a joyous Thanksgiving after all.

As all Americans know, the very first Thanksgiving was celebrated by the colonists at Plymouth to give thanks for their first harvest. We may not all know how the legal holiday of Thanksgiving came about.

Before 1879, each colony chose a date for a Thanksgiving celebration. In 1879, President George Washington issued a proclamation decreeing that November 26 would be a day of Thanksgiving. In spite of this, Thanksgiving continued to be observed on different days in different states.

The editor of the popular *Godey's Lady's Book*, Sarah Josepha Hale, decided to do something about this. She began to write letters to governors and presidents asking them to declare Thanksgiving Day a national holiday. She spent thirty years at this task.

On October 3, 1863, President Abraham Lincoln issued a proclamation that called for the observance of the fourth Tuesday of November as a national holiday. The president urged prayers to "implore the interposition of the Almighty to heal the wounds of the nations" and to give thanks for the "blessing of fruitful fields and healthful skies."

In 1939, President Franklin D. Roosevelt moved Thanksgiving to the third Thursday in November in order to boost the economy by prolonging the Christmas shopping season. After many protests to this move, he changed the holiday to the fourth Thursday in 1941. Also in 1941, Congress made Thanksgiving Day a legal holiday.

It is Benjamin Franklin we have to thank for the tradition of serving turkey on Thanksgiving Day. Pumpkin pie is a more recent addition to the traditional feast. What is not new is the giving of thanks on the part of those who observe this holiday.

Some time ago, the story was told of twenty-nine-year-old police officer Harry S. Van Meter, the first Fresno policeman to die in the line of duty. The date was February 21, 1907. A short time later, another twenty-nine-year-old man was hired to take his place. His name was Steele Davis and, when he was sworn in, he was given Van Meter's star which he proudly wore until he retired in 1921.

Davis was a large man. He was over six feet tall and weighed more than two hundred pounds. He had a loud, booming voice that could carry a great distance and, over his long career, was responsible for scaring more than a few criminals into giving up. He carried a number of scars earned in gun battles; a bullet lodged in his chest from an encounter in Chinatown remained with him forever. This last wound caused the department to transfer him to another duty—that of court bailiff.

Davis' memories of his years on the force painted a picture of the enduring struggles of the tenderloin district. Since Chinatown had been his beat, he was well acquainted with all the colorful characters—some of whom lived outside the law—that resided in that part of Fresno. One night during a raid on an opium den and a gambling parlor at China Alley and Tulare Street, Davis and other officers surrounded two buildings. Davis' foghorn voice ordered the men to come out. When they refused, the officers entered the buildings and arrested fifty men, handcuffed them, and marched them in pairs right through downtown to the city jail. In the days before a police patrol, officers were required to march their prisoners to jail. Amazingly, few escaped.

Davis remembered the days when the police would raid opium parlors and carry thousands of dollars worth of drugs and opium pipes to police headquarters—often without bothering to get a search warrant. One night Davis and two other officers saw seven men enter a building rather surreptitiously. The officers followed the men inside and searched the building—it was empty. Davis fell to his knees and began to touch the wood floor. He soon touched a spring that raised a fake wall. There were the seven men hiding behind it.

At the time of Steele Davis' retirement in 1921, a grateful city awarded him a pension for his years of service to the community. Van Meter's star was one of his most treasured possessions and he would proudly share Van Meter's story with all who asked.

# Angus Marion Clark

In the early hours of December 1, 1907, death brought to an end the life of one of Fresno County's earliest pioneers. Angus Marion Clark died at his home on I Street (Broadway) surrounded by his wife and four children.

*A. M. Clark was Fresno County clerk from 1873 to 1884. Courtesy of Robert M. Wash*

Clark was born on August 31, 1831, in Madison County, Mississippi, into a farming family. Clark received his early education in a log cabin schoolhouse. Like so many others, Clark came west in 1850 and tried his luck in the gold mining camps of the California foothills. In 1867, Clark came to Millerton and got involved in the Buchanan Copper Mine near Raymond.

In 1873, Clark was elected to the combined post of Fresno County clerk and recorder—a job he would hold for eleven years. When the county seat moved from Millerton to Fresno in the fall of 1874, it was Clark's responsibility to transfer all the county records to Fresno. A year later, he took part in laying the cornerstone for the historic courthouse.

In 1878, he formed an abstract business with William H. McKenzie—Clark & McKenzie. The successful partnership lasted for many years. In 1884, the business of the office of county clerk and recorder had increased so much that it was made into two positions. Clark resigned and, with his partner McKenzie, bought a controlling interest in the Fresno Loan and Savings Bank—one of the most successful of such institutions in Fresno. In 1885, Clark was elected to the California State Assembly where he served one term. He also served on the Fresno school board, the city's board of trustees, and as city recorder.

He never lost his love for mining. He and two partners organized the Harrow Gold Mining Company. Their mines were located in the foothills near Millerton and produced well for many years.

Angus Clark's first wife and mother of his four children, Emma Gildon, died in 1880. His second wife, Sarah Bemis, survived him.

Many of our tales of the Valley have talked about Fresno's Chinatown. How did the Chinese first come to California and then to Fresno?

In 1844, two men and a woman servant stepped off a boat in San Francisco—they were first Chinese immigrants in California. By 1850, the Gold Rush had brought hordes of Chinese to the gold fields of the California foothills—poverty and famine in China caused these men to leave their families and to come to California to seek their fortune. Their family associations or tongs supported these men until they found gold—the tongs expected to be repaid.

Many of the miners resented these newcomers, often forcing them to work claims that had been abandoned by someone else. A large group of Chinese miners drifted south to Rootville (Millerton) on the San Joaquin River. The same situation existed here, but the Chinese miners patiently worked the abandoned claims and often found gold that had been overlooked. By 1878, three hundred Chinese miners were working both sides of a thirty-mile stretch of the San Joaquin River.

There were several Chinese businessmen who had established stores in Millerton. Tong Sing and Hop Wo had each built a brick building in the center of the community—alongside the businesses run by white businessmen. In 1867, some of the influential white businessmen decided the Chinese, with their odd dress and unfamiliar customs, should not be allowed to live or do business in Millerton. The Fresno County Board of Supervisors passed a law that forced the Chinese to move to an area up river from Millerton. Ironically, this was a profitable move for the Chinese. They were nearer Fort Miller, making their stores much more convenient shopping places for the soldiers.

This story of segregation is a sad chapter in the history of Fresno County. Our story will continue...

# A Sad New Year's Eve

While the inhabitants of other foothill communities might be involved in planning and celebrating the arrival of the New Year, the citizens of Millerton were busy doing something else.

On the evening of December 30, 1867, a meeting was called to discuss a topic that seemed to be uppermost in the minds of Millerton residents—the relocation of the Chinese population to an area outside the town and the rebuilding of that part of the town they had formerly occupied.

J. Scott Ashman was appointed chairman and William Faymonville secretary of the meeting. Jefferson Shannon made a motion that a committee of five be chosen to "ascertain and define the limits of Millerton within which no Chinese inhabitants shall be allowed to reside" and that a reconstruction plan for Millerton be drafted. C. H. Hart, Ira Stroud, Lewis Leach, Jefferson Shannon, and Otto Froelich were chosen to serve on the committee by a unanimous vote. They were instructed to report the next evening at a meeting at the courthouse.

At precisely 7 p.m. on December 31, 1867, the second meeting was called to order. The committee presented the following resolution: "That all persons wishing to erect buildings for the occupation of Chinese be requested to build on the west side of the first creek below Shannon's House." They also suggested that a road be established that would run from the fourth post on the east side of Shannon's fence to a stake below Greiersen's adobe house. The road would continue in a straight line to Denny's brick store. The resolutions were unanimously adopted. A motion was made to request that all Chinese female inhabitants move to the new area "as soon as the same can be effected without serious detriment to themselves or to those whose property they are at present occupying."

The meeting was adjourned. It was not a happy New Year for the Chinese living along the San Joaquin River.

# Fresno's Chinatown–The First Chapter

When the Central Pacific Railroad line reached Fresno Station in April 1872, it was due to the manual labor of hundreds of Chinese immigrants and their white overseers. The railroad continued south, but later many of these Chinese returned and settled in Fresno.

Ah Kit, a blacksmith, was one in the first group of Chinese to move from Millerton to Fresno. He built a new shop on I (Broadway) Street. Two other Chinese businessmen built their stores nearby. In a repeat performance of the situation at Millerton, a town meeting was called. Everyone attended and signed a pledge not to sell land east of the railroad tracks to anyone who was Chinese. Ah Kit, whose best friend and business partner was Jefferson Shannon, land agent for the railroad, was not forced to move. But, he soon chose to join other Chinese businessmen and moved west of the tracks where he could buy land. This was the beginning of Fresno's Chinatown.

Tong Duck, also known as Sam Chee, made a business out of hauling the property of many of Millerton's citizens to Fresno. He then built a building at 1035 G Street. Lew Yick relocated his butcher shop from Millerton to Fresno. He later built a building in the 900 block of G Street that housed the Bow On Tong Association and their Kong Chow joss house.

Tong Sing and Tong Duck, who headed the Sam Yup Company, built a joss house on China Alley in 1889. Another former Millerton resident, laundry owner Hi Loy Wong, built a brick building in the 900 block of G Street that later housed the Rescue Mission. He also was a teacher of Confucianism.

Our story will continue…

As other Chinese residents moved into Chinatown, the neighborhood took on a color and mystique that other areas of Fresno lacked. Narrow China Alley between F and G and Inyo and Tulare streets had an atmosphere all its own. Many of the one- and two-story brick buildings had rooflines that extended over the walkways, cutting off the sun. The windows of these buildings had long vertical iron bars and metal shutters to protect the valuable merchandise inside, not the least of which was the gold that was stored there. It would never see the inside of a bank vault.

China Alley was quiet during the day, the street dotted only with a few elderly men sitting by open doors, but, at night, the alley came alive, bustling with activity. Games of mahjong and dominos brought men into some of the storefronts. Shop windows filled with silk kimonos, jade, and teakwood offered another kind of allure. The pioneer herbalist shop of Bow Tsee Hong was located at 1018 China Alley. Opium dens and gambling parlors were prevalent throughout Chinatown—they managed to stay just outside of the law—barring their doors to the police when necessary.

One enterprising merchant, Al Ming, fostered a story about a huge underground tunnel that honeycombed the city. Visitors from other parts of Fresno and other valley towns would come to Chinatown hoping to be given the tour. The myth exists to this day.

Through the years of World War I, Chinatown continued to be a community apart. Then many of the residents either began to go back to China or their children became assimilated into the greater Fresno community. Other nationalities had begun to move into West Fresno at or just before the turn of the century. California's second largest Chinatown became a mosaic of many cultures.

# A Fire on China Alley

China Alley, in 1908, was a colorful street with buildings clustered as close together as possible—it was a veritable rabbit warren of buildings—some built in back of others crowding into any available space on F and G streets. Many of the structures were brick, with interiors that were partitioned with wood. Other buildings were wood shanties. It was a fire chief's nightmare just waiting to happen.

Since the 1880s, a Chinese theater had occupied a place in the middle of the east side of the block between Mariposa and Tulare streets. The three-story building, owned by Tong Duck, had been used for Chinese plays. In recent years, it had been vacant save for three families living in its basement. The fire department had declared it a dangerous building.

On the night of August 16, 1908, a fire alarm was set off at Box 13 on Tulare and F streets. By the time Fire Chief Ward and his men arrived, flames were shooting upward from the Chinese theater. China Alley was filled with crowds of people trampling over each other as they tried to flee the flames. The families of Wong Fu and Sam Wing lived in close proximity to the theater and were among those running from the scene.

Chief Ward ordered his men to run a fire hose through the rooms of the Chinese Reform Association on G Street to the back of the theater. Deputy Chief Polson and his men took up positions in front of the building, turning the full force of water on the flames. After a grueling hour of battling the conflagration, the fire was put out.

The next morning, China Alley was the scene of clean-up activity and of great relief that things hadn't been worse. The Fresno Gas & Electric works, located across the street from the theater, had not caught fire. That would truly have been a spectacular sight, but not the kind of event any sane person would want to witness. It seems that God was watching over Chinatown on that hot August night.

# A Christmas Tree for Fresno

The first Christmas season in Fresno Station was one devoid of any special celebrations. The rain fell continually in December 1872, beating a constant rhythm on the roofs of the few frame houses and stores. The dirt streets were muddy and, in places, almost impassable. There were no trees in sight—indeed the nearest tree was twenty miles away. It was a dismal scene—the only joy seemed to be in the eyes of those who were winning at the gaming tables and standing at the bar in the saloons.

By Christmas 1874, Fresno was the county seat and more families had moved to Fresno Station. However, no one stepped forward to arrange any type of Christmas activities. Fresno was still without a church building. Any celebrations that took place were done quietly in the home.

By December 1875, a budding feeling of civic pride among the citizenry was in the air. It was decided that Fresno needed to have a public Christmas tree and a Christmas program. The only problem was that there were no evergreen trees nearby.

Two brothers, ages thirteen and fifteen, were given the job of going to the hills, selecting a tree, cutting it down, and bringing it to Fresno. They trudged across the bare fields and climbed the sloping foothills to Millerton. On the grounds of old Fort Miller they found a suitable tree—a digger pine. They actually found two large trees, cut them down, and prepared for the journey home.

Sam Brown, who had moved many Millerton residents to Fresno, had arranged to meet the boys. The three fellows loaded the trees on his wagon and by nightfall had reached Len Farrar's Magnolia Saloon on Fresno's Front Street (H Street). They carried the larger of the trees up the stairs to the large room over the saloon called Magnolia Hall. Here Fresno's first community Christmas tree was decorated and strung with gifts. Christmas had finally come to Fresno Station.

# Fresno's First General Election

The first general election in the new county seat of Fresno took place on September 1, 1875. There were a total of twenty precincts in the entire county—in places as far-flung as Millerton, Firebaugh, Jones' Store, Kingston, Liberty, and Centerville. Many of the voters would have to travel to cast their vote, so every buckboard, buggy, and stagecoach was readied for a journey. Horses were watered and shod. Lunches were packed and children were scrubbed and dressed in their Sunday clothes. Everyone was excited about the adventure. Of course, only the men could vote. Native Americans, women, and the insane were not allowed to cast ballots.

Fresno was the largest of the towns to be named a precinct and, here, the day took on a holiday tone. The stores were filled with tempting merchandise and the saloons were prepared for a larger than usual number of visitors. They were not disappointed.

As soon as the polls opened, the dirt streets began to fill with horse-drawn vehicles of all kinds. The women sat in the buggies with their children while their men folk went inside to cast their votes for a whole slate of offices—from the governor of California, secretary of state, and assemblyman, through all the county officers. When the men came outside, the women and children visited the shops of Fresno and the men retired to the saloons. When tired of shopping, the women sat on benches waiting for their men to return. Lunch or dinner at one of the local eateries capped off the day.

In this first general election, the Democrat ticket won. William Irwin became governor of California and P. D. Wigginton was elected to Congress. On the county level, James D. Collins was elected assemblyman; Scott Ashman, sheriff; and J. A. Stroud, assessor. The day was very different from election days now and is well worth visiting in the tales of our Valley.

# A Dodge City Christmas

Christmas was first truly celebrated in Fresno in 1875. In spite of its Dodge City atmosphere, the stores of Fresno geared up for a profitable sales period. Kutner & Goldstein ordered a wide array of elegant dress goods, hats, and fans for the ladies. Fanning & Brother had toys and books, focusing much of their merchandise on items for children. Bishop & Co. had vases, smoking sets, and other gift items. Vellguth's drug and variety store had a wide range of merchandise. Silverman & Einstein featured Japanese inlaid tables, toys, and ladies' goods. There were many things to tempt the Christmas shopper.

The community party in Magnolia Hall on Christmas night was well attended. Excellent music filled the hall, much to the enjoyment of many couples who danced until well after midnight. Dancing was not the only source of entertainment. Bowls of eggnog not only at Magnolia Hall, but also in all the many saloons in Fresno, were enjoyed with great gusto. Many a glass was lifted on that memorable night.

Unfortunately, as reported in *The Fresno Expositor* a few days later, many of the tipplers had trouble finding their way home and ended up sleeping off their holiday cheer in the by-ways of the town.

One gentleman, so full of cheer that he could hardly contain himself, found his way into Bishop & Co.'s store. Sitting atop one of the showcases was a bottle filled with a large number of tarantulas, scorpions, snakes, and assorted vermin, all preserved in alcohol. Fascinated by the bottle and its contents, he suddenly felt the need to once again quench his thirst. He pulled out the cork, took a swig of the contents into his mouth, wiped his face with his sleeve, and exited the store. The horrified clerk watched him stagger into the street and begin the long process of trying to wend his way home. Most likely, he would join the others who had fallen along the way.

# A New Year's Ball at Magnolia Hall

New Year's Eve in Fresno Station took on special meaning in 1874. Not only was the population of the town growing rapidly, but the town was also now the seat of county government. Fresno was on the way to fulfilling Leland Stanford's vision—it would one day be the largest city in the Central Valley.

The town was two—almost three years old. New businesses were opening up and homes were being built. A glimpse of civic pride was being seen on the faces of some Fresno residents. Concerns were being voiced as well. With all the frame buildings in the new town, there was just approximately two hundred dollars in the fire protection fund. The fund needed to grow so some sort of fire-fighting equipment could be purchased.

The populace was in the mood to hold a celebration so why not have a New Year's Eve party and use it to raise money for the fire protection fund? The idea caught hold. A committee consisting of men from all the Valley communities, including Merced, drew up an invitation list, booked Magnolia Hall for the night of December 31, 1874, and arranged for musicians. As word of the party spread, everyone began to make plans to attend.

On New Year's Eve 1874, several establishments—Pryce's Restaurant, Fresno Restaurant, and California Hall—offered special suppers to those who would later attend the ball at Magnolia Hall. By eight o'clock that evening, Magnolia Hall was filled to capacity with 120 ladies and gentlemen in their best evening attire. They danced to the music of Doyle, Glenn & Horn's Band until five the next morning. It was an evening of great merriment.

When the proceeds were counted, the fire protection fund was richer by one hundred seventy dollars. The money was deposited with Barth & Froelich, bankers. It had been a most successful evening in every respect—one well worth remembering in the tales of our Valley.

## Laura Winchell's Mince Pie

On a cold November day in 1866, just a week before Thanksgiving, Laura Winchell made a neighborly call on one of two recent arrivals in Millerton. There were two small houses near Greiersen's store and in each house was a new bride just arrived from Denmark. Although well educated in their homeland, the new arrivals did not speak English and had not yet learned the customs of their new country. Mrs. George Greiersen was the recipient of Mrs. Winchell's hospitable welcome to Millerton.

As soon as Mrs. Winchell left, Mrs. Greiersen called to her neighbor, Mrs. Francesco Jensen, to come quickly to her kitchen. Soon, the two women were staring in wonder at an object on the kitchen table. It was a mince pie made by Mrs. Winchell herself. Neither woman had ever heard of a mince pie, much less seen one. In fact, they were not familiar with pies at all. They wondered aloud how it should be served. Mrs. Greiersen raised a small edge of the crust to see what was inside. The flaky crust broke to reveal pieces of apple, raisins, and citron. The smell that emanated from the warm pie was truly aromatic. "Spices, peach brandy, and sherry must have been used," the ladies surmised. "Should we serve this hot or cold?" they asked each other. "Should we use spoons or forks?"

Mrs. Greiersen finally said, "Mrs. Jensen, will you and your husband have dinner with us tonight? Perhaps, our husbands will know better than we what should be done with this mince pie."

That night, after the two couples had partaken of a good meal, it was time for dessert. The mince pie was placed in the middle of the table. The young wives told their husbands that they did not know how to serve this mince pie that smelled so good. Amid some gentle laughter, Mr. Greiersen took a spoon and dipped a portion of the pie onto his plate. He likewise served the others.

Mrs. Winchell would surely have been horrified to see the mess that was made of her mince pie, but she certainly would have been pleased by the exclamations of delight that followed each bite.

# Fancy Equipages in 1880s Fresno

During the mid-1920s, the pages of *The Fresno Morning Republican* were made even more readable by a weekly column written by Ernestine Winchell. Called "Fresno Memories," it contained tidbits of remembered events at Millerton and in early Fresno—two communities where Ernestine and her husband, Lilibourne Winchell, had been pioneers. In one column, Mrs. Winchell reminisced about the "Equipages of the Eighties."

During the 1880s financial boom period a number of fortunes were made—mostly in real estate development. Just about everyone had a piece of land to sell and, with newcomers constantly settling in the Fresno area, the land sold for good prices. With their new wealth a number of Fresnans began to purchase fancy buggies and beautiful horses—their presence on the streets of the town brought a touch of elegance to the pioneer community.

Mrs. H. C. Warner's rather conservative carriage was drawn by a dappled gray mare. Mrs. Lewis Leach rode in a canopy-top phaeton pulled by a chestnut black trotter. Mrs. A. B. Butler drove into town "in an elegant, low swung vehicle shaded by a scalloped and fringed linen canopy." Mrs. Butler was usually accompanied by her children, her maid, and the driver, who sat perched on the box at the front of the carriage.

Not to be outdone, the men presented an even more interesting sight. Jim Northcraft's buggy was finished in highly polished natural wood. Other vehicles, of various sizes, featured eye-catching colors, gooseneck shafts, flared fenders, and decorations of all kinds. S. N. Griffith and David Terry each had a pair of horses with knotted tails and dangling chains pulling their fancy equipages. They made such an impression on the male population that they were soon being copied by those who could afford this extravagance.

The early 1880s were colorful in many ways—not the least of which was the passing parade on the streets of Fresno.

West Park Colony
School, with the
entire student body,
in 1900.

*Courtesy of the
members of the West
Park Thursday Club.*

# West Park Colony

Developer Bernard Marks, in partnership with William Chapman and William H. Martin, laid out the Central California Colony in 1877. Located south and west of Fresno, this was one of the earliest, and most successful, colony ventures. A few years later, in 1884, Marks—this time in partnership with Moses J. Church—developed a new colony on Bank of California lands just west of the Central California Colony. This new tract was bounded by Church Avenue on the north, Bryan Avenue to the west, American Avenue to the south, and West Avenue to the east. It was called West Park Colony.

The area grew quickly and, within a year, a school was needed. Moses J. Church donated ten acres of land for a school site. The West Park District was organized on May 4, 1885, and plans for a schoolhouse were immediately underway. Until the building was completed in the fall of 1885, classes were held in the home of Edith Luella Staub, the district's first teacher. Her class consisted of ten boys and nine girls.

The first school building cost $1,600 and was paid for in U.S. gold coin. The enrollment increased to such an extent that by 1899 a second teacher was hired and, in 1902, a third teacher was necessary. Three new buildings were added at the school site at North and Valentine avenues.

Over the years, two other schools were built on this site to meet the ever-increasing enrollment of the district. In 1953, two new wings were added to the present-day building giving the school "a total of fifteen classrooms, two kindergartens, a multipurpose room, and offices." Today, the school operates on a year-round basis.

Home of Mrs. John S. Dore where the first meeting of the West Park Thursday Club was held. Taken in 1890. The Dore family is gathered on the front porch. *Courtesy of the members of the West Park Thursday Club.*

# West Park Thursday Club

The women who lived in the West Park Colony, located in the Easton area, usually took their children and went to Santa Cruz and Pacific Grove for a few weeks during the hottest part of the summer. It was a hard trip. A large wagon was packed with tents and all the essentials for a vacation at the coast. The trip overland to the Coast Range Mountains and the rather harrowing journey on the stage road over Pacheco Pass to the coast took three days.

One summer the ladies decided to stay home, but they felt isolated. There were no telephones or radios in the late 1890s and they lived some distance from Fresno. Mrs. J. S. Dore decided to send out invitations to all the ladies in West Park to come to her home on Thursday afternoon, June 2, 1897. On the appointed day twenty-one ladies gathered at Mrs. Dore's house. As they talked they realized that they all wanted to see each other regularly. They were all eager to improve their minds through the study of a variety of topics and they wanted to communicate with each other about all that they were learning.

What day would they meet? They decided to meet on Thursday because it was the only day of the week they were free from major chores—Monday was wash day, Tuesday was ironing day, Wednesday was house cleaning day, and Friday was reserved for preparing for the weekend.

On that Thursday afternoon in June 1897, these twenty-one ladies organized the West Park Thursday Club. They elected the following officers: Mrs. H. W. Staub, president; Mrs. Hill, vice-president; Mrs. E. M. Lindsay, secretary; and Mrs. H. N. Burleigh, treasurer.

The descendants of the original founders are still involved in the West Park Thursday Club. Like the members of other study clubs throughout the Central Valley, these generations of women have played an important role in the development of the life of Fresno County and, as such, are remembered in the tales of our Valley.

Mrs. J. J. Bowen, Molly Burleigh, Edith Staub, Sadie Burleigh McNeil, and Lucy Angel (left to right), all charter members, gather at the fiftieth anniversay of the West Park Thursday Club in 1949. *Courtesy of the members of the West Park Thursday Club.*

# A Literary Afternoon in West Park

Our tales of the Valley have told the stories of many of the early study clubs for women. However, we have never paid a visit to one. In order to rectify this state of affairs, our story today will center on a meeting of the West Park Thursday Club.

It is June 1, 1899, and you are all invited into the home of Mrs. Bowen in West Park Colony. As roll is called, each lady answers with a quotation from literature appropriate to the topic of the day. This accomplished, Mrs. West opens the meeting with a short talk on "Concord, Historical and Political Associations." She is followed by Mrs. David Barnwell reading the "Concord Hymn." Mrs. Hill then rises to discuss the Brooks-Farm Community. Five-minute talks about Amos Bronson Alcott, Margaret Fuller, and Emerson by Mrs. Holcolm, Mrs. Levitt, and Mrs. Perkins follow.

The meeting ends with the query box. Members drop a question in this box and then, at the next meeting, they are answered by the club. Since refreshments are not usually served—unless the members vote to do so—after some visiting, the ladies retire to their homes wishing each other a good day. It has been a pleasant afternoon.

Over the years, the West Park Thursday Club ladies raised money for a number of admirable causes. One early project was to buy a suit of clothes for the minister of the West Park Church, the Reverend Del Webb, so that he could perform weddings, funerals, and services appropriately attired.

As the years progressed, the topics discussed reflected the times. At the meeting on March 5, 1913, two of the speeches were "Traditional Notions of Woman's Sphere" and "Effect of Franchise on Woman's Home Life." Roll call was to be answered by telling "Why I Want to Vote." The ladies were moving beyond literature and exploring the forces that were shaping their lives.

# John Ephraim Bugg

In the early spring of 1922, one of the legendary teamsters of the Sierra passed away at his ranch on Willow Creek in Madera County. John Bugg's amazing life began on February 26, 1839, in Williamson County, Tennessee. Within a few years, his family moved to Missouri.

In 1852, when he was thirteen years old, Bugg was hired by Jefferson James to help him run cattle across the plains. They left the stock in Nevada and came across the Sierra to California, settling at James' 25 Ranch near present-day Tranquillity. In the spring of 1853, they returned to Nevada and drove the cattle to the Valley. Bugg worked as a vaquero for James for several years.

In his late teens, Bugg bought a large wagon and a team of oxen and began hauling supplies from Sacramento and Stockton to the mining camps of the Sierra foothills. With the discovery of the Comstock Lode, Bugg began hauling freight over the Emigrant Trail to Nevada. There were so many wagons making this trip that, at night, the entire trail was alight with lanterns from the teamsters' campfires. In the early 1860s, Bugg began hauling logs over the notoriously steep road into Crane Valley—today Bass Lake. Bugg was known as the best teamster in the area.

John Bugg moved to Jonesville (Friant) to work for J. R. Jones, who ran an extensive stock ranch, trading post, and ferry on the San Joaquin River. He worked for Jones for many years. Bugg purchased the Lewis Ranch on Willow Creek at O'Neals and brought his bride, Mary Cramer, there in 1870. Over the course of their long life together, they would have seven children.

The couple raised cattle on their ranch for many years. Bugg served as an undersheriff and, in 1893, served as a member of the Madera County Board of Supervisors. With John Bugg's passing in 1922, one more of the great pioneers of our Valley was gone.

I n the last tale of our Valley, we told the story of John Bugg, teamster and cattleman. His strength, determination, and fiery temper were characteristics that stood him in good stead for the life that he chose for himself.

While working at J. R. Jones' trading post in Jonesville (Friant), Bugg had some interesting experiences. Christmas Eve 1867 saw a massive flood of the San Joaquin River that wiped out most of Millerton. On Christmas morning, Bugg and Alex Kennedy, Jones' bookkeeper, stood outside watching the debris-filled river roar past. All at once a chicken coop, with a huge rooster perched precariously on top, came bouncing by. The rooster crowed loudly, causing Kennedy to say, "Got a heap o' gall, ain't he?"

On a day in late autumn, Bugg and nine other men were gathered in Jones' store. Clerk Smith Norris was behind the counter, eight of the men were playing cards at two tables, and one man was watching the proceedings. With no warning at all, a voice yelled into the store, "Put up your hands!" Looking up at both doors, the men saw four Mexicans and the barrels of four six-shooters pointing directly at them—the Tiburcio Vasquez gang had come to Jonesville!

Never lowering their guns for a moment, the gang came into the store and forced the men to lie down. They tied their hands behind their backs and proceeded to rob the men and to take all sorts of items from the store.

The gang members got their loot stowed on their horses and, as they jumped onto their saddles and rode away, they called to their captives, "Adios, caballeros, hasta otro dia." (Goodbye, fellows, until another day). They pushed their horses forward and headed west over the Valley.

Bugg, whose well-known temper was really hot by this time, freed himself and notified Sheriff Ashman at Millerton. He signed on as part of the posse that headed out after the gang. They rode up to the Cantua home of Vasquez' sister, who appeared on the porch and swore at Bugg. She told him there wasn't a rope made that could hang her brother, that they could never catch him and should go home. Later, they found out that Vazquez and his men were hiding not quite three miles from there.

Bugg and the posse returned to Millerton empty handed, but not many years later, in 1875, Tiburcio Vasquez was arrested, tried, and convicted for his crimes.

On March 18, 1875, Vasquez was hanged—a rope was finally found to do the job.

# Moses Mock

One of the early lumbermen of the foothills was Moses Mock. Except for the fact that he was born in Pennsylvania about 1830, nothing is known about his early life. At some point he came to California and settled in Mariposa. Here he met John Humphreys. The two became partners in the lumber business. They came to Fresno County in the mid-1860s to see the road the Woods brothers were building up Sarver's Mountain—the Tollhouse Road—and to see what the timber prospects might be in the Tollhouse area of the Sierra.

The men felt the Woods brothers had chosen the wrong route for their road and pointed out another more advantageous path. Even though their suggestions were ignored, the visit was worthwhile because, in 1867, Mock and the Humphreys family moved to Tollhouse.

Unhappy with the slow progress of the road crew, Mock, with the supplies he needed on his back, followed Indian trails up the mountain until he reached the sugar pine forest at a place that is now known as Pine Ridge. He chose a site for a sawmill and set up camp in a shelter he made of bark. He cut down young cedar trees and began to fashion timbers for the future mill. By the time the Humphreys family and their mill crew arrived, all the wood that would be needed to build the mill was ready. The machinery that was needed for the mill came on heavy wooden-wheeled wagons drawn by teams of oxen. Pulling that load up the Tollhouse grade was an arduous journey.

Moses Mock and John Humphreys' partnership in the lumber industry lasted for thirty years. Their deep friendship was an important component of this partnership. Mock bought land adjoining Humphreys' holdings at Humphreys' Station. Here he built a home that he lived in for many years.

Moses Mock became one of the legends of the early timber industry of the area. He died at his mountain home in 1913.

# Moses Mock's Steam Wagon

Almost twenty years before a car was seen on the streets of Fresno, pioneer lumberman Moses Mock drove the first motorized vehicle up the treacherous Tollhouse Road. How was this possible?

Mock was a very skillful mechanic—a true genius when it came to working with metals and wood. He was also something of an inventor. He built a workshop on his property and experimented with his ideas in secret. He had long dreamed of some kind of horseless mechanized transport that could carry freight up Tollhouse Road. He developed a small working model of a steam-powered wagon crafted entirely of copper and brass. It was just eighteen inches long and worked perfectly. Mock began to work on a full-sized wagon. Unfortunately, when finished, it did not work as well as he had hoped. After a year of experimenting, he sent his drawings to an Eastern manufacturer and asked what it would cost to produce his wagon. The reply was a staggering figure for the time—$6,000. He would later learn that the company took his plans, made a few changes, took out a patent, manufactured the result, and made a fortune.

Mock persisted. This time he ordered one of the steam engines that were just coming on the market. In 1887, Moses Mock, with Tom Williams' help, took the steam wagon all the way up the Tollhouse and Pine Ridge grades to the Bonanza Mill—the first time a vehicle made this trip under its own power.

Although the steam wagon made the trip, it proved to be an inferior way to haul logs—ox teams proved better. Getting the huge wagon down the mountain was so hard that Mock sold the steam wagon to Clovis Cole. Cole used it for various tasks on his extensive grain ranch, but found it to be undependable and expensive.

Cole finally sold the steam wagon to the Fresno Vineyard Company. They sent it up to North Fork for a load of wood and there is no record of its ever returning. Like Mock's dream—it just vanished.

# Religion and the Central School

In spite of the Dodge City atmosphere in the earliest days of the little village of Fresno Station, there was always a segment of the populace who believed in attending church every Sunday. Since there were no church buildings, where did these small congregations meet? The Methodist Episcopal Church South congregation met in a room over the Magnolia Saloon. As soon as a school was established, some groups met in the school room. Other congregations met in private homes.

In 1879, when the Central School was built on the site of the present-day Veterans Memorial Auditorium, many of the religious groups including the Baptists, Methodists, and Congregationalists chose this as a meeting site until they could build their own churches.

The Episcopal mission was organized in 1879 and held services in Magnolia Hall before moving them to the Central School. On April 11, 1880, the Reverend Douglas O. Kelley, the missionary priest assigned to the congregation, presented the first confirmation class in Fresno to Bishop William Ingraham Kip. On that Sunday morning, in the Central School, Susan Adele Davis, Ella Guard, Mary Josephine Lovejoy, Lucy Jule Anderson, Helen Johnson Vendergau, Annie Foster, Emma Foster, Alba Stephens, and Mary Jane Stephens became confirmed according to the rites of the Episcopal Church.

Not only were Sunday morning services held at the school, but it was also a place for Sunday evening services. Since this was the era when young ladies could not attend events alone, many came in pairs—walking along the dirt streets and wagon paths and up the hill to the schoolhouse. Young men would be lined up waiting to offer an arm to a pretty girl. At meeting's end, many of these couples made their way home in the moonlight—undoubtedly making it a longer journey than the earlier one. Many a match was made on nights such as these. The Central School held many memories for the pioneer families of Fresno Station.

# Christmas in Fresno Station, 1872

After an autumn of almost drought-like conditions, on December 22, 1872, the heavens opened up and drenched the little village of Fresno Station. Five inches of rain fell that day, turning the dirt streets into a muddy, flooded bog. The next day was dry. Rain fell again on Christmas Eve and Christmas Day. For the inhabitants of the small village, it was a cold and very wet holiday.

There wasn't a lot of holiday spirit that year—with the exception of the liquid variety that could be found in the numerous saloons dotted through the town. The commercialism of the big cities had not found its way to Fresno Station—that was yet to come. There were few gifts exchanged between the adults—perhaps a new pair of galoshes and a plug of tobacco for dad, and for mom, an apron, a book, or a new wringer for the washtub.

For the children of the family, the most they could expect on Christmas morning was that their stockings would contain some fruit and, possibly, some candy. It must have seemed as though Santa Claus was neglecting the new town on the plains of Fresno County—perhaps he had yet to be told that it existed.

In the late afternoon of Christmas Eve, the rain stopped briefly. Emerging from the darkening mist that seemed to hover on the outskirts of the town, a team of horses came into view. The driver of the wagon, postmaster Russell Fleming, urging his team forward, yelled, "Giddap, you!" He directed the horses down Mariposa Street between the two rows of wooden buildings that lined the street. He pulled his team to a stop at the corner of J (Fulton) Street. Fleming jumped down and walked around to the back of the wagon. He pulled out two pouches of mail—one was only half full—and headed inside the store to sort the mail into the primitive wooden box that served as Fresno Station's post office. There were a number of Christmas messages placed in the box that day. Those who heard Fleming's call to his team—probably everyone in the small town—made their way to the post office to gather their mail.

On that rainy Christmas Eve of 1872, postmaster Russell

Fleming, in his unofficial role as Santa Claus, brought the only holiday mail into town. Many years later he would remember this day with fondness and so shall we now that it has been recorded in the tales of our Valley.

# The Fog of Winter 1874

Today, when the treacherous tule fog of winter wraps its cloak around our Valley it seems as though the pace of life should slow down a bit, but it rarely does. Electricity makes our homes as bright as on a summer day and large vehicles with powerful headlights make it possible to travel our Valley roads—although, if truth be told, the high-beam lights are less effective than the low-beam and, if one were truly wise, one would just stay at home until the fog lifts.

One hundred and thirty-one years ago—the winter of 1874—the tule fog arrived and decided to prolong its visit. Day after day the fog remained, enveloping the young town of Fresno and all the flatlands around stretching to the mountain ranges of the east and west in its cold, wet, dense shroud. It was a miserable time.

On one memorable December morning of that year, John Bass, who lived at Dahl's Camp west of Fresno, set out to tend his sheep at six o'clock in the morning. The fog was so thick that, although he knew the countryside like the back of his hand, he got thoroughly lost and couldn't find his way home—he ended up in Fresno at eight o'clock that evening, rather amazed and confused. His flocks of sheep were also confused by the fog and got thoroughly mixed up with Dr. Estelle's sheep—a rancher who lived nearby. Estelle, feeling the need to check on his flock, left his home around noon and, after wandering around for hours in the dense fog trying to find them, was forced to sleep outdoors. When he woke in the morning, he tried again to find his sheep. He wandered into Dahl's Camp around noon. He and Bass finally found their flocks. It took hours to try to separate them in the fog.

Mr. Turlock, the man who provided milk for Fresno's citizens, was also troubled by the dense blanket of fog. He got lost coming into town and spent six hours going from his dairy to Fresno.

The winter of 1874 was a memorable one for the pioneers of our Valley, who hoped that they would never again experience such dense tule fog. Were they ever in for a surprise!

# Abe Lincoln Teaches Sunday School

For one Kerman rancher, the memories of his boyhood in rural Illinois were highlighted by a friendship between his father and a young lawyer from Springfield that began in the Blue Ridge Mountains of Virginia when the two were very young. When they got older, the two boys headed west and, working side by side, split rails, worked on farms, and in country stores—taking any job that they could find.

James Henderson owned a farm midway between the county seat of Sullivan, Illinois, and Springfield. One Saturday evening, a rig and horse kicked up a lot of dust on the dirt road leading to the farm. The family gathered on the porch, happily anticipating the arrival of the young man who often stayed overnight when legal business took him to Sullivan. One of the sons, eight-year-old Paris, worshipped the gangling, awkward young man who always regaled them with wonderful stories. Paris was delighted that young Abraham Lincoln was paying them a visit.

The next morning, James Henderson was not feeling well so Lincoln offered to take the family to church. When they arrived, they found that Paris' Sunday school teacher was also ill that day. Lincoln said he would teach the class. On that magical Sunday morning, with the children gathered around him, Lincoln made the Bible come alive for a group of eight-year-olds.

Paris Henderson also remembered sitting on a platform with his father listening to Lincoln debate the free state question with Andy Thornton, who would later become a general during the Civil War.

Paris Henderson came west in 1908, settling in Kingsburg, where he was active in forming the first Sun-Maid raisin cooperative. Later, he moved to Kerman. Henderson's memories of Lincoln remained strong. "Even as a small boy I realized that Lincoln was a great man," Henderson said, "and I have always tried to pattern my life after his."

# The President's Last Address

In February 1927, Mr. J. M. Bell of Fresno gave an interview to a reporter for *The Fresno Morning Republican*. The story that appeared the next day contained events that are well worth chronicling.

Bell, who grew up in Elkhart, Indiana, met Abraham Lincoln on numerous occasions when Lincoln would stop by their home to visit Bell's father. A number of years would pass until Bell saw Lincoln again.

As the Civil War was ending, Bell and his brother went to Washington, D.C., to meet a third brother who was being mustered out of the Union Army. They no sooner linked up with their brother than word began to circulate that Confederate General Robert E. Lee had surrendered. People began to appear on the streets of the capital, pouring out of their homes and businesses. By nightfall the jubilant crowds gathered at the White House. According to Bell, "There were thousands in the crowd, stretching for blocks, and consisting of both soldiers and civilians. In answer to the calls of the people, Lincoln…came to the steps with a few loose sheets of paper in one hand and a candle in the other." Lincoln made a brief address recounting the events of the last few days and told them that the country and the capital were safe—that peace had truly come.

Bell said he would never forget President Lincoln's concluding statement. "Now I am about to call upon the band for a selection that our adversaries have endeavored to appropriate but we fairly captured it yesterday and the attorney general has given me his legal opinion that it is now our property, so I ask the band to play 'Dixie.'"

The next evening, the Lincolns attended Ford's Theatre. The tragedy of that night turned Washington D.C. into a place of fear—the residents were worried that another rebellion would break out.

Bell would never forget Lincoln's last public address and his last wish that the song that had been the martial song of the Confederate South would become a symbol of a united nation.

There is a small Finnish community in rural South Dakota near the town of Frederick. It was here that Arne Nixon was born in 1927, the youngest of four children. A birth defect that affected his legs also affected his growth. He didn't grow as tall as his siblings. His mother realized her youngest son was not cut out to be a farmer like his father—his size made heavy farm work difficult. Books became Nixon's companions and opened a window to the outside world. The often-brooding, dark Norse tales told to him by his grandfather introduced him to the great oral tradition of storytelling. The only language he knew as a child was Finnish.

The first school Nixon attended was a one-room schoolhouse. When he was in the eighth grade, he entered an elocution contest at the State Normal and Industrial College in Ellendale, North Dakota. Mr. McMillan, president of the college, was so impressed with Nixon's presentation that he invited the young man to live with his family and attend the high school that was held in the college. Without McMillan's help, Nixon's family could not have afforded to send him from their rural farm to a high school. Nixon lived with the McMillan family, graduated from high school, and continued his education at the State Normal and Industrial College, receiving an associate of arts degree. Later, in an expression of gratitude for the generosity of the McMillans, Nixon established a scholarship for teacher education students at California State University, Fresno in their name.

Nixon's first teaching position was a one-room school (grades 1-8) in Guchlock, North Dakota. He had to drive the school bus, sweep out the school each day, fire up the coal stove, and teach all the grades. He soon returned to college and completed his bachelor of arts degree.

His second teaching position was with the Bureau of Indian Affairs on a reservation on the Olympic Peninsula in Washington. While there, he earned a master of arts degree from Western Washington State University. He went on to Columbia University as a

Arne Nixon (about six years old) and his brother Edwin in South Dakota.
*Courtesy of Dr. Maurice Eash.*

Arne Nixon (center) with two of his classmates at the State Normal and Industrial College in North Dakota in 1944.
*Courtesy of Dr. Maurice Eash.*

Marshall Field Fellow and completed his Ph.D. in education in 1959. His dissertation topic was a study of young children and reading.

At Columbia, one of his professors, Leland Jacobs, taught him the art of storytelling. "The key," Jacobs said, "is to think of Charles Laughton." Jacobs became a true mentor—many of Jacobs' mannerisms found their way into Nixon's storytelling persona.

A teaching job in Tulare brought Arne Nixon to California where he served as a principal and assistant superintendent. In 1961, he joined a project of the U.S. Agency of International Development engaged in teacher education in the African country of Sudan. After two years, he accepted a position at what was then Fresno State College, teaching storytelling and children's literature—a position he would hold for thirty years.

During his tenure, he would not only be a tremendous influence on the young people he taught, but his storytelling abilities would also make an impact on the larger Fresno community. He spoke to numerous groups—his programs became the stuff of legend. It was his interaction with children, however, that brought special joy. His close friend Maurice Eash said of Nixon, "There was an early stigmata of genius in him in the way he related to children." His ability to get children to listen and to talk to him might have been partly related to his small stature, but most likely it was because he looked them in the eye and listened to what they had to say.

Nixon's philosophy was that the significance of children's literature is in character, not in plot. He said there were only seven or eight plots, but the characters had infinite permutations. He also saw a bipolarity in children's literature. On one hand, there are stories that tell the happy, golden side of life that is joyful and safe; on the other there is the darker side where children are threatened and vulnerable. The latter is often found in the folktales of cultures that have been handed down by oral tradition.

He was a great believer in offering children opportunities to read widely. He felt there was a voice in children that needed to express itself—giving them the chance to read a variety of books would allow them to find expression for that voice.

Arne Nixon was raised in a strong but narrow church tradition—an upbringing that gave him an extensive knowledge of biblical literature. As an adult and a rationalist he was not given to supernaturalism. A wonderfully free spirit, he wandered widely through many countries of the world—always making lifelong friends along the way. A man of keen insights into human behavior, he, above all, disliked the pretentious.

In his travels he collected vast numbers of children's books and their related toys and story plates. Two years before he died, he gifted his large library to California State University, Fresno to establish the center that now bears his name—the Arne Nixon Center for the Study of Children's Literature. His death in 1997 brought to an end a life well lived and left for the future a rich legacy for children and teachers of these children.

Arne Nixon (right) in 1947 with his first through fourth grade students in Guchlock, North Dakota. His first teaching assignment was in this one-room school house.
*Courtesy of Dr. Maurice Eash.*

# The Arne Nixon Center

The Henry Madden Library on the California State University, Fresno campus offers students and scholars an excellent environment in which to study and to do research. But did you know that, within its walls, is a separate and unique library—a one-of-a-kind in the Far West library—that is a treasure trove for those who are studying children's literature?

In 1995, Dr. Arne Nixon, who taught children's literature and storytelling at the university for more than thirty years, donated his personal collection of approximately 22,000 volumes to the Henry Madden Library. This gift founded the Arne Nixon Center for the Study of Children's Literature. His gift came with a condition—that these books would be preserved as a resource for those who wanted to do research in the field of children's literature. The collection would be non-circulating. For the next two years Dr. Nixon worked with the center and helped to establish the basic principles for the use of the materials in the collection. When Dr. Nixon died in 1997, he left a generous bequest so that the work of the center would be perpetuated.

In 1999, Angelica Carpenter, who holds master of arts degrees in library science and in education and has published four biographies for young people, was hired as curator. Since that time the collections of the center have grown. A number of authors and illustrators have donated copies of their books and papers. The oldest book in this unique library is an 1865 edition of *Alice's Adventures in Wonderland* that is part of a 2,000-piece donation of Lewis Carroll's works. The library's large collection of multi-cultural literature gives another important focus for researchers and reflects another one of Dr. Nixon's interests.

The glass cupboards in the reading room are filled with books and ceramic pieces that change according to the subjects addressed by speakers hosted by the center. The artwork of Fresno native and author Leo Politi grace the walls of the library.

The Arne Nixon Center's collection now totals approximately 38,000 books. It has gained an international reputation as the finest and largest library of children's literature in the Far West and is a mecca for teachers, librarians, writers, and researchers who are studying the history and literary analysis of children's literature.

The Arne Nixon Center is a unique and important place in the city of Fresno—it is fitting that its early history is recorded in the tales of our Valley as it begins its journey. A visit to this library touches something in all of us who hold treasured memories of a well-loved book from our childhood.

Arne Nixon in 1949 at age twenty-two.
*Courtesy of Dr. Maurice Each.*

# A Flag Raising

On a morning in late March of 1892, a large number of parents, teachers, children, and guests filled the hall of the Fresno Colony School. Situated on the southwest corner of Jensen and Fig avenues, land for the school had been donated by Thomas Hughes, founder of the Fresno Colony. The students and faculty of the one-story school building were celebrating the purchase of a new flag and flagpole. The flagpole, which soared to a height of seventy-four feet, came from Oregon. The new flag, which measured ten by sixteen feet, came from Chicago. Its bright colors generated many admiring comments.

At the appointed hour, Principal Charles E. Taylor strode to the podium and welcomed the overflow crowd. After a prayer by Trustee C. B. Kimble, four little girls unveiled the new flag, which was hung across the front of the room. Numerous recitations, quotations, and songs—all pertaining to the flag—were given by several of the students. The final offering in this part of the program was a flag drill given by eight boys and eight girls. Their precision was so skillful that the audience clapped loudly and they repeated their performance. Superintendent Kirk spoke to the assembled throng about the importance of the flag as an emblem of our country and impressed on them the importance of raising children to love their country and their flag.

Then it was Dr. Chester Rowell's turn to speak. He walked to the podium and turned to face the flag. He talked about "Old Glory" and, as he spoke, his stirring words filled the room with his sense of patriotism. He turned back to the audience and, looking directly into the eyes of the children, told them how important it was for them to love their country and their flag—that it would make them better citizens. When Dr. Rowell finished his remarks, the meeting adjourned to the area in front of the school. Two students, Beulah Bell and Harry Ewing, assisted by Maggie Kemble and Roy Wharton, attached the flag to the new flagpole. As the flag was raised a breeze caught it so that it furled grandly, adding much enjoyment to the moment. Three cheers went up. Everyone went home filled with patriotic thoughts of flag and of country.

# The Dashaway Literary Association

Just a few short months after Fresno had become the county seat—in November of 1874 to be exact—a temperance organization was founded by a few citizens of the new city. A committee to draft a constitution for this group—the Dashaway Literary Association—had been formed and met early in the month to undertake its task.

A week later, on a Sunday evening, the organizational meeting at Shannon & Hughes Hall drew a large number of people— many of them ladies. Mrs. E. C. Phillips, John J. Boyle, and Frank Horn provided instrumental music to usher in the evening's entertainments. This was followed by a choir singing a song entitled "Sparkling and Bright." W. J. Young walked to the front of the hall to deliver an address on the "Heroism of the Pacific." A number of musical selections, including a song by the Misses Waterman, and a recitation by Miss Alice Shanklin followed.

Members of the Constitution Committee made their report. When the vote was called for, those present voted to unanimously accept the document. As outlined in the constitution, the aims of the Dashaway Literary Association were "to promote intellectual improvement, social enjoyment and moral advancement; and in furtherance of these objects the members are pledged not to use as a beverage, nor buy nor sell, on their own account, any spirituous or malt liquors, wine or cider." When called upon, thirteen gentlemen and seven ladies came forward, signed the document, and publicly took a pledge to uphold the tenets laid out in the constitution.

With this accomplished, the meeting was adjourned until the following week when the meeting would begin with the election of officers—Elisha Cotton Winchell would serve as the group's first president.

In a town with numerous saloons, this was the first temperance group to form—showing that not everyone in Fresno approved of the Dodge City atmosphere of the town.

This view of Fresno in 1877 was taken from the top floor of the Fresno County Courthouse. The photo shows K Street south of Mariposa. The Henry Hotel is the large building on the left. *Author's collection.*

# Party Politics in 1892 Fresno

In the early days of the city, Fresno was divided into five political wards. Each ward had a seat on the board of trustees that governed the city. Trustees were nominated at local party conventions and ran for office on party tickets. After the city election, the party that won the majority on the board was in control. It was a colorful system that ultimately let to various types of corruption. The trustee from the Fifth Ward represented all of Chinatown and the rest of the Tenderloin area. He wielded tremendous political power. It all led to some rough and tumble situations.

Firman Church served as district attorney from 1892 to 1894. He also served on Fresno's board of trustees. *Courtesy of Robert M. Wash.*

Late in March of 1892, the Democrats of the First Ward were represented by an honest man—Firman Church. They decided they wanted to form a Democrat Club that would be made up only of Democrats from the First Ward. They selected a night for their meeting and planned to elect Trustee Church the president of their new club. Word leaked out and soon the other trustees and influential men from the Fourth and Fifth wards learned of the meeting. They met and decided to take over the meeting and do everything they could to keep Trustee Church from being elected to this office.

Dan Levinson, Dan Mahoney, and Mollie Livingstone—three of the most powerful figures in the Tenderloin, along with Boss Fahey from the Fourth Ward and Boss Alford from the Third Ward, persuaded as many people as possible from their wards to attend the meeting. They also convinced Justice of the Peace Crichton to allow his name to be put in nomination for president of the First Ward club. Since he was soon to run for election and didn't dare lose any votes, he agreed. When the Democrats of the First Ward heard the news, they approached Crichton and made him promise he wouldn't begin the meeting until 8:00 p.m. Unfortunately, Crichton made the promise before he found out that the bosses had already told their followers to be in Quimby's Hall at 7:30.

At 7:30 P.M. of the appointed evening, Quimby's Hall was filled to capacity. By the time the First Ward Democrats arrived they could barely squeeze through the throng. Only five made it inside; the rest went home. During the boisterous meeting that followed, Judge Crichton was elected president of the new club—the corrupt forces of the city had won another victory.

The honest Democrats of the First Ward vowed to try again, but, unfortunately, nothing changed until 1901 when a new city charter brought reform government to Fresno.

# Martha Ann Humphreys

In the spring of 1940—when wildflowers were carpeting the foothills of our great Central Valley—the little community of Tollhouse was plunged into mourning. On April 19, Martha Ann Humphreys, the ninety-seven-year-old widow of John W. Humphreys and the first white woman to live in the area, died on the ranch that had been her home for more than seventy years. She had only been ill for ten days.

Martha Ann Flinn was born in Jackson, Missouri, on February 23, 1843. She crossed the prairie in a covered wagon with her parents, William E. and Emily Rebecca Flinn, in 1856. They settled in the town of El Monte, near Los Angeles. She met and married sawmill owner John W. Humphreys in 1863 when she was twenty years old. They moved to Mariposa where he had established his business. Ten children eventually would be born to the couple.

In 1867, John and Martha and their two children moved his business to the Pine Ridge area near Tollhouse. During that first summer, they lived in a small shack while Humphreys helped to build the toll road up Sarver's Mountain that would be called the Tollhouse Grade. In the fall, with the road completed, he purchased the rights to the Cornstalk Ranch below the toll gate—now the site of the community of Tollhouse. This would be Martha Humphreys' home for the rest of her life. It was here, in 1868, that Martha Flinn Humphreys became the first white child born in the area. In those days, all children in the mountain communities were born at home. It was sometimes dangerous because, if complications arose, the nearest doctor was thirty miles away in Centerville.

When Martha Ann Flinn Humphreys died in 1940, her friend Ernestine Winchell eulogized her as a "capable, courageous pioneer." Although she had not had much formal education, she was a cultivated woman of great intelligence and strong character. She was interested in world events—she read and listened to the news and enjoyed discussing it. She was a student of the Bible and was an authority on the history of the Tollhouse area.

It is fitting to add the name of Martha Ann Humphreys to the roster of pioneers in the tales of our Valley.

Our story today centers around a school and a parcel of land bounded by Fresno, O, Merced, and N streets. Today, the Veterans Memorial Auditorium is on this site, but in 1872, when Fresno Station was established, it was part of a four-block parcel the Central Pacific Railroad owners hoped would be the site for a courthouse and other county buildings. The citizens of Fresno requested four blocks at Mariposa and L streets instead.

By 1878, the city had grown so much that Fresno's only school, located near Tulare and M streets, was filled to overflowing—one class had to meet in the Methodist Church. It was obvious that another school was needed. California's legislature authorized the school district to issue $15,000 in bonds. The district hired contractors Frank and C. P. Peck to design and build the new school on the little hill where the courthouse might have stood. The two-story white frame building had almost identical entrances on both O and N streets, was capped by a tower, and was called the White or the Central school.

The new school opened in September 1879 and, by 1885, had reached its capacity of 400 students. The city continued to grow—another school was needed.

The Central School is the large white building in the center of this 1884 photo. *Author's collection.*

In 1902, the Central School was moved to the Merced Street side of the site, another story was added to the building and it was renamed the Hawthorne School. Another building was built—this one of brick—on another part of the parcel, the corner of Fresno and O Streets. This school was named Washington Grammar School. By 1913, a new Washington Grammar School was built on Glenn Avenue so the brick building on Fresno and O streets was renamed the Hawthorne School and the white frame building behind it became the Luther Burbank School.

It may sound confusing today, but to the residents of Fresno in the early part of the twentieth century it seemed to make sense. By whatever name it was called, the old white frame building had become, next to the courthouse, the most cherished building in the city. For almost everyone in Fresno the old schoolhouse evoked memories.

This 1920 photo shows the Central School in its new location (white building) and the Hawthorne School across from the WaterTower. *Author's collection.*

This 1913 photo, taken on the steps of the Hawthorne School, is the sixth grade class. Snow White Brown, their teacher, is seated on the left.
*Courtesy of Mary Helen McKay.*

# Saint Patrick's Day, 1923

March 17, 1923, was a day that created lasting memories for those Fresnans of Irish lineage. It was Saint Patrick's Day—a day that was filled with activities both sacred and social.

By 12 noon, there was scarcely a seat to be had in Saint John's Cathedral—it was filled to overflowing. The early comers were treated to something unusual—the organist, after playing a quiet prelude, launched into a series of lively Irish airs. There were smiles on every face. At exactly 12 noon, the High Mass began with the singing of the "Kyrie" by soloists Alice Murphy and Mrs. William Gibson. The dean of Saint John's Cathedral, P. J. McGrath, was the celebrant of the Mass. The offertory selection was a "Hymn to Saint Patrick" sung by Catherine Balthus. At the conclusion of the service, the congregation was once again treated to Irish folk music as they left the cathedral.

The program for the day had just begun. Many preparations for the evening's festivities still had to be finished. The members of the Saint Patrick's Day committee were joined in this undertaking by the Knights of Columbus, the local chapter of the Catholic Daughters of America, the Catholic Ladies Aid Society, the Young Men's Institute, and the Yupka Club. Months of planning had gone into arrangements for the Grand Ball that was going to be held that evening at the Fresno Civic Auditorium.

At eight o'clock that evening, ball goers were greeted at the door by three charming young women, Cecelia St. Louis, Margaret Palva, and Margaret Gart, members of the Yupka Club. The orchestra, conducted by Harry Nolan, filled the air with Irish music. Grayce Mooney and Margaret Matthey, dressed in Irish costume, dispensed liquid refreshments. Many dance cards were filled, many toasts to Saint Patrick were made—a good time was had by all.

For several years, the ministers of Fresno churches had hoped that the day would come when Fresno merchants would voluntarily close their stores for three hours on Good Friday. There had not been a formal effort to achieve this, but, nonetheless, it was a quiet dream in the hearts of the clergy.

By 1923, other communities in California—San Francisco, San Diego, and Sacramento—and many large cities throughout the United States were observing Good Friday in this manner. It was no surprise to anyone when three clergymen, the Reverend F. G. H. Stevens of the Methodist Episcopal Church, Dean D. E. G. MacDonald of Saint James' Pro Cathedral, and Father Joseph Howard of Saint John's Cathedral, submitted a proposal to the Fresno Merchants Association asking them to consider closing businesses between 12 noon and 3:00 P.M. on Good Friday. The ministers also outlined plans to hold joint services for the community at the Strand Theater. Many churches would also hold their own services during the same three-hour period.

On Wednesday evening, March 15, the board of directors of the Fresno Merchants Association held its monthly meeting. The members seriously considered the ministers' proposal and acted upon it. The next day, association secretary Lawson J. Allen, made a public announcement of the board's decision. Allen said that community services were being planned between the hours of 12 noon and 3:00 P.M. on Good Friday and that the merchants would close their stores during those hours so that everyone who wanted to could attend. "It is something that should be done in every community for the moral good of the people," Allen said. "Fresno is following the steps of (other) cities in this movement." He said it was important for people in this fast-paced world of 1923 to stop occasionally and think of serious things.

The Fresno ministers were very happy with this outcome. Dean MacDonald said that the community services were going to focus on fellowship and brotherly love rather than doctrinal matters.

# Sarah Jane Ellis Davis

In this Valley legend we honor the memory of a pioneer woman of great strength and tenacity, Sarah Jane Ellis Davis.

Sarah Jane was born in Missouri, the eldest of thirteen children. Her father, Dr. T. O. Ellis, was not only a fine physician, but also a man of great intelligence and dignity. As the eldest child, Sarah Jane emulated her father, but she also inherited her mother's practicality.

In 1857, Sarah Jane married William Hale Davis. They began a farming and stock raising operation that lasted until 1867 when a flood wiped out their ranch. He moved his remaining stock to Watts Valley. He built a frame cabin for his family, which now included five sons and a daughter. In 1871, William died, leaving Sarah Jane to raise their children and run their ranch. Money was in short supply, but there was plenty of water and wood.

With the knowledge of medicine learned from her father, Sarah Jane was called upon to tend the sick and help with the births and deaths in the small communities nearby. Compensations for this took many forms and helped her growing family.

The boys earned what they could. When they were older and strong enough, they took their father's rifle and looked for wild game. The old Yager was a muzzle-loader that was so heavy it took two boys to carry it. When they spotted an animal, they would place a forked stick in the ground, one boy would put the muzzle of the gun into the fork to support it and the other boy would operate the hammer. They managed to shoot enough wild game to feed the family.

Sarah Jane and her children cleared enough land to plant wheat. When the crop was harvested, they took it to Centerville to be ground into flour. On one occasion, the local Indians were helping with the harvest. Rain clouds began to gather and the Indians decided to leave. Sarah Jane told her son Willie to put the Yager in place. She posted son Jeff near the door with another gun. Holding another pistol, this tall, dignified woman walked up to the chief and, pointing the gun at him, told him to order his tribesmen back to work or she would kill him. The chief decided to comply and all the wheat was safely under cover before the rain began.

For all the hardships she suffered, Sarah Jane Davis' dignity, precise speech, and good manners remained a part of who she was. She lived to the great age of ninety years. Sarah Jane Ellis Davis was a true legend of our Valley.

# The Hedges Home

Today, the northeast corner of Fresno and O streets is a parking lot. Nothing remains here that tells the story of a home that once graced this corner—a home that housed a family for two generations. H. P. and Mary Hedges came to Fresno from the Midwest in 1881. Mr. Hedges built a home for his wife and three daughters on M Street just south of the Mill Ditch that ran the length of Fresno Street. After the horrible flood of 1884 that inundated not only the Hedges' home, but also all the other homes and businesses in Fresno, Mrs. Hedges asked her husband if they could please move to higher ground.

There was only one place in the young town of Fresno that fit that description—the knoll at Fresno and O streets where the railroad owners had hoped the Fresno County Courthouse would be built. The Central School was across the street on the northwest corner, but the northeast corner was empty—that whole block was empty. Dr. Chester Rowell owned this property and was glad to sell it to Mr. and Mrs. Hedges. From their new property, the Hedges family could see everything for miles around. They built a two-story white frame house that featured a covered veranda that ran along three sides of the house. The house faced O Street, but steps from both streets led up to it. Orange trees from the M Street home were transplanted into the front yard landscape.

The interior of the first floor contained a large entry hall with double parlors to the left and a large dining room to the right. The fourteen-foot ceilings of the first floor rooms gave a feeling of spaciousness. The upstairs contained bedrooms for the family. In this era before indoor conveniences several outbuildings, including a carriage house, were also on the property.

After the death of Mr. Hedges in 1906, and Mrs. Hedges in 1916, their daughter, Mrs. J. H. Pefley, continued to live in the home. Mr. Hedges owned quite a bit of property north of Olive Avenue that he subdivided into colony lots. Hedges Avenue bears his name. The Hedges home was torn down many years ago for a parking lot. Like so many other historic buildings it exists only in the memories of the elders of our community.

# A Joyous 50th Anniversary

In the afternoon and evening of June 8, 1900, the home of Mr. and Mrs. A. T. Stevens was filled to overflowing with a steady stream of family and friends. It was a notable occasion. They had all come to celebrate the fiftieth wedding anniversary of Mr. and Mrs. H. P. Hedges. The party was given not only by Mrs. Stevens, the eldest daughter of the honorees, but also by her sisters, Mrs. J. H. Pefley and Mrs. William Shaw.

The parlors of the Stevenses' spacious Queen Anne home on the southwest corner of N and Merced streets were decorated with flowers, evergreens, and gold streamers. In the large dining room, with its Birdseye Maple paneling and built-in sideboard, several young women in dainty spring gowns played hostess to relays of twenty-five people who enjoyed their refreshments in this elegant setting.

H. P. Hedges was born in Chestertown, New York, on August 20, 1824. He married Mary Hunt on June 8, 1850, in Cayuga County, New York. The couple moved to Saukville, Wisconsin, a community twenty-five miles north of Milwaukee. In 1865, they moved to Waubeek, Iowa, where Mr. Hedges engaged in the mercantile business. In 1881, they came west to Fresno, bringing their family with them. In 1900, in addition to their three daughters, their descendants included nine grandchildren and one great-grandchild.

H. P. and Mary Hedges were well-respected members of the Fresno community. They were also a couple for whom many felt great affection. The reporter from *The Republican*, who attended the party, reflected that is was not often that Fresnans had the opportunity to celebrate a Golden Anniversary "and still more rare are the occasions when a multitude of friends gather to offer congratulations so sincere and generous as those bestowed upon Mr. and Mrs. Hedges" that day. Over five hundred people attended— to honor a couple that had earned the respect and good will of their community.

# A Most Romantic Love Story

The new year of 1900 was hardly begun when the halls of the Fresno County Courthouse fairly rang with joyful news of a most romantic sort.

Fresno County Recorder James M. Kerr seemed to many to be a confirmed bachelor. He was good-looking and charming with a fine job—he seemed to have all the qualifications of a good husband, but, as far as the people of Fresno could tell, matrimony had not entered his thoughts.

Surely, before the nineteenth century became the twentieth, Mr. Kerr would choose one of the lovely girls of Fresno as his wife. At least that was the thinking of one of Kerr's deputies. In the fall of 1899, the deputy made a bet with James Wade, one of Kerr's best friends, that Mr. Kerr would marry before midnight on December 31, 1899. He also stated the name of the Fresno woman he would marry. Wade felt a twinge of guilt about making the bet because he knew a secret no one else in Fresno was privy to.

James Kerr grew up in Danville, California. In his youth, one of his classmates was a charming girl named Emma McPherson. They not only attended school together, but they also were in the same Sunday school class. Even at their young age, they fell in love. The years went by and they made a pledge to each other. Then, in 1885, the unthinkable happened. James' parents decided to move to Fresno. The young people had to tell each other goodbye.

Fifteen years later James Kerr was in San Francisco on business. Quite by chance, he ran into William McPherson, Emma's brother. Their visit resulted in an invitation to visit the McPherson home. For the first time in fifteen years, James and Emma were reunited. The spark of love that had burned so brightly was still there. A few days after the twentieth century began James boarded a train for Oakland where he quietly married Emma. The minister who officiated had been their Sunday school teacher all those years ago.

As word spread through the Fresno Courthouse of this most romantic love story and its happy ending, the only person not smiling was the poor deputy who had lost his bet.

The editor of *The Fresno Morning Republican* assigned a re-porter to the city hall beat. Part of this assignment in-cluded attending the meetings of the board of trustees and report-ing on them for the readers of the newspaper.

On the evening of June 4, 1900, the trustees' meeting went on for a very long time. In the words of the reporter, "there was the usual long winded discussion on matters of minor importance." It seems some things don't change.

The residents of Blackstone Avenue were requesting two fire hydrants, but Trustee Joe Spinney said that since the people of this ward had not yet paid city taxes they should not be given the hy-drants. The matter was referred to the fire and water committee. Several saloon licenses were granted including one to Dan Maloney, one of the shady characters of Chinatown. An extension of thirty days was given to complete the grading of Blackstone Avenue.

The most interesting item—aside from Spinney denouncing the city dogcatcher because of the smells emanating from the pound—concerned the city's library. Spinney suggested that $150 dollars from the city's coffers be transferred to the library so they could buy more books. Spinney, who was illiterate and signed docu-ments with an "X," said that although he was not much of a reader, he liked to see institutions like the library flourish for the good of the community. Trustee Albin made the motion to transfer the money. Chairman Craycroft opposed the transfer of money, stat-ing that if the library trustees were as good businessmen as the city trustees, they could get along without the money to buy books. When the vote was taken, the motion to transfer the money passed by three to two. However, Joe Spinney had more to say about the library. He said that, since the library existed for the benefit of small boys, a way should be found to compel them "to partake of the benefits." He moved that a curfew be rung every evening at eight o'clock that would warn all young boys to get off the streets. The motion passed, leaving the reader of today envisioning all the small boys of Fresno running into their houses at eight every night and grabbing a book to read. Ah—would that it were so!

In late May and early June of 1900, a committee of Fresno High School graduates was busy planning for a special event—a reunion of all the graduates of the school. This event would not only serve as a social occasion, but it would also be an organizational meeting of the newly formed Fresno High Alumni Association.

The committee had been busy soliciting memberships and, so far fifty-eight Fresno High graduates had joined the group. Since that number represented not quite one third of the graduates of the school, articles about the event were placed in *The Fresno Morning Republican* with the hope of attracting more members.

On the evening of June 8, 1900, about one hundred people walked through the front door of Fresno High School, located at Stanislaus and O streets. It was a festive occasion as members of the various classes met and talked about their memories of their days at Fresno High.

Promptly at 9:00 P.M., Alumni President Harry Latimer, class of 1896, welcomed the alumni, teachers, guests, and members of the class of 1900 who had graduated the night before. After a program of musical selections by the Fresno High School orchestra, the business meeting got underway in earnest.

The first order of business was a speech given by Clarence Edwards, class of 1897, to welcome the members of the class of 1900 into the alumni association. Henry Dewell rose to respond on behalf of the class of 1900. Secretary Oscar Baker read the constitution as proposed by the executive committee. It was adopted by the group.

Officers were duly elected, and an executive committee appointed. Superintendent of Schools C. L. McLane gave a short speech commending the alumni association on its method of organization.

After the program, the members of the Fresno High School Alumni Association made their way to the third floor of the building where the hall was filled with beautifully decorated tables done by the ladies of Saint Paul's M.E. Church. A sumptuous repast was served. The evening ended at midnight with a rousing rendition of the Fresno High yell that brought the alumni to their feet:

> "Zooligan, Zooligan, Hiloway, Holm!
> Goodizen, Goodizen, Bim, Bom, Bohm!
> Soqui, Soqui, Ha, Ha, Ha!
> Fresno High School, Zip, Boom Bah!"

At the turn of the nineteenth century, when Fresno High was still a small school, a number of charming traditions developed. One of them was kept on the evening of May 12, 1900, when the entire senior class, consisting of thirteen young ladies and four young gentlemen, arrived at the P Street residence of C. L. McLane, superintendent of schools. They were greeted by their hosts and hostesses for the evening: their principal, Osmer Abbott, Mrs. Abbott, and all of their teachers and their spouses.

The gardens of the McLane home were decorated with Chinese lanterns. Inside, the rooms were tastefully decorated with spring flowers, greens, and streamers.

The teachers had planned many entertainments for the evening. Several games were played including the "Prince of Wales Guessing Cap," "Clothespins," and a game created by the teachers in which cards were distributed with the teachers' pictures on them. Then one of the teachers stood in front of a curtain and by using his hands, eyes, or the shadows cast on the curtain as clues, the students had to guess which teacher he was depicting. Much merriment was elicited by this game.

The guests retired to the dining room where an elegant dinner was served. At each place were a name card and a puzzle that had to be guessed during the meal.

After dinner, a program of musical selections and recitations were performed by the teachers. Duets in German and Hawaiian were greatly enjoyed. But the high point of the program was a recitation by Miss Ella Reed and Miss Lena Redington based on their memories of school days.

The festive evening ended and the senior class departed, agreeing that this evening had been one of the high points of their years at Fresno High School.

# The Story of Two Saloons

There were two saloons, one at Millerton and one in Centerville, whose owners and establishments would become intertwined as their histories played out in the 1860s and 1870s.

In 1860s Millerton, Fritz Friedman ran the Tom Allen Saloon, located near the courthouse, which made it a favorite libation spot for all the locals. During the same years, Len Farrar opened a saloon in Centerville. This establishment, however, had a second story room that was reached by an outside stairway. This became a popular setting for dances and other public gatherings. Music was provided by a local string band made up of Myers and Minkler on the violins, Winter on the guitar, and Uncle Billy Hutchison, the favorite local fiddler.

After Fresno Station was established in 1872, Farrar decided to move to the new town. He sold his business to Friedman, who left Millerton to try his luck in Centerville. Farrar built the Magnolia Saloon on H Street between Tulare and Mariposa streets. The building had a second floor—it was called Magnolia Hall and was the setting for church services, plays, dances, and, in 1875, the first community Christmas tree.

Meanwhile, Centerville now took second place to Fresno and Friedman's business did not do well. He lost the business and the building became the property of J. A. Blasingame in 1876. Blasingame had the building dismantled and moved to Fresno. It was rebuilt on the west side of I Street (Broadway) behind the Magnolia Saloon. He named it Metropolitan Hall. He added an outside stairway to allow access to the ballroom on the second floor. The first floor had a large room with a stage at one end. Plays and political conventions were held here. There were two small rooms on each side of the building—one housed a saloon and the other the courtroom for Justice of the Peace Spence Hill. For this reason, the building was popularly called "City Hall."

Ironically, on the same night, July 27, 1882, these two buildings—both tied to Len Farrar—burned to the ground. On that night, Fresno's most popular halls were gone forever.

# *Fire on a Summer Afternoon*

The afternoon of July 27, 1882, was one of those mid-summer afternoons when the heat outside and the heat inside homes and businesses was about the same—just plain hot. The pioneer village of Fresno Station did not yet know the joys of air conditioning. The saloons were doing a brisk trade—the streets were busy, too.

About a quarter of six, someone noticed that smoke was trailing upward from behind the Metropolitan Hall on I Street (Broadway). A gun fired, then another gun went off—the volunteers were being summoned to fight the fire. In the blink of an eye, the smoke turned to tongues of flame hideously lashing upward. Crowds began to gather—at first standing transfixed with horror—then quickly moving to help save the buildings nearby.

Unfortunately, there wasn't adequate water available nor were there enough ladders to reach the second stories and roofs of the buildings. A wind began to blow from the northwest, fanning the flames still further. Magnolia Hall, located on H Street behind the Metropolitan Hall, was next to feel the flames' wrath. Before long, both buildings—the two main social halls where dances and plays were enjoyed—were totally destroyed. They were not alone. The Ogle House, the French and Star hotels—all on H Street—were soon piles of ashes.

The flames leapt across I Street igniting Hughes Stables and Simpson's Blacksmith Shop. The horses, saddles, and harness were taken out and saved. Despite the herculean efforts of every citizen, forty-nine buildings were lost on that quiet Sunday afternoon. Most were insured—still, the loss was great.

But these folk were pioneers—they had known hardship before. Within a couple of days, they were all talking of rebuilding. As the reporter for *The Republican* said, "Phoenix like, Fresno will rise from her ashes…a fire is more or less disastrous, but a thriving and prosperous town like Fresno does not clothe herself in sackcloth simply because she has plenty of ashes."

In 1940, the seed of a dream began to take root. At the Pacific District Conference of the Mennonite Brethren Churches, a committee was formed to explore religious education. The following year, the young people of the church passed a resolution asking for the establishment of an accredited Bible institute. By 1942, it was decided that such an institution would be located in Fresno. A fundraising campaign brought in thousands of dollars. The project that would be the fulfillment of the dream was well underway.

By January 1, 1944, a general plan of the organization of the school and the requirements that would need to be met by both students and teachers had been accepted. It was hoped that the school could be near Fresno State College, then located at Van Ness and University avenues, so that its students could also take advantage of the secular subjects offered there.

After much prayer, a building was found near Fresno State and was purchased by the school committee. The home, at 1095 North Van Ness, was built by Albert Munger in 1911. The beautiful Greek Revival home became the first location of the Pacific Bible Institute.

In a few years, the institute moved its campus to Tuolumne Street. During this time the school had grown, but it was not growing at a great speed. The idea of a Bible college in the 1940s was a very acceptable one to many local Mennonite families, but, by the 1950s, many young people wanted a college degree from an accredited academic institution. Enrollment began to decline.

In the late 1950s, fifty-three acres were purchased at the corner of Chestnut and Butler avenues. The vision of the school was beginning to shift—it would come to fruition at this new campus site.

Our story will continue...

# Fresno Pacific University

By May 1959, the first classroom on the new campus of the Pacific Bible Institute had been completed. The new site at Chestnut and Butler avenues was truly open for business. Some classes were still being taught at the old campus on Tuolumne Street in downtown Fresno. Not only were religion classes offered, but a junior college program, with a separate enrollment, was in place as well. There were problems—enrollment in religious studies was declining.

Arthur Wiebe, who had served as an administrator for eight years at Immanuel Academy, a Mennonite Brethren high school in Reedley, was in the first year of his doctoral program at Stanford University. He was invited to attend a meeting with members of the West Coast Mennonite Brethren Board of Education to discuss the future of the Pacific Bible Institute. The outcome of the meeting was that Wiebe would make a thorough study of the institute. When his study was complete, he met with the board to present his findings and outline a direction for the school. In April 1960, Wiebe was hired as the Institute's president.

Wiebe's plan was to gradually move the institution to a first rate liberal arts college with a strong Bible program. The first steps in reaching this goal were to hire well-qualified faculty members, build the enrollment, broaden the selection of the classes offered, and to realize the accreditation of the junior college program. With board members such as E. J. Peters, P. A. Enns, M. S. Gaede, and Peter Funk firmly committed to this plan, things moved ahead. In 1961, accreditation was achieved and the school's name was changed to Pacific College.

In 1965, Pacific College became an accredited four-year school. In 1974, it also became a graduate school. Two more name changes were in the college's future—Fresno Pacific College and, today, Fresno Pacific University.

# *Ladies Who Love Learning*

In case one might think that the Fresno women of 1900 were solely pursing homemaking, needlework, and socializing, it's interesting to note that many study clubs were forming. These groups were established because women wanted to expand their horizons through learning.

Fresno's oldest study club, the Wednesday Club, formed in 1889, has a long-standing tradition. At the final meeting in May of each year, program books listing all the topics to be covered in the next year (October through May) are given to the members. The program committee keeps its selections a secret until that very moment. As the ladies look through their books, they see what their assignments are and how long they have to prepare their papers.

During 1900 and 1901, the Wednesday Club ladies were undertaking a course of study relating to Spain. Some of the topics included "Modern Spanish Literature," "Spanish Colonial System," "Modern Spanish Artists," "In New Spain," and "Modern Spanish Statesman." Papers would also be given on Emilio Castellar, Serreno, and Sagasta.

Midway through the year, the focus would turn to the Netherlands. Papers were given on Rembrandt, Rubens, Van Dyke, "The Moral Influence of Art," "Dutch Industries," "Pottery, Tapestries, and Lace," and "Dutch Literature Day," which would include discussions of Erasmus, Melanethon, and Dutch poets and recent writers.

At this time the ladies were meeting every week. The serious papers were given on alternate Wednesdays, and on the other Wednesdays lighter topics were offered. Some of the topics included "What Books Shall a Busy Woman Read" and "Illusions of Life."

The twenty-five members of the Wednesday Club were busy indeed. It may be safe to assume that they all had Fresno Public Library cards and, rather than drinking tea with their friends, were spending many of their afternoons doing research in the library.

# Sarah Elizabeth McCardle

O ne of the pioneers of our Valley was also a great contributor to one of its finest institutions.

Sarah Elizabeth McCardle was born at Millerton on February 25, 1873. Her mother, Ellen Baley McCardle, came west with her parents, Gillum and Permelia Baley, and other members of her family on a horrendous journey over the Santa Fe Trail, finally reaching Millerton in 1860. Her father, James McCardle, was born in Belfast, Ireland, and made his way to California on a ship that journeyed around Cape Horn. He had signed on as a sailor, but left the ship in San Francisco and headed to the gold fields. The year was 1848. He later raised stock in Fresno County.

Sarah Elizabeth McCardle. *Courtesy of Robert M. Wash.*

In 1874, the family moved to Fresno. It was here that Sarah lived for the rest of her life.

In 1908, Sarah joined the staff of the Fresno Public Library. On January 11, 1911, when Miss Jean Baird resigned as Fresno County librarian, Sarah McCardle was named to the post. There were two goals in her mind: to establish an adequate fund from which to purchase books and to open branch libraries throughout Fresno County. By April 1913, thirteen branches had been established— many housed in school buildings. On July 11, 1917, the county board of supervisors voted "to incorporate the City Library into the county system." The result was the establishment of the Fresno County Free Library—Sarah was at the helm. She tried to visit the branches often—a policy that meant sometimes riding on a logging wagon to get to the mountain libraries.

Sarah McCardle served in her post until her retirement on December 31, 1945. During her tenure she had overseen tremendous growth of the library system. When she died on October 15, 1952, the Central Library and all the branch libraries closed between nine and eleven that morning to pay tribute to her. Sarah McCardle was truly one of the legends of our Valley.

# The Mayor of Chinatown

A story in the pages of the November 27, 1921, *Fresno Morning Republican* paid tribute to Fresno's longest serving police officer, E. B. Bradley. In 1897, before the 1901 City Charter created a real police department, Bradley was appointed to serve as a patrol cop. In 1900, he became part of the West Fresno patrol. So successful did he become in tracking down and catching criminals, the underworld elements, who had always operated freely in Chinatown, gave him a nickname—the Mayor of Chinatown.

Gunfights, knifings, and chasing criminals became his everyday job. As he reflected on his career, certain episodes stood out. During one China Alley fight, Bradley knocked out the ringleader, who didn't wake up until three weeks later in the Fresno County Hospital. During the Bing Kong-Suey On Tong War of October 1900, a gun battle that began on G Street ended in China Alley with the murder of nine men. Bradley, who said gambling was the cause of the fight, saw the whole thing.

During his long career, he tried to save several "fallen women" by turning them over to the newly formed Fresno Rescue Society, but they all chose to go back to their lives in Chinatown.

Arrested criminals were walked through the streets of Fresno to jail or taken there in a dog wagon or wheelbarrow. On one memorable day, Priscilla Duffey, an underworld character of note, was arrested for intoxication and disturbing the peace. As Bradley wheeled her through downtown in a dogcart, she screamed at him and tried to stab him with a hatpin—much to the delight of onlookers.

Running gun battles were very much a part of his police experience. On many occasions, people had to hide in doorways to escape danger as Bradley chased murderers and robbers through West Fresno, exchanging gunshots with the culprits.

As he approached retirement, Bradley was the oldest member of the Fresno police force. No longer in service in Chinatown, he was now custodian of the Free Market that surrounded two sides of Courthouse Park on certain days of the week. For the rest of his life, he loved to share his memories of the wild days when he was called the Mayor of Chinatown.

# The Antics of the Annex

The Leisure Hour Club, the second oldest women's study club in Fresno, had a delightful tradition. Once a year they would invite their husbands, whom they playfully referred to as "The Annex," to an evening social. For their February 24, 1900, gathering, they asked The Annex to provide the entertainment.

The husbands had a grand time preparing what would be a total surprise to their wives—they were going to present a parody of a meeting of the Leisure Hour Club. For this one evening the officers would be: John E. F. Edwards, intellectual president; John C. Cooper, intellectual vice president; L. O. Stephens, intellectual scribe; T. Calvin White, intellectual keeper of records; and T. G. Hart, intellectual peace officer.

On the appointed evening, the ladies and their husbands gathered at the home of Dr. and Mrs. John C. Cooper. The meeting began with the election and installation of the officers for the evening. The reading of the minutes of the previous meeting, as seen through the eyes of The Annex, followed. The final paragraph, written by Intellectual Scribe L. O. Stephens read as follows: "After installation, the club repaired to the banquet room, where the culinary artist had prepared multigenerous viands and draughts to sooth their edacious media, and cause them to give forth sundry spiritual adumbrations of wit and wisdom neither evanescent nor fugacious, but tangible entities of materialistic value to every lover of lore, which the august potentiality of the club does greatly revere."

This was followed by the usual order of business and included a letter from Colonel Chisholm apologizing for not being able to "materialize at the anticipation." A bill for a suspiciously large number of oysters was presented.

The program for the evening then began. Henry Tupper gave a solo performance of "Raccoon on the Rail" accompanied by a chorus of The Annex. Dr. Cooper sang his rendition of a song entitled "The Pussy Cat," also accompanied by the chorus. Dr. Cooper then presented a learned treatise on the subject of "Mary's Little Lamb"—"its historical inerrancy and dramatic force." The scientific offering by John E. F. Edwards in "Astrological Observations" was an emotional recitation of "Twinkle, Twinkle Little Star." Henry Tupper offered an overview of Spanish history to show that Mrs. Tupper's study of the subject had not been for naught. The program ended with L. O. Stephens' learned discussion of Jack and Jill drawing from it many moral truths about marriage and domestic bliss.

As the ladies of the Leisure Hour Club and their husbands bid their hosts good night, it was unanimously agreed that the evening had provided much merriment and had been a great success.

# Paderewski at the Barton

On the night of Wednesday, April 4, 1900, carriages began pulling up in front of the Barton Opera House. As the beautifully dressed men and women alighted from their equipages and moved inside, a growing sense of excitement pervaded the scene. The loges, balcony, gallery, and orchestra seats began to fill. Soon the house lights were dimmed and a hush fell over the audience. The curtain went up to reveal a bare stage—save for a large concert grand piano. Anticipation grew—then, to stage left, the curtains moved. A man strode out and walked to the piano. The wildness of his hair, which stood up all over his head, belied his great genius, but it underscored a wildness of spirit that pervaded his musical interpretations. From the moment he took his seat at the piano, Ignace Paderewski, the greatest pianist of his time, held his audience enthralled.

Paderewski was born in Poland in 1860, the son of a shop steward. He entered the Warsaw Conservatory at age twelve to study piano. He later studied in Vienna.

From the time of his first concert in 1887, he held his audiences in an almost mystical devotion. Critics in Europe and the United States hailed his piano virtuosity.

The concert at the Barton began with Schumann's "Etudes Symphoniques," opus 13, followed by Beethoven's "Sonata in F Minor," the Appassionata, that was played with such great feeling the audience felt complete rapport with the artist. Following the brilliancy of his playing of Schubert's "Hark, Hark, the Lark," Paderewski received a huge ovation. It was his mastery of the four works of Chopin—an etude, a valse, a nocturne, and a ballade—that brought the audience to their feet. The "Nocturne in D Flat" was played with such an exquisite intensity of expression, Arthur Alan, *The Republican*'s music critic, rated it the finest of the program. Ovations and encores completed the evening. It would be a while before Fresnans would be treated to the presence of such genius again.

In early February of 1900, two of Fresno's well-known citizens—Gustav Eisen, agricultural expert, and Jake Hermann, haberdasher to Fresno's 400—decided to take a trip to the south valley to view some property in which they had invested. It was hoped that oil would be found on their land and that their investment would make them rich. Their trip was very successful—they not only saw their property and were assured of the potential it held, but they also were having one whale of a good time.

Eisen and Hermann left Bakersfield and began the journey north. The conversation turned from serious matters to subjects of a more jovial nature. By the time they reached Hanford, they were in such a cheery state of mind that a happier pair would be hard to find. They decided that a stop at the Arestia Hotel would be a good idea since they were in need of a cool drink and a good meal.

In their search for the dining room, they wandered into the hotel's saloon. A nice cocktail before dinner was in order. It was so pleasant an experience that a delicious dinner, accompanied by a fine wine, was followed by a return to the bar for a little more liquid refreshment. By this time, their spirits were high, indeed. They struck up a conversation with the bartender who seemed to them a man of great character who ran a fine establishment. The two men offered to buy the saloon—lock, stock, and barrel. The bartender accepted their offer of $2,000 and Eisen's check for $100 to seal the deal. The trip home was accomplished just as successfully.

It's too bad that the same couldn't be said for the morning after. Both men awoke to the horrible realization that they owned a saloon in Hanford that they didn't want. Hermann high-tailed it to Hanford. He walked into the saloon with a smile on his face and approached the bartender. Laughing, Hermann explained to the man that it was all a joke and asked for a return of the $100. The bartender, who seemingly had no sense of humor at all, refused, saying a deal was a deal. Finally, Hermann offered to buy half the saloon for $1,000. The barkeep's sense of humor began to surface a little and he agreed to the deal. A few days later, Hermann had second thoughts and purchased the other half.

Now the full owner of a saloon in Hanford, Hermann was praying hard that oil would be found on his land in Bakersfield. An oil gusher would certainly help to pay for spirited libations in Hanford.

# The Bachelor's Send-off

On the evening of January 30, 1900, a group of gentlemen gathered in the private dining room of the Hughes Hotel. This was much more than a social gathering—it was a send-off for one of their own, Mr. Charles Riege, owner of a Fresno bookstore and one of the leading young businessmen of Fresno.

The men, who sat down at the large table set with a linen cloth and fine china, were all members of the Ancient Order of American Bachelors. At each place was a card that read: "Cholly Riege's Last Night on Earth." Mr. Riege was going to be married in just a few days—this was his bachelor party.

The men, all attired in black tie, enjoyed a twelve-course dinner—each course a delicious masterpiece and each beautifully served. It was a jolly time for all of them.

At dinner's end, Willis Pike, who acted as toastmaster for the evening, called on Judge Crichton, who rose to his feet and offered a toast in which he revealed many secrets to a happy married life. E. E. Manheim's toast centered around the topic of "Money and Its Influence on the Conjugal State." John Jonsen offered thoughts on the influences of literature upon matrimony. The legal aspects of the married state were offered by George Jones. Several other toasts followed.

Thomas Lynch offered a lengthy toast praising Riege and congratulating him on his wise decision to abandon "the state of single blessedness." Riege stood and thanked the assembled group—bachelors all—for their friendship and for the evening. Willis Pike made the final remarks, wishing a happy life for the future Mr. and Mrs. Charles Riege.

And, so, a traditional bachelor party in 1900 came to a close.

One of the most notable political figures at the turn of the twentieth century was William Jennings Bryan. Bryan was born in Salem, Illinois, on March 19, 1860. He graduated from Illinois College in Jacksonville and from Union Law School in Chicago. In 1890 and again in 1892, he was elected to Congress.

Blessed with a talent for moving an audience, he became one of the most eloquent orators of his time. At the 1896 Democratic Convention, he electrified the crowd with his speech in which he said, "You shall not press down upon the brow of labor this crown of thorns, you shall not crucify mankind upon a cross of gold."

Campaigning on a platform of free coinage of silver as opposed to the gold standard advocated by the Republican Party, Bryan won his party's nomination for president. His stance on the coinage issue was his only radical position. During this campaign, he traveled 13,000 miles taking his issue to large cities and small towns alike. He was the first political candidate to travel in this manner and to make hundreds of speeches blatantly seeking votes. His campaign was not enough to win, however, and William McKinley, his opponent, became president.

In 1900, Bryan again ran against McKinley and, again, lost. He would be the Democratic Party nominee a third time in 1908, but would lose to William Howard Taft. He supported the candidacy of Woodrow Wilson, in 1912, and was rewarded by being appointed Secretary of State.

Bryan failed to achieve some of the other issues he espoused—women's suffrage, prohibition, graduated income tax, and popular election of U.S. senators. These would later become law.

In 1925, he made headlines again for his role as an associate counsel in the trial of John Scopes, a teacher who was accused of teaching evolution in a public school. Bryan died on July 26, 1925.

In 1900, William Jennings Bryan made Fresno a stop on his campaign tour…that story will follow.

# Bryan at the Barton

Saturday, April 8, 1900, was a day of great excitement for the local leaders of the Democratic Party and for all the local voters of that persuasion. Perhaps, it would be more accurate to include most of Fresno in the excitement, for the gentleman who was about to grace the city with his presence was one of the most famous political leaders in the country. The Barton Opera House, where the great man would speak that evening, was decorated with flowers. Every seat had been sold for the event. All was in readiness.

At exactly 5:20 P.M., a train pulled into the Santa Fe station. Crowds lined the platform and the streets for as far as the eye could see. The train stopped, a porter opened the door and put down the stairs. Suddenly the doorway was filled by the appearance of a dark-haired, handsome man—William Jennings Bryan. The crowd went wild. Bryan and his party descended to the platform and, with great difficulty, moved through the crowd to the open carriage that awaited them.

Bryan, who would soon be a candidate for president on the Democratic ticket, waved to the crowds lining the streets as his carriage proceeded to the Hughes Hotel. Getting from the carriage to the registration desk of the Hughes was not an easy task, but, as soon he signed the register, he told his hosts that he wanted to take them up on their offer to see the countryside. Although darkness was approaching, they all climbed in the carriage and drove through some of the vineyards and farmlands just outside the city.

Later, during his speech at the Barton, Bryan, one of the greatest orators of his time, held the rapt attention of the crowd as he swept them along on a tidal wave of political issues—free silver, imperialism, trusts, and the changing face of the Republican Party. After an hour and a half, his speech finished, Bryan left for the Hughes Hotel and a good night's rest. Those who were present that evening would always remember the eloquence and the enthusiasm of William Jennings Bryan and the night he came to Fresno.

# William Walter Shipp

O n the morning of January 16, 1900, an elderly gentle-man, driving a team of mules, left his ranch at Big Dry Creek and began the journey to Fresno. By the time he turned his rig onto Blackstone Avenue it was nearing lunchtime. He contin-ued south on Blackstone and, just a mile from downtown, ap-proached the point where the Santa Fe Railway crossing was eas-ily discernible. He heard a train in the distance and urged his team forward. When they got onto the tracks, the mules froze in fear and wouldn't move. The train came ever onward—the engineer tried to stop the train in time, but could not. On that winter morn-ing, one of Fresno County's oldest pioneers, William Walter Shipp, was killed instantly.

William Walter Shipp was born in Holmes County, Missis-sippi. He married Mary Strother and together they would have ten children. When the Civil War broke out, Shipp joined the Con-federate Army and fought for four years in the cavalry. After the war, he owned a cotton plantation and gained a reputation as one of the most successful cotton farmers in the South, but the lure of California drew him west.

In 1868, W. W. Shipp and his family left their home in Durant, Mississippi, and traveled to New York. They joined the families of David Cowan Sample, Major Thomas P. Nelson, and others, boarded a ship, and came to San Francisco. After a short stay in Vacaville, the group purchased enough food for a year and, with the remainder of their funds, bought sheep. They came south, driv-ing their sheep with them, and settled at Big Dry Creek. Shipp and his family settled on government land. He became a noted sheep man in the county.

In 1887, he built a home in Fresno and, from that time on, he and his wife spent most of their time in the city. They attended the Methodist Episcopal Church South and had many friends.

It was with shock and great sadness that the news of William Walter Shipp's passing was received. The Fresno community mourned the passing of another of the great pioneers of Fresno County.

# Robbery at the French Bakery

In the wee hours of a summer morning—on June 19, 1904, to be exact—the staff of the French Bakery on K Street (Van Ness) were beginning their early morning chores. One of the bakers was tending the outdoor oven in the back yard of the building. Several other bakers were working in the indoor oven room, located at back of a long hallway. Another baker, awaiting his shift, was sound asleep in a room off the hall. This fellow had gone to bed at 8:00 p.m. knowing that he would be called to work about 1:00 a.m. A noise in the hallway roused him from his slumber. "Is it time to get up?" he called out. "No, not yet!" a voice answered. He went back to sleep.

The noise from the oven room at the back of the building was such that no one heard the entrance of four young men who had no business being there. They had been casing the building for several weeks—often coming in to buy doughnuts or bread and wandering through the building. Many rooms opened off the long hall that ran through the center of the building—the young men had become familiar with them all.

On this summer night, their thoughts were not on bakery goods, but on valuables. As the young men moved along the hallway, one of them answered the voice that called out to them asking if it was time to get up. They stood quietly—waiting to make sure the owner of the voice had fallen asleep again.

They tiptoed into one of the adjoining rooms where they knew a large trunk was stored. They moved the trunk into the hallway and positioned it in such a way that if someone came into the hall they would fall over it. They brazenly opened the truck, took out a number of fine pocket watches, silver watch chains, and ten dollars in cash. Then they hightailed it out of the building. A few hours later, one of the bakers stumbled over the trunk, discovered the robbery, and called the police. A police search was soon underway for the four men whom the baker suspected were involved. It was not a happy time for the staff of the French Bakery who had lost one kind of dough while tending to another.

# A Grand Parade

On October 5, 1896, people poured into Fresno from all over the state. From Hanford, Visalia, Modesto, Merced, the colonies around Fresno and from as far away as Sacramento and San Francisco they came. By 10:00 A.M., the streets of Fresno were so filled with people that one could hardly move. Excitement was the order of the day. At 1:30 P.M., the first train of the People's Railroad would arrive, but first a grand parade was about to start on the streets of downtown.

At precisely 12:30 P.M., the parade began. Leading off the march were the mounted police. Grand Marshal Fulton G. Berry, wearing a striking yellow sash and mounted on a beautiful horse, came next. Governor Budd, a splendid horseman, was a commanding presence as he and members of his staff—all on horseback—drew cheers from the crowd. Justy's band set a stirring tempo for horses and marchers alike.

Company E of Visalia, under the command of Captain Ward and marching in formation, were followed by a large delegation of Tulare County's leading citizens. Large delegations from Hanford and Visalia followed.

Many local businesses had floats—Fancher Creek Nursery; Fresno Agricultural Works; *The Fresno Republican*; Kohler & Chase music house; Kutner, Goldstein & Company; the Shaw Company; and W. Parker Lyon's furniture store, to name a few. Floats from the Eisen, St. George, and Centennial vineyards, corn and pumpkins from the Laguna de Tache grant, and figs from packer S. N. Mitrovich showcased the valley's produce.

The best was saved for last. Clovis Cole's mule teams, numbering nine, eight, ten, and twelve, hauled wagons filled with grain from the Cole Ranch. It was, indeed, impressive.

The parade over, the crowds headed for the barbecue and speeches at the Santa Fe Railway reservation. It was a most exciting day in the tales of our Valley.

# Mr. Spreckel's Railroad Comes to Town

The San Francisco and San Joaquin Valley Railway, between Stockton and Fresno, was established by Claus Spreckels and a group of capitalists in reaction to the monopoly that the Central Pacific Railroad had on the Valley's business. Prices to ship agricultural produce were constantly rising. The Central Pacific was making huge profits, but the Valley's farmers were suffering.

When the new rail line, popularly called "The People's Railroad," reached Fresno on October 2, 1896, it was a cause for celebration. On the morning of Monday, October 5, the largest parade that Fresno had ever seen wended its way through downtown, ending at the railroad reservation. The participants were soon joined by multitudes of people from all over the Central Valley. Excitement was in the air as they waited. Then, in the distance, the shriek of a railroad whistle could be heard. Suddenly, the first passenger train, called the Emancipator, rounded the corner from Diana to Q Street. A shout went up, "There she comes!" The cheering crowd went wild. After the dignitaries disembarked, a number of speeches were given—notably one by Claus Spreckels, president of this line. This was followed by a barbecue attended by an estimated 20,000 people. It was a hot October day, but the crowd was in a joyful, celebratory mood—no one seemed to mind the heat.

Not everyone was thrilled about the new line. Dr. T. R. Meux who, in 1889, had built a Queen Anne style home for his family at R and Tulare streets, now had trains running just outside his back yard. O. J. Woodward, Jacob Vogel, L. O. Stephens, and Ingvart Teilman, who all lived on Q Street, now had the train running down the middle of their street.

By 1898, the new rail line was completed as far south as Bakersfield. With trains soon scheduled to run on a regular basis, a passenger depot was needed.

After the grand parade had ended and the first train, the "Emancipator," had arrived on the Santa Fe tracks, several other events were held on this day of celebration—October 5, 1896.

Thousands of people attended the huge barbecue at the railroad reservation. The smell of roasting meat had made it hard for many of the attendees to listen to the speeches that preceded the meal. Finally, however, the twelve tables that were filled with cups, plates and silverware were also heaped with plates of food. The lines formed and several thousand people feasted on the following menu: Eau de Fresno (soup); Fromage de Valley Road, Boeuf au naturel, Mouton en deshabille, Cochon de San Joaquin Valley (entrees); and a variety of desserts. Three huge tanks of hot coffee awaited the diners. Since it was hot—in the words of one reporter, about 2,000 degrees—hot coffee seems an odd choice.

At eight in the evening, a parade of bicycles of every size, type, and color imaginable filled the streets. There were many cycling clubs in the area and they all participated.

Also that evening, a very elegant dinner was held at the Hughes Hotel. Hosted by the members of the Chamber of Commerce and the Hundred Thousand Club, it was given to honor the Committee of Ten who had planned the day and the distinguished guests, including Governor Budd and Claus Spreckels. Three hundred and fifty people sat down to a formal dinner. John Reichman acted as toastmaster for the evening. Many toasts were made, the most notable the one given by James D. Phelan, the Democratic nominee for mayor of San Francisco, that was clever and lent much merriment to the evening.

The next morning, when the story on the day's events appeared in *The Fresno Morning Republican*, the reporter added a few notes at the end: "Rah for Claus, Fresno did herself proud, the livery stables made lots of money, and…tired feelings in order today." It had been a fine time, indeed, in the tales of our Valley.

# The Santa Fe Depot

In 1899, construction began on a depot designed in the Mission style. Its red tile roof and white stucco would make a striking appearance for the exterior of the building and would become a prototype for other depots throughout the West.

By November, a reporter for *The Republican* was allowed to tour the building. He reported that the exterior was almost finished—all it needed was painting and sanding. The interior, he said, was not yet painted and the electrical wiring was not completed.

The southern one-story portion of the building would house Wells Fargo & Co. A sliding window at the southern end and a sliding door opening to the west would allow wagons to unload their goods at either place. Large scales were in place just inside the door. The floors of this area were asphalt.

The main section of the building was two stories high with a one-room attic—for the superintendent's use. The main feature of the interior of this section was two waiting rooms—one for ladies and one for gentlemen—and between these two rooms was a tiled vestibule leading to the ticket office which was on the east side of the building. Windows opening from this office to the outside allowed passengers to purchase their tickets without going inside.

On July 1, 1900, regular passenger service began and the Santa Fe Depot opened its doors for the first time.

Now, after a massive restoration project, the Santa Fe Depot looks just as it did in 1900. It was dedicated for the first time in its history on February 12, 2005. Once again it will be used as a passenger depot and will provide another touchstone to the history of our great Valley.

In 1869 there was a ferry crossing on the San Joaquin River just ten miles downstream from Jones' Ferry. The ferry boat itself, actually a large flatboat, had torn apart from its moorings at Jones' Ferry during the horrific flood of 1868 and was carried on the flood waters until it reached this spot, where it went ashore. It was such an unwieldy craft that to try to move it back was almost impossible.

Charles E. Strivens found the craft and dragged it to a nearby spot on the river. He started operating it as a ferry—the first in the area on the Valley floor.

Soon afterward Strivens married Mary Parker, daughter of W. H. Parker, who operated a store twenty miles farther down river. The couple built a home on the south bank of the San Joaquin. From here they could operate their ferry. Eventually, they opened a trading post.

In March 1872, the Central Pacific Railroad line reached the Strivens' land. A post office was opened with Charles Strivens as the postmaster. The name given to the little settlement was Sycamore.

The couple, thinking that a bridge would never be built over the river, built a new ferry. They were hoping that they would make a great deal of money as traffic increased due to the new towns being developed by the railroad.

A school district was formed and the couple was allowed to name it for their first child—Lorena.

For a few years all was well. Then, in the 1880s, the railroad changed the name of the Sycamore post office to the Herndon post office in honor of one of the railroad's section bosses. The name of the school district was also changed to Herndon.

As the years went by, a bridge and a highway replaced the ferry. Today, the settlement of Sycamore is gone—the only traces of its existence are the stately Sycamore trees that stand on the bluffs of the south bank of the San Joaquin River.

# Converse Ferry

In the very earliest days of Fresno County, three ferry crossings were the first to be licensed on the San Joaquin River—one in Millerton in August 1856 for Ira McCray, one for Stephen Gaster at Mono City, and one in November 1856 for Charles Converse.

Charles Converse was drawn to the mines of the upper San Joaquin River and left his Mariposa diggings in the early 1850s. After spending a little time in the area, he became aware of the difficulties the river posed for transportation at certain times of the year. When the river was low, horses and wagons could cross the river easily; but when the river was full or at flood stage, crossing was impossible.

Seeing an easier way to make money than mining, Converse chose a spot on the river downstream from Millerton. It was at the base of the foothills and on the stage road that traversed the Valley from Fort Tejon to Centerville to Stockton. At this point, the road "went down the earth bank on one side and up on the other before winding down the shore and…across the plains." Converse took advantage of this route and placed his ferry at this spot.

He placed posts hewn from massive tree trunks on each bank of the river. To these, he attached heavy cables. Using a pulley and slips, he rigged them to a huge scow—a flatboat—that was heavy enough to transport the largest of freight wagons with a team of sixteen to twenty animals.

Converse, like other ferry operators, had to pay a monthly fee of eight dollars and was under a bond of $3,000. As more people came into the area, the ferry operator found his business a profitable one.

During the flood of 1867-68, the ferry was wrenched from its moorings and ended up at Sycamore. Converse rigged a new vessel out of pontoons. He operated his ferry until 1869 when he sold it to J. R. Jones. Today, this site on the San Joaquin River is the town of Friant.

# Redheads Ruled the Day

Anyone walking near Theater Fresno on the afternoon of March 18, 1916, was greeted by an interesting sight. Red-haired women of every possible hue—from auburn to strawberry blond—were lined up outside waiting to walk through the theater doors. Not a person with brunette or blond hair, or for that matter, any men were allowed inside for this particular matinee. "What prompted such an event?" one may ask. It happened in this manner.

Miss Virginia Brissac, a well-known actress of the time, was appearing in a play entitled "Alma, Where Do You Live?" It was a musical farce—an enjoyable, light-hearted play. Miss Brissac was blessed with auburn hair. The road company with which she performed, the Brissac Players, traveled throughout the United States. She had long wanted to hold a special event for redheaded ladies on her birthday, which was March 18, but she had never been to a city where she saw a large number of redheads. Then the company came to Fresno. Everywhere she went she was struck by the fact that there was an abundance of red-haired ladies.

One day early in March 1916, she was walking down a street in Fresno and saw a group of beautiful red-haired girls looking at her picture in a shop window. At that moment she decided that Fresno was the place where she would celebrate her birthday in the way of which she had dreamed.

The advertisements went out. Every red-haired woman in Fresno—regardless of age—was invited to attend the matinee free of charge. On that March afternoon, Miss Virginia Brissac celebrated her birthday with every red-haired woman in the city of Fresno. A glorious time was had by all on this most unusual occasion.

# A Man and His Ads

Ah, spring…that time of year when the thoughts of many turn to love. In the world of the irrepressible W. Parker Lyon, thoughts turned to advertising.

It's been a while since we have visited Mr. Lyon's creative ads…these have been gleaned from the pages of *The Fresno Morning Republican*.

March 19, 1903… "The Kicker…There's a kicker in this town, a jolly good fellow, nit; Who reads my ads with chronic frown, While others throw a fit." "This man came into my store last week and asked if I would furnish a house for him, buy the house and lot for him, pay the interest on the debt and feed the dog. Yes, I'll do anything to sustain my reputation as Fresno's leading philanthropist and furniture dispenser."

December 2, 1898… "A Recipe for Lemon Pie is: 'Sit on a hot stove and stir constantly.' Just as if one could sit on a hot stove without stirring constantly."

One of the popular buildings in turn-of-the-twentieth-century Fresno was a four-plex called a flat. There were two apartments upstairs and two downstairs. One feature of many of these flats was a Murphy bed. It folded into the wall when not in use. It was often faced with a large glass mirror so, when it was folded up, the mirror provided a decorative element for the room.

February 23, 1902… "A Folding Bed Story. Did you ever live in a flat? Well, I did and it was a flat failure. The only mirror in the house was in the front of the folding bed and when my wife got up late for breakfast, I had to lay flat on my back on the floor under the bed to put on my necktie. W. Parker Lyon…Flats in wallpaper. The latest fad. All kinds of picture frames made to order by Professor Kiesker, former framer to his Majesty, King Edward VII."

Ah, W. Parker Lyon—truly a colorful character for any season!

# Thomas W. Patterson

On the morning of March 15, 1914, flags in Fresno were flying at half mast out of respect for one of Fresno's leading citizens who had died in San Francisco the day before. There was a true outpouring of grief throughout the city.

Thomas W. Patterson was born in Perry, New York, on August 3, 1859. He was a direct descendant of Captain Thomas Patterson, a distinguished Revolutionary War soldier. After completing his education, he became involved in the mercantile business in Rochester and Buffalo before coming to Fresno in 1888.

At that time, Fresno was in the midst of an economic "boom" period. Patterson became involved in the real estate and loan business and did well. He purchased vineyards, orchards, and parcels of land in the city.

On November 16, 1892, Patterson married Elizabeth Bernhard. They had a son and a daughter.

Patterson became a stockholder in the Fresno National Bank in 1897 and, in March 1900, became its president. Under his vigorous leadership, the bank became a strong institution.

Patterson had other interests as well. He owned the northeast and southeast corners of Tulare and J (Fulton) streets. He also purchased the mansion once owned by developer Marcus Pollasky. This home sat on land bounded by U, Mariposa, Divisadero, and Tulare streets.

In 1908, Patterson became involved in developing land in Stanislaus County. He and his cousin, John D. Patterson, laid out a town site on land inherited from their uncle. Today, it is the city of Patterson.

In early 1914, Patterson became ill with what was diagnosed as a stomach ulcer. After the first operation in San Francisco, he seemed to be recovering—then he relapsed. The second operation proved fatal. His death at age fifty-four left Fresnans mourning a man who had contributed so much to the economic growth of Fresno.

Thomas W. Patterson.
*Courtesy of California History and Genealogy Room,
Fresno County Free Library.*

Patterson Block, Fresno, Cal.

First Patterson building on the northeast corner of J (Fulton) and Tulare streets. *Author's collection.*

# T. W. Patterson Building

Among the real estate holdings of Thomas W. Patterson were two downtown parcels across the street from each other—the northeast and southeast corners of Tulare and J (Fulton) streets. He built a two-story building on the northeast corner that was called the Patterson Building. Hans Graff and Company, a hardware and grocery store, occupied the ground level space for many years. This property would later come under the ownership of Louis Einstein's heirs.

The southeast corner was purchased in 1899. In 1900, the title was transferred to the Central Land and Trust Company of which Patterson, Colonel William Forsyth, and Captain W. A. Neville were equal partners. In 1903, a four-story building, called the Forsyth Building, was built on this property. Eventually, Patterson became the sole owner. In 1921, the building was destroyed in a massive fire.

Thomas W. Patterson died in 1914. In 1923, his heirs built an eight-story, steel framed office building on the site for $1,250,000. In an interview with a reporter for *The Fresno Morning Republican*, architect R. F. Felchlin, whose company was also constructing the building, told about the progress of the project. Felchlin said that the fastest elevator of any building in the country, save the Union Bank building in Los Angeles, was being installed. It would go from the top of the building to the bottom in eleven seconds. Every room in the building would have both hot and ice water. Vertical airshafts that connected to every room would provide forced air circulation. Felchlin said that if a satisfactory air system was invented, the building would be ready to receive it.

When completed, the Patterson Building was the largest office building in Fresno. One unique feature of the building was that the entire eighth floor was reserved for the Sequoia Club. They had the one of the finest clubrooms in California.

Today, the T. W. Patterson building still stands—a reminder of a man who contributed a great deal to the early growth of Fresno's business community.

# April Tidbits—1900 Style

In the early part of the twentieth century, there was a column in *The Fresno Morning Republican* called "The Man About Town." It was filled with tidbits of news—the sort of stories that are humorous or thoughtful, but not important enough to fill a regular space. On April 15, 1900, two items appeared that are worth noting.

A few days before this column appeared, William Jennings Bryan had been in Fresno—it seems everyone had seen him. Another well-known gentleman also was in town—Morris E. Dailey. Mr. Dailey had been superintendent of Fresno schools from 1897 to 1899. He now was the vice principal of the San Jose Normal School. He decided to pay a visit to the C Street school for "old times sake." He talked to the teachers and then stopped by one of the lower grade classrooms. He visited with the children and, after a few minutes, went on his way. After he was gone, the teacher asked the children who that distinguished, dark-haired gentleman was. No one could tell her. Finally, a hand went up in the back of the room. When called upon, a very small boy got up from his desk, stood up to his full height, and, in the loudest voice he could muster said, "That gentleman was William Jennings Bryan."

The other story took place in Sanger. A Sanger attorney by the name of Cureton needed to have a certain woman in the community make an affidavit. Most people in this situation would make an appointment with the aforesaid party so that a time convenient to both persons could be agreed upon. For some unknown reason, Barrister Cureton decided to forgo this professional nicety and, instead, bring an element of surprise into the equation. At midnight, when all of Sanger was fast asleep, he appeared at the woman's door demanding she get up and make the affidavit then and there. She called the authorities. Mr. Cureton was soon serving forty days in jail for his surprise visit—plenty of time for him to think about matters of etiquette and jurisprudence.

# Joseph Dobbins Davidson

On the morning of December 7, 1908, the life of one of Fresno's top surgeons drew to a close. Dr. Joseph D. Davidson passed away quietly at 5:50 a.m. at his home at 1762 K (Van Ness) Street

In 1862, Joseph Dobbins Davidson was born in Columbia, Tennessee. His father was a practicing physician. Joseph, deciding to follow in his father's footsteps, graduated from Vanderbilt Medical School at nineteen years of age.

In 1886, he came to Kingsburg and built up a good medical practice there. Four years later, he moved to Fresno and went into partnership with Dr. Deardorff, who had his offices in the Fresno Loan and Savings Bank building.

Shortly after settling in Fresno, Davidson was named county physician. During this time, he decided to devote more of his practice to surgery. In 1897, Davidson, along with four other physicians, George Aiken, J. L. Maupin, W. T. Maupin, and D. H. Trowbridge, formed the Burnett Sanitarium in the former boarding house of Mrs. Celia Burnett. On May 16, 1900, the hospital was incorporated. From the time of its organization until his death, Davidson served as president of the hospital.

As Davidson devoted more and more of his practice to surgery, he took a post-graduate course in modern surgery in New York and spent a summer traveling and studying in Europe. On his return, he visited the leading hospitals in the country to learn their surgical techniques. In 1901, on a visit to Tennessee, he married Mrs. Louise Peden of Nashville.

In 1903, Davidson was diagnosed with heart disease. He seemed to be doing well and led an active life until October 1908. He went to San Francisco for treatment and was admitted to a hospital in that city. His condition worsened. In accordance with his wishes, he was brought back to Fresno, where he died on the morning of December 7, 1908, with his wife at his side.

# Burns' Night—1892

On Monday, January 25, 1892, the dining room of the Hotel Pleasanton in downtown Fresno filled with a colorful group of men, all members of the St. Andrew's Society. For on this evening, in this place, a birthday was to be celebrated—the birthday of Scotland's poet Robert Burns.

Bagpipe music filled the room—it could be heard out on the street as well—and kilted laddies, one hundred fifty strong, gathered to pay tribute to the poet of their hearts. The whiskey flowed that night…laughter and tears flowed as well. It was a night also to pay tribute to the homeland of some and the ancestral homeland of many who were here together in Fresno.

Judge Crichton, Fresno leading authority on Burns' poetry, having committed most of it to memory, was present and was to give the address. He was not feeling well and made only a few remarks. It was left to members of the St. Andrew's Society to carry out the program.

Bob Baird sang "There was a Lad was Born in Kyle" with great gusto. Then A. D. Spence walked to the front of the room. He began to recite Burns' immortal poem "Tam O'Shanter." "He made the fire gleam; the winds roar: the witches dance and leap; the 'old Nick' blow loud and louder; the dancers fly quick and quicker; the race; the escape; and the moral"—Spence's delivery was perfect; his mastery of the Doric (the Scots dialect) was perfect. He made it all come alive. The audience rose to their feet applauding.

The program continued with songs, poems, and dance. No mention was made of food. Perhaps no one had a recipe for haggis, the traditional centerpiece for any Burns' Night supper. Even without the haggis, the evening was a great success—everyone went home happily humming the songs of Robert Burns.

# William Walker Phillips—The Early Years

On July 20, 1851, one of Fresno County's pioneers, William Walker Phillips, was born in Yazoo, Mississippi. His parents, Seaborn Moses Phillips and Emily C. Phillips, were delighted to welcome their first son—five more children would follow. His earliest memory was of the presidential election of 1860. Abraham Lincoln won and, soon after, eleven Southern states seceded from the Union.

Seaborn Phillips, a veteran of the Mexican War, organized a company of soldiers and became their captain. Young William remembered how they drilled every night and how he would march alongside the drummer boy. When his father left with his unit to fight for the Confederacy, he begged to go, too. He was only ten years old when, in February 1862, he and most of his town watched the soldiers board the steamer *The Yazoo City* and sail away. His father was elected a colonel of the Tenth Mississippi Regiment, but he died of pneumonia just three months after leaving home.

William Phillips' grandfather, who owned a plantation in Madison County, sent a four-mule team to collect the remainder of the family and move them nearer his home. William would make the eight-mile trip to Canton to collect the mail. One of the pieces of news he brought home during those years was the assassination of President Lincoln on April 14, 1865.

Phillips attended a school about a mile from his home. It was very primitive with hard wooden benches. A dozen hickory switches were in the corner waiting to be used in the punishment of those who had not done their homework. He left school at age thirteen.

When the war ended, Phillips found a position as a clerk in a store in Canton run by J. B. Otto. During this time, former President of the Confederacy Jefferson Davis and his cousin, General Joe Davis, visited the town. Otto instructed Phillips to call on them at their hotel and present them with two quart bottles of brandy from his private cellar. Phillips, remembering that the general and his father had been friends, was thrilled to comply. The memory of this visit would remain with him for the rest of his life.

Our story will continue…

William Walker Phillips, at one time the owner of the Riverview Ranch that is now the Coke Hallowell Center for River Studies.
*Courtesy of David Phillips.*

# William Walker Phillips—A Joyous Welcome

We continue the story of Fresno County pioneer William Walker Phillips who, after serving as a page in the Mississippi State Legislature, battling illness, and facing the difficulties of finding a job after the Civil War, made a life-changing decision. He wrote to his cousin Harry Dixon, who had gone west and was living in the Alabama settlement near present-day Madera. He told Dixon his problems and asked if work could be found in California. Dixon wrote back and said he had found a position for him in a mercantile store in Centerville. Enclosed in the letter was a bank draft for $250.

Phillips, in a narrative he wrote for his grandchildren, said he packed his "carpet sack and with a blanket I headed for California." He took the train to Stockton. At the Webber Hotel in Stockton he met Zack Hall, a beau of his sister's. Hall told him he could borrow his horse to travel the remaining eighty miles to the settlement. The horse was at the Ashe Ranch, twelve miles from Stockton—Hall gave him an order to give to the ranch foreman.

Phillips couldn't afford to rent a horse so he walked six miles to Knight's Landing. The next morning he walked the remaining miles to the Ashe Ranch only to find that the bridle and saddle were at another ranch twenty miles away. Phillips, who was still weak from the aftermath of a fever, simply could not walk that additional distance. The foreman rigged up a bridle with snaffer bits and baling rope. Phillips threw his blanket over the horse and headed out for the Alabama settlement.

Phillips arrived at his uncle's house in the Alabama settlement on New Year's Day 1871 at two o'clock in the afternoon. Everyone was out making New Year's calls so the Chinese servant gave him dinner. When the family returned, a joyous welcome was given to the young man who had traveled so far. William Walker Phillips had arrived in Fresno County.

# William Walker Phillips—The Fresno Years

We have been following the story of William Walker Phillips as he journeyed from Mississippi to the Alabama settlement. Our story today will tell of his life in Fresno County.

The illness that had plagued Phillips for several years hit him once again after his long trip west. With the help of his family, Dr. Graves' medicine, and a month of recuperation, Phillips was finally well enough to take up a position at a merchandise store in Centerville. After two and a half years, he was offered a job at Kutner & Goldstein in Fresno. He did very well and, at the end of two years, he was offered a partnership and was asked to find a place to start a new store. Phillips chose Centerville and was soon managing Kutner & Goldstein's new store in that town. After four and a half years, Phillips was reporting profits to Mr. Kutner—the store was doing very well.

Kutner wanted to start a bank in Fresno, using the profits from the store, and wanted Phillips to run it. Phillips told Kutner that he knew nothing about the banking business. Kutner said to him, "You are a good bookkeeper, you know the values of land, and you know the people, and you know who to trust. You can learn the business in a week." Phillips went to Santa Rosa for ten days and studied the bookkeeping system used by a bank in that city. He came home and on March 1, 1882, opened the Farmers Bank of Fresno.

Two years earlier, Phillips married Bettie Pressley, whose father was Judge Pressley of Sonoma County. Three children were born to the couple. In 1893, W. W. Phillips purchased the Riverview Ranch on the San Joaquin River, and moved his family there. During the two years they lived there, he turned it into a successful ranching operation.

About this time, Phillips got involved in politics and was elected a delegate to the Democratic National Convention in Chicago in 1893. He was an ardent supporter of Grover Cleveland, who became the party's nominee, and then was elected president.

Not long after the death of his wife in 1916, W. W. Phillips moved to San Francisco where he lived until his death on January 21, 1935.

During his long life he made significant contributions to the community of Fresno through volunteer work. He helped establish the Fresno Ice Works in 1874, helped organize and served as a director of the Fresno Gas Light Company, served as a director of the Fresno Water Company, and as the first secretary of the Fair Grounds Association.

A true legend of our Valley was William Walker Phillips.

Elizabeth Pressley Phillips.
*Courtesy of David Phillips.*

# Elizabeth Pressley Phillips

At four o'clock in the afternoon of March 17, 1916, the pews of Saint James' Episcopal Church at Fresno and N streets were filled. The organist was playing softly as the shocked and grieving friends of Elizabeth Pressley Phillips sat quietly, listening to the music. Bishop L. C. Stanford, Dean G. R. MacDonald, and the Reverend G. I. McNalty walked down the center aisle, ahead of the coffin, intoning the comforting words of the Episcopal funeral rite, "I am the resurrection and the life, saith the Lord; he that believeth in me, though he were dead, yet shall he live..." The choir sang "Jesus, Lover of My Soul" and "Rock of Ages." When the service ended, pallbearers W. H. Coates, S. L. Strother, W. D. Creighton, Judge M. K. Harris, W. H. Issacs, and Dr. J. C. Cooper carried the coffin to the waiting hearse. It was a sad day for the friends of Mr. William Walker Phillips and his late wife, Elizabeth.

Only the day before, Elizabeth Phillips had been in good health and looking forward to attending a luncheon at the home of Mrs. E. D. Edwards. Mr. Phillips had left home early to go to his ranch on the San Joaquin River. His son, John, had gone there earlier and, after a while, Mrs. Phillips called to see if her husband had arrived. She received a caller, Mrs. Adeline Thornton, in the late morning. When Mrs. Thornton left, Mrs. Phillips called to her maid and was suddenly stricken by a brain hemorrhage. She died that evening without regaining consciousness.

The Fresno County Chamber of Commerce issued the following resolution: "Whereas, Mrs. W. W. Phillips, wife of our [former] president, has been called hence; and Whereas, Mrs. Phillips was an honored member of this community, a woman of fine personality, high intelligence, a good wife and mother, and one who enjoyed the affectionate regard of a large number of our best citizens; therefore be it Resolved, That the members of the board of directors of the Fresno County Chamber of Commerce desire to express their heartfelt sympathy with the bereaved husband and son and that the secretary be instructed to forward this resolution to Mr. Phillips, and that it be also recorded on [sic] the minutes of the Fresno County Chamber of Commerce."

# The Buried Treasure Hoax

At the witching hour of midnight July 19, 1900, some sinister figures materialized near a fence that surrounded a vacant lot on the alley behind K (Van Ness) Street. It was an odd time for well-dressed gentlemen to skulk about under the light of the moon in an alley downtown. What could be their purpose?

Two of the gentlemen, well-known attorneys in the Fresno court scene, told little white lies to their wives that night—they said they were going to a lodge meeting. They walked out their respective front doors without any feeling of guilt and met at the fence in question.

It seems that a vineyardist in Easton by the name of Fred Rosses had buried $5,000 in his yard. When he decided to dig it up, in the spring of 1900, it was gone—someone else got there first. Dismayed at this turn of events, Rosses got the word out but, to date, the money had not turned up.

Enter a fortune-teller by the name of Mrs. Dr. Jones. Jones, who seemingly was well known for her clairvoyant powers, claimed to have a vision. She could see a box filled with the $5,000 reposing quietly under several feet of dirt in a vacant lot behind the new Burnwell building on K Street. She felt it her duty, she told the attorneys, to let them know of this knowledge she possessed.

At the hour of midnight, they stood behind the fence, peering through the slats watching Mrs. Dr. Jones and a young boy she hired for the occasion digging for the treasure. Spade after spade of soil was removed, but, as the night wore on, no box was found. Finally, in desperation, the attorneys jumped the fence and began to join in the search—not knowing that another man, a hired detective, was watching them all.

No treasure was found. News of the event leaked out. The two attorneys had been the object of a major prank and had to undergo not only joshing by other members of the bar, but also a rather cold reception from their wives.

Midsummer in Fresno is always, to some extent, a season of quietude. It is too hot to have a tremendous amount of ambition. Staying home with a good book has an appeal to many. The swimming pool and air conditioning add greatly to the enjoyment of this season. What did people do when these amenities did not exist?

Fresno's midsummer season, in 1900, had a number of interesting activities. Wheeling parties were extremely popular. Young people would hop on their bicycles on a summer night and, in groups, head out in a number of directions. Wheeling east on Ventura Avenue, past the fairgrounds, cyclists would head out toward Sanger. Or they might choose a ride on Elm Avenue to Easton. The northern end of Blackstone Avenue with Lane's Bridge as a destination had great appeal, or a ride out to Chateau Fresno (Kearney Boulevard) offered romance and beauty under a full moon.

Many couples found that a melon party was a great way to spend an evening. Not, it should be explained, the kind of melon party that involved skulking in a melon patch only to find oneself gazing into the barrel of irate farmer's gun, but, rather, the kind of melon party that involved sitting on the front porch eating cantaloupe or watermelon and having a quiet tête-à-tête.

Gatherings that featured music were also popular. Sitting under the stars on a warm summer evening listening to the strains of a violin or coronet were magical events. The best of these evenings, however, was one in which someone brought his guitar and everyone sang along.

Midsummer in Fresno—in spite of the heat—has always had its own brand of charm.

# Midsummer in Courthouse Park

July in twenty-first-century Fresno conjures up all sorts of seasonal themes—patriotic celebrations, ice cream cones, intense heat, glorious evenings, pool parties, and outdoor barbecues. We enjoy air-conditioned homes, cars, and stores. There are so many ways to deal with the heat that it's not the problem it once was.

In 1900 it was very different.

Fresnans in 1900 celebrated the Fourth of July, enjoyed ice cream cones, and experienced the intense heat. What they didn't have were the modern ways of keeping cool that we have today. They did have something that we don't have today—a small town environment with a large Courthouse Park within walking distance of their homes.

The huge elm trees of Courthouse Park provided the perfect canopy of shade for young mothers and their children. By mid-morning, with her work well underway, the young Fresno mother would walk out her front door with her children and make the short walk to Courthouse Park. Here, she would join other young mothers and their children. While the children played on the grass, the mothers would gossip and visit—all under the marvelous shade of the trees.

At noontime, many of the office workers would bring their lunches to Courthouse Park, find a bench or a spot of grass, relax and eat under the large trees. Many a deal was made during such lunches, many a friendship was formed—business and pleasure could go hand in hand in the shade afforded by the park's trees. The heat didn't seem nearly as hard to bear when listening to the splashing water of the "Boy With the Leaking Boot" in his fountain at the park's edge.

Sunday band concerts filled the park with music and a festive air. Everyone in town came to sit under the trees and visit and listen to all kinds of music—from stirring to serene.

Oh, for the good old days, when Courthouse Park was a lively place—truly the heart of the city that grew up around it.

# A September Sunday at Millerton

In the pages of the *Weekly Merced Herald*, on Saturday, September 30, 1865, to be exact, a story appears that captures the attention of the reader because it gives a glimpse of life in Millerton.

The editor of the newspaper, P. D. Wigginton, decided to leave his office in Snelling, due north of present-day Merced, and travel to Millerton "in search of copper veins, old debts, old acquaintances, subscribers to the *Herald*, or almost anything that we could turn into ready cash or 'grub.'" He accepted a friend's offer of a seat in his carriage and they began their journey.

Travel by horse and buggy was slow. They left on a Saturday morning and arrived in Millerton late Sunday afternoon—actually making rather good time for that mode of transportation. They met a few friends along the way, but, thankfully, no bandits.

When they drove into Millerton, the stores were closed. They were terribly impressed that the residents of Fresno's county seat were such God-fearing people, until they learned that it had been four years since a religious service had been held in the town.

They were hungry and saw Ira McCray's Oak Hotel. Remembering that McCray always set a fine table, they tied their horses to the hitching post and went inside for libations and a meal. Since the meal was a good one and much enjoyed, they decided to postpone the libations until after dinner. A stroll to Gaster's Saloon provided an opportunity to partake of the aforementioned liquid refreshments.

The two men walked through the swinging doors of the saloon and saw a number of men sitting around enjoying Havanas and discussing the issues of the day including the copper question. They joined in the conversation, adding their own thoughts and perspectives.

It was a lazy autumn afternoon in the foothills of Fresno County—a little slice of life now recorded in the tales of our Valley.

# Culture and Elegance Come to Fresno

The tales of our Valley have occasionally taken place within the elegant ambience of the Barton Opera House. Graduations, concerts, plays, and other public events have been played out within its walls. The greatest musical artists and the finest actors of the time trod the boards of the Barton. But, on the night of September 29, 1890, this was all in the future for, on this night, the Barton Opera House was dedicated and open for its first performance.

Fresno society turned out in all its glory. According to a reporter for the *Daily Evening Expositor*, "The house was as perfect as art and artistic taste could make it...the boxes, loges, chairs and the foyer were decorated with a galaxy of beauty when the handsome and lovely ladies of Fresno arrived...handsome faces, lovely gowns and happy people—what more could be desired to make a theater-opening a success."

The eight boxes, perched on the sides of the house with four on each side, were near the stage and considered prime seats. For opening night they had been auctioned off to the highest bidder. Box A was Mr. Robert Barton's private box. Joining him were his wife and Mrs. C. M. Pyke and Miss Blanche Verdenal. Box B was occupied by Louis Einstein, Henry Gundelfinger, and A. Newhouse. Box C was hosted by Mr. and Mrs. A. B. Butler, who invited as their guests Mr. and Mrs. Louis McWhirter and H. M. Newhall.

Colonel and Mrs. William Forsyth, Mrs. Forsyth's mother, Mrs. D. F. Verdenal of New York, and George H. Malters enjoyed the evening's performance from Box D. Mr. and Mrs. W. W. Phillips, Mrs. Pressley, and J. B. Pressley occupied Box E. The remaining boxes, loges, and chairs were filled—the house had sold out for its first performance.

The ladies did not wear hats that evening—they had their hair dressed in elaborate styles and many, like Mrs. S. N. Griffith, tucked dazzling jewelry into their coiffures.

It was a night of elegance, beautiful music, a charming play, and social mingling among the guests—it was the beginning of many such nights and put Fresno on the map as a cultural center.

As the final bars of the opening overture were concluded, the audience broke into rapturous applause. At this first performance in the Barton Opera House, it was clear to everyone that the perfect acoustics of the house would draw to the Barton not only enthusiastic audiences, but also great artists.

Entering from stage left, Manager C. M. Pike and the Honorable George E. Church walked onto the stage. After Pike's brief introduction and words of welcome, Church began his dedicatory speech to the assembled throng. After all, this September 29, 1890, evening was the dedication of the Barton Opera House.

George E. Church, speaker at the opening of the Barton Opera House. *Courtesy of Robert M. Wash.*

George Church spoke of the great happiness he felt at being able to address such "an elegant audience in such a beautiful temple of art." He spoke of the public-spirited citizenry "who, with splendid audacity, with an audacity that challenges our admiration, has dared to conceive…has with rare munificence dared to build this splendid temple to art, to be devoted and dedicated to art—a temple that would be no discredit to the metropolitan cities of our land."

Church reminded his listeners of the criticisms often made by foreigners who say we have neither art nor artists, who ask, "Where is our music or our temples of music?" He elaborated considerably on these remarks and then told his audience that we have learned to work, but we have not learned to play. "All art is play," he said, "and all artists are players." He thanked Mr. Robert Barton, the man who built this "magnificent theater."

Church predicted that when a second railway made its way to Fresno (which it would six years later), Fresno "would be lifted out of our provincial condition to metropolitanism, others [would] follow his example and erect great temples of art and found great libraries. That time is coming. It is coming rapidly. Tonight we have a foreshadowing of it. And God be thanked for it all."

It is important to be reminded of Church's vision for Fresno from our vantage point one hundred and fifteen years later. It did happen as he said it would. Fresnans of 1890 yearned for culture and established the beginnings of it; Fresnans of 2005 enjoy the fruits of all the efforts in the years in between. Our vast library system, our theaters, our museums, our artists, our poets, our writers, our universities, our musicians, and all those who support and sustain them add richness to life in our great Central Valley to be enjoyed by us all.

# The Sinks of Dry Creek

For thousands of years, the plains and foothills of our great Central Valley were places of peace. In those halcyon days before the white man set foot within this realm, wild antelope and elk lived side by side with the coyote and the rabbit. The Yokuts peoples lived along the rivers of the Valley and the foothills. In spring, wildflowers carpeted the Valley floor—blue lupine, orange poppies, and pink alfilaria grew luxuriantly amid the native grasses.

In the heat of summer, the vegetation died and the floor of the Valley came into view. It could be seen that the areas between the two great rivers—they would later be named the Kings and the San Joaquin—sloped almost imperceptibly into a common center creating a natural bowl. When the Sierra snows melted, the rivers and creeks filled with water. Three of these natural streams—Red Bank, Dog, and Big Dry creeks—flowed down into the area that would become downtown Fresno and emptied their waters into this natural bowl that would later be known as the "Sinks of Dry Creek."

Exploration for mission sites and converts brought the Spanish into the Valley in the late eighteenth and early nineteenth centuries. The life of the Yokuts and foothill Native American tribes were disrupted—the white man brought disease and an element of fear. The Gold Rush of 1848 brought white men into the foothills, displacing the Native American from his land.

The building of the first canal in the late 1860s brought water from the Kings River onto the plains to irrigate wheat. More canals were built, some of them utilizing the natural channels of the creek beds.

When the railroad was built to Fresno in 1872, the land was fairly dry. There was a lot of rain that winter, but it wasn't until 1884 that heavy snows in the Sierra began to melt and heavy rains caused the three creeks flowing into downtown to wreak havoc with the populace. A flood of tremendous proportions filled and overflowed the Sinks of Dry Creek, causing people to use rowboats for transportation.

Today, flood control measures have been implemented, but,

when it rains in Fresno, water accumulates very quickly in the natural bowl that is our city center.

From time to time plans surface for a lake in downtown Fresno. "Why not?" one may ask. Just undo the flood control plans, let the rains come, and the lake will create itself just as Mother Nature permitted it to before man intervened.

# The Fire Whistle

On March 24, 1896, the Fresno Volunteer Fire Department held its monthly meeting at City Hall, a convenient location since the City Hall was also the headquarters for the fire department. The trustees met in the firemen's dormitory on the second floor of the building. Since ladies occasionally attended the trustees' meetings, an ordinance had been passed to make it mandatory that the firemen remain clothed during the meetings.

A number of things were discussed that night, but two of them were of primary importance. First was the matter of the appointment of the tillerman. A new, much longer fire truck was soon to arrive and a tillerman was needed. This person would guide the rear wheels of the fire truck when it had to make a sharp turn. The rear wheels were adjustable—it was a job requiring a qualified person because the slightest mistake could result in a serious accident.

The foreman of the hook and ladder company, M. Bilby, reported that the company had unanimously nominated W. J. McDonald for the position of tillerman. This recommendation went to the board of trustees, who appointed all city employees. However, traditionally, they always accepted the fire company's recommendations, so the firemen welcomed McDonald to his new job.

The other matter of importance involved fire alarms. The city was replacing many of the steam engines that ran various machines for various city businesses, with electric power. It seems the alarm bell at City Hall was not loud enough to wake the whole city and, therefore, the volunteer firemen had to rely on whistles that were located at several locations. The city's whistle at the Fresno Waterworks was the one most relied upon. There was just one potential problem with this whistle—since the waterworks would now be run by electric power, would there be any compressed air available to operate the whistle?

J. J. Seymour, president of the water company, assured the firemen that he would see to it that there was compressed air for this purpose. Said Mr. Seymour, "I'll provide the air, if the city furnishes the whistle." The city had come a long way from the days when gunshots were used to round up the volunteer firemen.

As one travels northwest from Merced on Highway 99, the next city one reaches has an interesting name—Atwater. What does that name mean? Does it mean the city was founded there because it was at the site of water? Or, is there another reason?

In the mid-nineteenth century, the name given to the area between the Tuolumne and the Merced rivers was known as Paradise Valley. John W. Mitchell had taken possession of 100,000 acres of government land in this region. After using his herds of sheep to clear the land, he planted wheat in the now barren soil. By 1870, Mitchell's acreage was a golden wheat field.

In 1869, cattleman Marshall D. Atwater began to farm part of Mitchell's holdings and purchased 6,000 acres of his own. When the Central Pacific Railroad began to build their line south in 1870, they put in a switch so that Mitchell and Atwater could ship their grain to market. It was called the Cuba Switch.

Marshall Atwater was not only a farmer, but also an inventor—his enormous grain harvester pulled by twenty-four horses was one of his inventions.

After Mitchell's death, his estate was handled by the Fin De Siecle Investment Company, created for this express purpose. One of Mitchell's nieces, who was married to George Bloss, Sr., inherited the bulk of the estate. In 1887, Bloss and Henry F. Greer created the Atwater Colony on 480 acres of the land, which was subdivided into twenty-acre parcels. In 1888, a town was laid out on the site by the Merced Land and Fruit Company. Lots were sold at auction and the town was named Atwater.

The town began to grow and, by 1900, it boasted a population of one hundred. A weekly newspaper was started in 1911. When the Fin De Siecle Investment Company was liquidated, George Bloss, Sr., used his one-third share to build a library and a hospital for the town. In 1922, Atwater was incorporated. The former Castle Air Force Base, located nearby, brought business and people to Atwater. Today, Atwater is one of the fast-growing cities in our great Central Valley.

Atwater in the 1890s. J. B. Osborn, General Merchandise, is on the right. *Courtesy of Merced County Historical Society Archives.*

# Mr. Cearley Clearly Can't Sing

In 1890s Fresno there was a man named C. T. Cearley who had a store on J (Fulton) Street. It was a stationery store stocked with everything one could need for the office or for the home. He also sold books, magazines, and newspapers from all over the world.

Mr. Cearley, himself, was a delightful conversationalist—able to visit on every subject imaginable. He and wife were popular members of Fresno society. This personable, engaging man had one minor flaw—he could not carry a tune.

Hardly a week went by that Cearley was not approached by one of the women in town and asked if he would be a part of some gathering at which singing would be required. He would always politely take the lady aside and explain to her his inability to sing a single note on key—let alone an entire song. The lady would not ask again, but there was always another woman who, not knowing of his lack of musical gifts, would ask the question of him.

Knowing this, when the reporter who wrote the "Man About Town" column for *The Fresno Morning Republican*, heard about the following conversation between Mr. Cearley and his daughter, he felt compelled to share it with his readers.

Just before Christmas of 1897, a young lady looked up into Cearley's eyes and said, "Papa, sing."

Poor Mr. Cearley. "I can't, dear," he said. He looked into the eyes of his daughter and realized that, this time, he had no choice but to make the effort of his life and to try to sing a song. She would not understand if he told her that on one occasion when he sang a song, a nearby gas meter exploded. She also wouldn't understand if she was told that her mother stayed at his mother-in-law's house for two weeks because in a reckless moment he had sung "Sweet Genevieve."

He asked his daughter to sit down while he searched the house from cellar to attic while making sure no one else was home. He closed the windows that were open and prepared to sing. He stood in front of his daughter, opened his mouth and began the first notes of "In the Gloaming." The little girl listened intently, with ever-widening eyes, to her father's "gurgling, groaning, squeaking, rasping voice" as he sang the song to its very end.

Cearley stood patiently awaiting her verdict. After a long pause, she said, with the utmost conviction, "Papa, you can't sing."

608 — ROSE COVERED RESIDENCE "MINNEWAWA" NEAR FRESNO, CAL.

The home of Minna Eshleman on the Minnewawa Ranch. *Author's collection.*

# Wednesday Club's Eighth Optional

Each year Wednesday Club members enjoy a unique celebration at their last meeting in May—just before the club takes a hiatus for the summer. They have an "optional." At this event, instead of presenting papers, each member is called upon to perform for the group—she has an "option" to choose what she will do.

The occasion of the club's eighth Optional, in 1897, was looked forward to with great anticipation. Miss Minna Eshleman invited her fellow members to have their meeting at her home—the Minnewawa farm. At this party each member was allowed to bring a guest. What the ladies did not know was that Miss Eshleman had a special surprise in store.

A few minutes after everyone arrived at the Minnewawa and were enjoying visiting in Miss Eshleman's beautiful home, a tooting of horns and a ringing of cowbells brought everyone to the front door. Some sort of conveyance was making its way up her drive. The largest carriage in Fresno came into view. It pulled up in front of the house and, as the ladies squealed with delight, their husbands—who were supposed to be busy at their offices—arrived. Miss Eshleman informed them that this was her part of the entertainment.

After much visiting and a great deal of laughter, the program began. Mrs. C. L. Walter, the Wednesday Club president, opened the meeting. What followed was an afternoon of recitations, readings, and quotations—both serious and humorous—interspersed with music, both instrumental and vocal.

When the program ended, the ladies and their husbands and guests went outdoors where the members of the Ladies Aid Society of the First Christian Church had set tables beneath the spreading trees. After partaking of delicious refreshments, everyone toured the Minnewawa creamery and exclaimed over its cleanliness and the manner in which it was operated.

The Wednesday Club's Eighth Optional was a memorable day, indeed!

# The Thimble Club

The young lady of the mid-1890s was in an interesting situation. Better educated than the generation before hers, she had the opportunity to go to college or to obtain a job if she wished—however, all this was not as important as obtaining a husband. Marriage was the goal of most young women. For them, even if she had a job, once married, she would stay home and make a home for her husband and her children.

In the spring of 1896, a group of young, unmarried society women belonged to the Thimble Club. They had meetings once a week—their purposes were social improvement and enjoyment. The subject of their meetings was always a secret. Woe be unto anyone who would be so uncivil as to divulge their discussions!

It seems that one day someone did leak some rather fascinating information to the newspaper. It was spring and thoughts of love and marriage were definitely in the air. For several meetings the young ladies had been discussing and rating the eligible young men of Fresno at some length. Imagine their surprise when, on the morning of March 11, 1896, their opinions made the pages of *The Fresno Morning Republican*.

Thomas Lynch was the subject of an entire meeting. The ladies had unanimously decided that he was a model young man. Not quite so lucky was G. D. Tucker. His spirited way of dancing was not appreciated by some of the ladies; other felt it was evidence of "a lively and jovial nature." There was much discussion about Ed White. Some of the ladies felt he "had a graceful form and records gas meters correctly." His abilities as a dancer, vocalist, and conversationalist were given high marks. They all agreed that Captain George W. Jones was the handsomest man in Fresno. His bashfulness was a challenge that they were all willing to help him overcome.

There were many red faces in Fresno on that spring morning. There were also a few men walking to work with smiles on their faces. Ah, springtime in Fresno!

# Women's Suffrage Takes Center Stage

In 1848, at the Seneca Falls Convention, "The Declaration of Sentiments" was passed. Based on the Declaration of Independence, it laid out the numerous demands of the early activists who were striving to obtain voting rights for women. By the late nineteenth century, the Women's Suffrage movement was gaining support all over the country.

On March 20, 1896, in Fresno, one of its forceful advocates, Mrs. Gougar, gave a speech at the First Baptist Church.

Crowds of people came. Even after Mrs. Gougar started speaking, more people came. By intermission, seventy-five more chairs were brought in. Men and women both crowded the church, filling it beyond capacity.

After a hymn was sung, Miss Sadie Whistler offered a prayer. Then the Reverend J. W. Webb rose to introduce Mrs. Gougar, who addressed the crowd for two full hours. She held their rapt attention as, according to the reporter for *The Fresno Morning Republican*, she, "with logic, history, wit, and sarcasm," good-naturedly, but keenly, discussed the issues of women's suffrage. There was no attack on the "tyrant male," the reporter continued, only a move "to help good men to good government." She spoke of the women who pay taxes, yet are not allowed to vote—this is taxation without representation. Because women are not allowed this basic right, she said, they are not part "of government by the people."

Mrs. Gougar discussed the temperance issues, too. She pointed out that women would support the Prohibition ticket. Since now only a woman's husband and brothers represent her at the polls, she asked all those in audience who would vote the Prohibition ticket to stand. No one stood. "Sisters," she said, "look back and see how you would be represented." Much laughter followed that remark. Mrs. Gougar said, "Suffrage needs the woman and her moral force much more than woman needs the suffrage."

Mrs. Gougar asked the members of the audience who planned to vote for the pending amendment for suffrage that would be on the November ballot in California to stand. Everyone in the audience stood, the Doxology was sung, and everyone filed out of the church.

The constitutional amendment that would give women the right to vote was not passed until 1920. But, on this March evening in 1896, Mrs. Gougar had given the people of Fresno much to consider.

# The San Joaquin Valley Medical Society

Two years before the incorporation of Fresno as a full-fledged city, a group of doctors formed the Fresno County Medical Society. They met in the parlors of the Grand Central Hotel, the date was December 29, 1883, and Dr. Chester Rowell was elected the first president.

Thirteen years later, on March 24, 1896, another assemblage of doctors gathered to create one more medical society. This one would encompass the entire Central Valley and would give doctors an opportunity to share information and ideas for the mutual improvement of their profession. The all-day meeting took place at Spinney Hall.

Dr. A. J. Pedlar not only led the organizational meeting of the San Joaquin Valley Medical Society, but also served as mayor of Fresno.
*Courtesy of Robert M. Wash.*

The opening meeting was called to order at 9:00 A.M. by Dr. A. J. Pedlar of Fresno. Dr. L. E. Felton of Hanford was chosen temporary chairman and Dr. C. A. Rogers of Bakersfield was asked to be temporary secretary. Drs. Jessie Hare, George Hare, and W. T. Maupin, all of Fresno, and C. A. Rogers of Bakersfield, J. B. Rossen of Tulare, and W. N. Sherman of Merced were selected to serve as an organizational committee. They presented a slate of officers: Dr. L. E. Felton, chairman; Dr. W. N. Sherman, first vice president; Dr. T. E. Taggart of Bakersfield, second vice president; Dr. W. B. Charles of Lemoore, third vice president; Dr. C. A. Rogers, secretary, Dr. E. C. Dunn of Fresno, assistant secretary; and Dr. W. T. Maupin, treasurer. They were all elected by acclamation.

Drs. Chester Rowell, W. T. Maupin, and W. H. Miller of Hanford were instructed to write a constitution and by-laws and have them ready for the afternoon session.

The afternoon was filled with a number of papers presented by the members. "The Bacillus of Tuberculosis—Methods of Examination," "Autotoxin in Diphtheria," and "Thoughts on Anesthesia," were only a few of the papers given. The constitution and by-laws were read and accepted with a few changes. It was decided that the group would meet twice a year—in March and in October.

The evening session consisted of more papers and, after the members adjourned to the dining hall, an elegant dinner was provided by the ladies guild of Saint James' Episcopal Church. Justy's Orchestra provided music, toasts were given, and the first meeting of the San Joaquin Valley Medical Society drew to a close.

# J. W. Ferguson

A great shock greeted the readers of *The Fresno Morning Republican* on the morning of July 27, 1900. The death of County Assessor John Wilson Ferguson, just before midnight the night before rated a full column story. He had been in perfect health on Tuesday, took sick at work, and expired on Thursday night of acute pneumonia.

J. W. Ferguson was born in Kentucky on October 4, 1841. He came west and settled in Sacramento before he came to the Selma area where he was hired by sheepmen Dusy and Collier. He later purchased a quarter section of land from his employers, which he farmed for a number of years. Before he came west he had been married and had a daughter, Mary, who came west with her father. Ferguson married Carrie Ross, the sister of Mrs. Frank Dusy. They had three children.

While in Selma, Ferguson was an active member of the Methodist Episcopal Church South and served as superintendent of the Sunday school for a number of years. He also became interested in politics and was a Populist candidate for a number of political offices. His campaigns didn't result in a win until 1898, when he was elected to the position of county assessor. Holding this office necessitated a move to Fresno where the family immediately became active with the Methodist Episcopal Church South congregation in that city. He served the office faithfully and well and it was while he was attending to the duties of this post that he became ill.

Mrs. Ferguson and the children were at Kenyon's at Pine Ridge to escape the Valley heat when word was sent to them to return to Fresno. A stage and team were dispatched to bring them home, but, due to miscommunication, Mrs. Ferguson and her children packed their belongings into their rig and headed home down the treacherous grade. They arrived just three minutes before Ferguson died. It was a terrible shock.

The people of Fresno County mourned the death of this good man who had been a faithful servant of the people.

# A Most Incredible Concert

The evening of May 4, 1931, was a memorable one not only for the piano ensemble classes at Fresno State College, but also for all those who attended their annual concert. Music lovers in the community looked forward to these concerts performed by the advanced piano students. Their professor, Elizabeth Petersen Carnine, had the ability to inspire her students to reach their potential in a way that is usually the preserve of only the finest private teachers.

On this evening, six concert grand pianos graced the stage of the Fresno State College auditorium. Only one other time in the history of music in Fresno could concertgoers remember such an occasion—a Fresno Musical Club concert.

The audience filed in—a hush went over the filled house as sixteen advanced piano students in lovely tea gowns walked onto the stage. It was a night of great anticipation, but also a night of sadness. Mrs. Carnine was very ill and could not direct the performance. This duty fell to Helen Roberts, the voice teacher at the college, and to Frances McLaughlin, the student president of the piano department. Mrs. Carnine, however, was backstage—this knowledge inspired her students to reach new heights.

The first three numbers were played by twelve women—two at each piano. The allegro con brio movement from Beethoven's "Fifth Symphony," Liszt's second "Hungarian Rhapsody," and the allegro molto-vivace movement from Tchaikovsky's "Pathetique Symphony" were played, according to Mitchell P. Briggs, reviewer for *The Fresno Bee*, with "clarity and delicacy." The rest of the concert consisted of twenty-four-hand, twelve-hand, and four-hand selections from the finest of the world's piano literature.

At the concert's end, the applause brought the students back to the stage several times. It was clear that the audience knew they had heard a concert of rare quality. Mrs. Carnine was helped to the stage to pay tribute to her students and to receive the applause of the audience. The young women knew their beloved teacher was dying—it was not long after this night that she passed away. They had played their hearts out for her.

For these young women—Arthayda Stiner, Madelon Carper, Ruth Elaine Williams, Anne Aaronson, Helen Schorling, Lorraine Anderson, Ruth Christensen, Catherine McKay, Frances Mc-Laughlin, Augusta Niles, Ivah Fullerton, Ruby Neufeld, Gaye Hibbard, Mildred Armstrong, Sue Bell Browne, and Clarice Roberts—it was a night they would remember for the rest of their lives.

Elizabeth Carnine, left, and Helen Roberts surrounded by the piano ensemble students.
*Author's collection.*

There are occasions when it takes the stranger in our midst to open our eyes to the beauty around us. So it was when Sheriff J. T. Umstattd, from Paris, Missouri, arrived in Fresno on March 31, 1896, to pick up an escaped convict who was being held at the county jail.

Jay Scott served as Fresno County sheriff from 1892 to 1898. *Courtesy of Robert M. Wash.*

It seems that Ben Crawford was arrested on a charge of stealing sixty chickens and placed in the Paris jail. While awaiting the Grand Jury's indictment, he broke out of jail, swam across the river that flows near the town, and, before the law could catch up with him, began a journey that ended in Fresno. A telegram from Umstattd to Fresno County Sheriff Jay Scott resulted in Crawford's arrest in Fresno.

When Sheriff Umstattd arrived in Fresno, Sheriff Scott met him at the train and decided to make his visit more pleasant by taking him for a drive east of the city to visit the vineyards and wineries. They stopped at one winery and had a glass of port wine. Umstattd thought it was far more delicious than any port he had ever tasted in Missouri. He was fascinated by the irrigation system that was used to water the farms. He had never seen canals used in that way and thought it was amazing.

A reporter for *The Republican* called on Umstattd and asked him what he thought of Fresno. "[Today] is [sic] saw the grandest country I have ever seen…there is no comparison between it and Missouri. If I were not tied up in Missouri I would come to Fresno in as short a time as I could make it…[I like] the vim and energy of the California people…yes, I have seen the finest country today in the United States, and I am almost glad that Ben Crawford gave me the chase out here." More wonders were in store for Sheriff Umstattd—Sheriff Scott was planning to take him on a drive through the colonies south of Fresno before he had to leave. It must have been a happy day for both men—a chance to share and to enjoy the beauties of Fresno County.

# Needlework in the 1880s

By the mid-1880s, the ladies of Fresno were moving beyond the hard life they had known as pioneers. More stores offering specialty items were opening in the business district; bakeries were selling a variety of breads and rolls so the homemaker no longer had to make her own. The wives of successful businessmen had household help which gave them leisure time. They filled this time calling on their friends, engaging in charitable works, joining study clubs, and doing needlework.

In the 1870s, needlework in Fresno was somewhat confined to sewing clothes and making quilts—both necessary items for family and home. By the 1880s and the 1890s, needlework was taking on more interesting forms. The detailed quilts of the 1860s, that are so collectable today, were replaced by crazy quilts which consisted of irregular pieces of satin, velvet, ribbon, and silk of every possible color that were stitched together and decorated with a variety of embroidery stitches, also in many different colors. The richness of the fabrics and colors along with the diversity of the stitches allowed the lady a showcase for her needlework talents.

Kensington embroidery, which was made popular by the girls at the Kensington School in England, was very much a favorite for the needle worker. Using red cotton floss that had been created in Turkey—the first colorfast floss on the market—the lady would use her needle and floss to outline designs that had been drawn on the cloth. One of the stitches she used was a spilt stitch, also called a Kensington stitch. As she outlined, she would bring the needle up into the previous stitch thus splitting the yarn.

Laces were also made by hand. With her tatting kit close by, the lady would create delicate, breathtaking works of art from fine thread.

Today, some of these arts have not been passed down; others are still popular. Needlepoint, cross stitch embroidery, and quilting are still popular with Fresno ladies who manage to squeeze time from their busy lives to carry on the traditions that their mothers enjoyed.

# A Bicentennial Spectacular

It's been twenty-nine years since the celebration of our nation's bicentennial. It was an exciting time. "Bicentennial Minutes," short stories about United States history, aired on television stations every day for a year or more before July 4, 1976. Other special programs appeared throughout the year. By the time the day arrived, Americans had received a thorough history course reminding them of the forces and of the brave men and women who created the United States of America.

In Fresno, as in communities all across the country, unique ways of commemorating the event were carried out. Board of Supervisor Chairman John Ventura and Mayor Ted C. Wills planted a Virginia Oak tree in Courthouse Park. A marker, designating it as the Bicentennial Oak, stands nearby. The restoration of the historic Meux Home was undertaken as Fresno's Bicentennial project. The students, parents, and staff of the Enchanted Forest, a special education school in Fresno, created a large papier-mâché replica of the Statue of Liberty.

On Saturday morning, July 3, 1976, a huge parade threaded its way through downtown Fresno. Bands, floats, historical figures, and dignitaries made up the three-hour parade.

On Sunday morning, July Fourth, every church bell in the Valley rang out at eleven o'clock—the moment designated by President Gerald Ford for every church bell in the country to ring—ushering in the third century of our nation.

On Saturday and Sunday evenings, 14,000 people flocked to the Fresno County Fairgrounds to witness "From Redcoats to the Red Planet," a two-hour pageant that told 200 years of American history. With 1,200 volunteer participants and a massive fireworks display, the pageant brought out feelings of patriotism in all who witnessed it.

For that weekend in our Valley's history, we were all reminded of the sacrifices of those who made our republic possible.

# Patricia Marion Baker Fey

On July 19, 1929, Patricia Marion Baker was born in Kankakee, Illinois. Her interests included tap dancing and playing the piano. Her happy childhood in this northeastern Illinois city gave her solid Midwestern values and a joyful outlook on life.

In 1951, Pat graduated from the University of Illinois with a bachelor of arts degree in political science. She decided that she was ready for some adventure outside of the classroom and signed up for an archaeological dig in Arizona in late summer. The expedition's photographer, Russell Fey, offered her a ride. They had never met and when he picked her up, his girl friend was in the front seat, so Pat climbed in the back. Somewhere along the way, the girl friend decided to return home and Pat moved to the front seat. By summer's end, Pat and Russ had fallen in love.

After their marriage in the summer of 1952, they piled all their belongings into the trunk of their Mercury coupe and drove to Berkeley, California, where Russ was embarking on a graduate degree in urban planning at the University of California. Pat supported him through school working at a housewares import store called Fraser's.

After Russ obtained his degree, job opportunities took them to several different cities—Tacoma, Richmond, Fresno, Modesto, and, finally, back to Fresno in 1969 so Russ could teach in the newly formed Department of Urban Planning at California State University, Fresno. By now, the couple had been blessed with three children—Sarah, David, and Ellen.

It was in Fresno that the couple became an active part of the grassroots efforts to preserve the city's historic architecture. For Pat, it was the first step on a new path that would result in her becoming the finest textile conservator in Central California. In addition to the training she received in this field, her natural gifts of patience and attention to detail set her apart. With needle in hand, she would approach her restoration efforts with respect for the garment before her—for the craftsmanship of the original sewer and for the fabric itself—and she would proceed with gentleness and reverence. A costume exhibit, curated and mounted by Pat at the Metropolitan Museum, at Kearney Mansion, at the Kings County Museum at Burris Park, or at the Meux Home was a work of art. All these museums are in her debt.

Pat Fey was the first president of the Meux Home Museum Corporation—she worked hard with the committee that worked on the restoration of the home in 1976. She also served as registrar for the Fresno Historical Society and, later, as curator of the Kings County Museum in Burris Park.

The last two years of Pat's life were overshadowed by a recurrence of cancer. The dignity with which she faced this illness was matched only by her courage. Her death on May 25, 1998, ended the life of a woman who had enriched her community beyond measure.

Pat Baker, left, and Russ Fey, right, on the archaeological dig in Arizona in the summer of 1951.
*Courtesy of Ellen Fey.*

Pat Baker on the Arizona dig in the summer of 1951.
*Courtesy of Ellen Fey.*

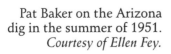

Pat Baker and Russ Fey on the University of Illinois campus in 1951 shortly after they announced their engagement. *Courtesy of Ellen Fey.*

Pat Fey in their MG convertible, 1952.
*Courtesy of Ellen Fey.*

# Citrus, Citrus Everywhere

Armory Hall was a beehive of activity on the afternoon of Friday, January 3, 1896. Men and women were busy setting up displays featuring every kind of citrus crop imaginable. In the center of the room was a large circular stand meant to represent a well, complete with a rustic beam and oaken bucket. The entire rim of the "well" was decorated with oranges. Thirty incandescent lights would be placed around the circle in the evening.

The four corners of the room were being worked on by such notables as Gustav Eisen, Dr. George Hare, G. H. Miller and representatives from the Barton estate. Along the sides of the hall, other citrus exhibits were being put together...and overseeing everything was the chairman of Fresno County's very first Citrus Fair, Fulton G. Berry.

It was mid-afternoon and still not all was in readiness for the 6:00 P.M. opening. George C. Roeding was not worried at all as he stacked his oranges into a huge pyramid that could be seen from all over the hall. Mrs. A. H. Powers of Centerville was arranging her jars of homemade orange marmalade in a decorative fashion.

Two enormous cylindrical glass vessels were placed on either side of the well. Fulton G. Berry was busy filling them with pomelos grown on his farm. He explained that pomelo seeds found their way into a bag with orange seeds that he purchased. They grew into fine trees with delicious fruit. He now wished he had more of them.

Each exhibit booth had a sign or two spelling out its name in oranges. Exhibitors tried to outdo each other in creating these unusual signs.

On the north side of the hall space had been left for a large platform. It was here that Justy's orchestra would play and the dignitaries would speak. It would soon be 6:00 P.M. Armory Hall had become a fragrant sea of citrus. The fun was about to begin.

# The First Ever Citrus Fair

At the precise hour of 6:00 P.M. on January 3, 1896, the doors of Armory Hall opened and people began to arrive. Those early arrivals were greeted by the scent of oranges and the sight of every kind of citrus imaginable in exhibits throughout the hall. Those who walked up to the second floor gallery and looked down on the scene were rewarded with a look at the overall effect of the exhibits. Fresno County's first Citrus Fair was underway.

Justy's six-piece orchestra, with M. M. Meyer on the piano, began to play. More and more people arrived—soon Armory Hall was standing room only.

At nine o'clock, Nick Justy drew everyone's attention by blowing a bugle call. The crowd grew quiet. Alex Goldman, the president of the Fresno County Chamber of Commerce, walked to the front of the platform. As he addressed the crowd, he told them that there was no question about it—the Citrus Fair was a success. Next, D. T. Fowler gave a short history of citrus culture in Fresno County. He said that, at first, people thought citrus could not be grown here except in select places near the foothills. He talked about the first oranges that were grown at Judge Hart's place in Millerton. Hart bought oranges from a peddler from Merced, planted some of the seeds, and they grew into fine producing trees. Fowler told about Yank Hazelton and the orange seeds he brought from Mexico and the oranges that were grown on the Eggers vineyard. "[Now], for the first time," he said, "Fresno County is ranked as a citrus grower in the commercial world."

After the opening remarks were over, the crowd continued to enjoy the exhibits. In the center of the room, a lady dressed in costume was selling lemonade at ten cents a glass. The proceeds went to charity.

The fair was such a success that it was extended for two more days to allow all the outlying communities an opportunity to see the exhibits. Fresno County was on its way to becoming known not only for grapes, but also for citrus.

# Alma's Birdcage

For the historian in search of a good story, an afternoon at the microfilm machine pouring over old newspapers from the 1880s is a wonderful experience—and, once in a while, a headline just reaches out from the pages and grabs one's attention to such an extent that one must not only stop and read it, but print it out as well.

So it was with the Sunday edition of *The Daily Republican*, July 21, 1889. This story had not one headline, but several. "Alma's Bird-cage...Gilded Nests of Soiled Doves Among Coffins...The Palace of Sin Over the Abode of Death"—an attention grabber for sure. One might also assume that the aforementioned doves were not birds of flight—or, perhaps, on occasion, they were.

It seems that a tall, brunette businesswoman named Miss Alma was operating her establishment in the upper floors of the Phillips Building on J (Fulton) Street in a very respectable part of downtown. The first floor of this building was occupied by Williams undertaking parlors.

Three weeks before this article was published, the editor of *The Republican* warned Miss Alma that he would be watching her and, if she did not cease her operations, he would see to it that she was shut down. Miss Alma met with two reporters and told them that she had dismissed her employees and was going to reform and, from now on, would live respectably.

A few days later, a reporter, watching from the building across the street, saw that Miss Alma's business was up and running once again. The reporter decided to visit her establishment and see for himself what was going on. He entered the door over which was a sign reading "Furnished Rooms." As he turned the knob, a bell rang for several seconds at the head of the stairs. Miss Alma appeared on the landing and looked her visitor over. Deciding he was a person who was "all right," she asked him to come upstairs and ushered him into a reception room.

As the next few minutes unfolded, the reporter was convinced that her place of business was anything but respectable and, after hearing the bell ring at least thirty times in as many minutes, he decided two things—that Miss Alma's place was very popular and that it would be wise for him to leave. And, leave he did—just hoping that no one was watching his departure from the building across the street.

Investigative journalism is always a tricky business!

# Russell Harrison Fleming

On December 14, 1928, the life of a gentleman who was revered as one of the first residents of Fresno Station drew to a close. The writer for *The Fresno Morning Republican* said that he had "reached the end of his trail"—a most appropriate statement because Russell Harrison Fleming had been one of the foremost stagecoach drivers in Fresno County.

Fleming was born in Wilkes-Barre, Pennsylvania, on April 12, 1832. He made the journey to California in January 1854. He sailed to Central America, crossed the Isthmus of Panama, and continued by boat to San Francisco. He left for the gold fields of Mariposa where he engaged in placer mining and also found employment in a retail establishment run by Sullivan and Cashman. During his time in Mariposa he also did some farming and conducted tours to Yosemite, which could be reached only by mountain trails.

In 1863, he married Elizabeth Emma Dorgan. Their marriage would last until her death just after their golden anniversary. In 1868, the Flemings moved to Millerton. Here, Fleming operated a stage line to Visalia. Among his experiences was a hold up enroute. Luckily, he had placed valuable Wells Fargo papers in his hat and, even though the robbers shot through his hat, the papers were safe.

When Fresno was founded in 1872, the Flemings moved to the new town, becoming one of the first families to settle there. Russell Fleming was named Fresno's first postmaster and operated a stage line between Fresno and Millerton. He also opened a livery stable on Front (H) Street.

At the age of eighty-eight, he drove a vintage stagecoach in the Raisin Day parade, drawing great applause and affection from all who were there. He handled the four-horse team like the professional he was.

A reserved, quiet man, Russell Fleming played an important role in the history of Fresno County. Known for his integrity and honest business dealings, he held the respect of all who knew him. There was great sadness throughout the county when he died in 1928.

# The Tile Layer's Lament

By 1892, Fresno County had grown to such an extent that the original Courthouse was becoming too small to house all the offices and records. It was decided to add on to the existing building. When it was completed in 1893, the building had two new wings, one on each side of the building. The architect also added wide granite steps and several impressive columns. The original cupola was removed and a new, large dome—sheathed in copper—replaced it. The new Courthouse was the pride of the county.

Even though most of the work was complete, some finishing work was still underway. Tiles were being laid on some of the floors and a few other projects were also being completed.

It was a warm autumn morning and Nathan Lafayette Bachman decided to walk up to the second floor of the Courthouse to take care of some business. Bachman, a very large, heavy man, was admiring all the work that had been done. He entered a hall that was covered with beautiful tile.

One of Bachman's dreams was to one day walk on the gold paved streets of the New Jerusalem. The floor reminded him of that dream. He put one of his extremely large feet down on the tile. It felt glorious. He put the other foot down and continued down the hall. He began to realize that the floor seemed a little buoyant—perhaps a little slushy. He hurried along until he reached the end of the hall, stopped, turned, looked back and with a horrified gaze realized he had left imprints that looked like a hippopotamus had come along behind him.

At that very moment, another very large, very angry man appeared and, with a roar that echoed to the Sierra itself, let forth with a stream of expletives that turned the air blue. Bachman ran into Judge Samuel Holmes' courtroom and hid until the angry tile layer had run past.

The tile man was heard to say, trowel in hand, that if he caught Bachman he would skin him alive. Bachman escaped across some scaffolding into the other part of the building all the while deciding he had learned the difference between the tiles of the Courthouse and the gold streets of the New Jerusalem.

# The Domes of the Courthouse

As the Fresno County Courthouse evolved into a much larger structure, so too did the dome. When the Courthouse was completed in 1875, the dome was impressive even though it was of a delicate Italianate design. It had two tiers—the bottom tier featured columns—and it was topped with a distinctive four-sided cap. It could be seen from any place in Fresno.

In 1895, the Courthouse was enlarged—two wings were added. The old dome was removed and, in its place, a very large dome, entirely sheathed in copper, was installed. The new dome was massive—it was a statement that this county was growing in wealth and population.

On the night of July 29, 1895, a fire broke out in the Courthouse roof just a few feet behind the dome. The resulting conflagration caused the copper to melt and, as reported in the *Fresno Daily Evening Expositor* on July 30, to "pour down in streams of red liquid from the portico in front, falling into the water on the porch with explosions that could be heard from afar. After a time, the ceiling of the portico began to give way and let down showers of sparks that were carried down and southward with most beautiful effect."

The dome collapsed onto the roof of the south wing of the building, where it burned until it was no more. Thousands of people gathered to watch the spectacular sight.

Once again, the county board of supervisors was called upon to restore the Courthouse. A third floor was added to the building and a new dome was designed. This one would be lighter in weight and would be fire proof. It was not as tall as the previous dome and was more symmetrical and designed to be more in keeping with the classical architecture of the structure. This dome would stay atop the building until it was torn down in 1966.

Unfortunately, there was one feature of the new dome that caused a problem—that story will follow.

# The Hideous Green Dome

After the disastrous fire that damaged the Fresno County Courthouse on July 29, 1895, and destroyed its new copper dome, a third floor was added to the building and a new dome was constructed and placed on top of the building. It was a magnificent dome. It was fireproof, symmetrical, classical in its proportions, a thing of beauty in every way except one—someone decided to paint it a hideous shade of green that slowly faded to pale yellow as it descended to the bottom of the dome. Since the Courthouse itself was pure white, the dome stuck out like the proverbial sore thumb.

By June of 1897, the citizens of Fresno had had enough. After all, this abomination could be seen for miles around. One couldn't get away from it. One of the reporters for *The Fresno Morning Republican* called it "a bilious monument to colicky misery." Obviously, something had to be done.

When a crisis presented itself, there was one man in Fresno who would always put himself forward to solve the problem. Camelot had King Arthur. Fresno had W. Parker Lyon.

Just before eight o'clock on the morning of July 24, 1897, the doors of *The Republican* office flew open. Mr. Lyon walked in carrying a large sheet of paper covered with paint samples. He stood before the desk of the gentleman who wrote "The Man About Town" column and said he had been sent by Supervisor Rose to ask him what color of paint should be used on the dome. (This columnist had been writing about the horrible color). The gentleman told Lyon that he was not "the guardian of public taste," but merely a voice of protest. As soon as Lyon left, another gentleman came in with paint samples to present to the columnist who was beginning to suspect one of Lyon's schemes. Getting into the mood of this, he told this man the dome should be painted scarlet. The man left and another man with paint appeared. To this man, he said, "Paint it red, white, and blue for all I care!" Another man and still another man appeared. Then the phone began to ring. The columnist recognized the poorly disguised voice of one of Lyon's employees.

In the space of an hour, the poor columnist had been bombarded with calls, callers, and paint samples. All the paint samples were the same—"dark lead, brick red, iron, brown, dark olive, yellow, orange, road-cart red, imperial blue, vermillion, coach green, and Quaker green." He felt that any of these would be an improvement over what was on the dome, but his eyes were bleary from looking at all these colors over and over again.

Lyon had his fun, but the point was made—something had to be done about the color of the dome. Eventually, it was painted the color of the building—pure white, but not before more protests and more years went by.

The original dome of the Courthouse built in 1875, the copper dome that replaced the original in 1895, and the third dome, built in late 1895 after a fire destroyed the copper dome (left to right).
*Courtesy of California History and Genealogy Room, Fresno County Free Library.*

# The Mighty Dome

The poor Courthouse dome—as if it hadn't suffered enough. In 1898, in spite of W. Parker Lyon's best efforts, it was still painted a very ugly green color and now the wind was blowing. Not just a gentle zephyr, mind you, but a true wind. By mid-morning it was blowing at twenty-one miles an hour and increasing by the minute.

By early afternoon, some of the county employees on the third floor were hearing creaks and groans—the dome was beginning to shake under the onslaught of the gale blowing outside. People began to get nervous, fearing that the poor dome was going to topple. It might just topple through the roof and onto the third floor itself. A number of the workers were suddenly reminded of urgent business downtown and exited their offices. The third floor grew ominously quiet save for the creaking and moaning of the dome.

Then the dome started to vibrate. A small group of people began to watch from across Van Ness Avenue—one man said he thought the dome was leaning six feet toward the southeast. Another man said there was no danger until it leaned seven feet in that direction. Both men left rather suddenly, perhaps not wanting to see what happened.

On and on the wind blew. Suddenly, one of the joints of the columns that encircled the colonnade of the dome came loose. The columns were made of galvanized iron and were just there for architectural effect. The loose column began to wave with the wind and, for a while, it looked like it would come hurtling to the ground. The janitor and his assistants went up into the tower and secured the column with bailing wire.

By nightfall, the wind had stopped. The dome remained in place for another sixty-four years. On the day that it was pulled down, April 7, 1966, it took many men and nine hours to accomplish what the forces of nature could not. What a sad day that was in the tales of our Valley!

# Harold Zinkin–Muscle Beach Era

In the mid-twentieth century, the movement toward physical fitness had not yet become part of our culture. A man who would become an important part of the Fresno community had joined a small group of people who were breaking new ground in physical fitness. They knew the importance of exercise and bodybuilding to physical well-being.

Harold Zinkin was born on May 11, 1922, in San Francisco. Five years later his family moved to Los Angeles. In the mid-1930s, when the Depression was at its height, Zinkin was a ninth grade student at Belvedere Junior High. One of his friends, Abe Regenbogen, was, like Zinkin, interested in gymnastics and tumbling. He took Zinkin to the beach at Santa Monica where athletes went through their exercise routines and performed impromptu shows for the crowds of thousands that gathered to watch. As soon as they arrived and saw what was taking place, they joined in—it was a day that changed Zinkin's life forever.

Zinkin became involved in football, track, and gymnastics at Los Angeles' Roosevelt High School and lettered in varsity sports, but, whenever he had the chance, he went to the beach and joined in the activities there. That first group of people was the core— the founders of what would become known as Muscle Beach. They honed their physical skills here, formed lasting friendships, and embarked on career paths that reached fruition as they educated people about physical fitness. It was at Muscle Beach that Zinkin met Jack LaLanne, Armand Tanny, and Steve Reeves, as well as other well-known athletes. He went to grade school with his life long friend Joe Gold, who would later found Gold's Gyms.

In 1939, Harold Zinkin began competing in light heavy weight lifting. He won first place for the state of California in 1939, first place in the tri-state in 1940, first place in western division in 1940, and, in 1949, won first place in the national competition.

In 1941, at age nineteen, Harold Zinkin won the first Mr. California title. In 1945, he was honored by becoming the first runner-up to Mr. America.

Our story will continue…

Muscle Beach is the setting for this photo showing Harold Zinkin (doing a backbend), DeForest Most (standing on top of him), Jack LaLanne (standing atop Most), and Gene Miller (on top). These men were the first to perform this stunt that later became world famous.

*Courtesy of DeWayne Zinkin, Sr.*

Above, Harold Zinkin performing a backbend on a high platform at Muscle Beach.

Left, Harold Zinkin locking in back tilt of Earl Eads, a friend and patient who was paralyzed from the waist down due to an injury suffered in World War II. Eads was able to do this stunt after undergoing physical therapy in Zinkin's physical services gym in the 1940s.

*Courtesy of DeWayne Zinkin, Sr.*

# Harold Zinkin—The Fresno Years

Our last story told of Harold Zinkin's early involvement in the unique culture of Muscle Beach where he honed his skills as an athlete. Taking those skills one step further, in 1943, he joined the United States Navy and was sent to the physical instructors school in Bainbridge, Maryland, where he soon was given a position as an instructor. He was selected for the Naval Rehabilitation Educational program in Rochester, New York, and went on to serve as a rehabilitation director assigned to Long Beach Naval Hospital. He worked on procedures for rehabilitation through physical therapy.

After World War II was over, Zinkin opened his first fitness gym in West Los Angeles. The year was 1947. His cutting edge concepts of therapy included not only bodybuilding, but also training in wheelchair and crutch skills. Zinkin's clients included many movie stars, but he still found time to keep training and competing in weight lifting contests at the national level.

By 1957, over fifty fitness gyms had been franchised throughout the country by the enterprising Zinkin, including one in Fresno that opened in 1951. He had been working for a long time on a total workout machine. In 1963, he perfected its design and had it patented. He began manufacturing his Universal Gym Machine and selling it throughout the world—there was even one purchased by the White House.

In 1985, Zinkin invented the Ultra Shaper, a home workout machine that was light enough for travel. It, too, was sold worldwide. By 1990, both companies had been sold and he continued to support fitness programs for youth. In 1999, Zinkin published a book of memoirs of the Muscle Beach years entitled *Remembering Muscle Beach…Where Hard Bodies Began*. He won many honors including induction into the United States Sports Acrobatics Hall of Fame in Dayton, Ohio.

Harold Zinkin died in Fresno on September 22, 2004. His death brought an end to an illustrious career for one of Fresno's citizens.

These men are engaged in brick making at the brick plant where C. J. Craycroft worked in Illinois before coming to California in the late 1860s or early 1879s. Note the mule in the background pulling the long pole (attached to a log that goes into the ground) around. This grinds the clay so that it can be formed into bricks.

*Courtesy of Gary and Cathy Craycroft.*

Late 1860s or early 1870s photo of the brick plant in Illinois where C. J. Craycroft learned the craft of making bricks. Note the rows of bricks drying on the ground and the long poles (on the right side of the picture) used in grinding the clay.

*Courtesy of Gary and Cathy Craycroft.*

# Craycroft Brick Company—The Early Years

In 1880, Columbus Joel Craycroft, whose wife had recently died, and his young son Frank settled in the Panoche Valley, just west of Coalinga, where he had a herd of sheep and made a living hunting deer, quail, and dove—selling them to local stores. Two years later they moved to Fresno. Craycroft ran the old Fresno House, a hotel and rooming house at the corner of Tulare and M streets.

By the mid-1880s, the city of Fresno was growing. Bricks were needed to build structures that would be more fire resistant and structurally sound. Few of the town's original frame buildings remained. Most had burned to the ground.

In 1887, with the knowledge he had acquired working in a brick plant in his native Illinois and with equipment manufactured by his uncle, Craycroft opened Fresno's first brickyard. In these early years, the plant was located on Railroad Avenue—later the Sunland Oil Refinery would locate on this site. He had two business partners. The first was Mr. Herald; the second was Mr. McKnight. The business grew and, in a few years, the name of the company became C. J. Craycroft and Son. The plant moved to Orange and Jensen avenues.

A few more years went by and, in 1910, Craycroft and Son moved for the second and final time. The new site was at 2301 West Belmont Avenue—a 100-acre parcel adjacent to the historic Chinese cemetery. This location was ideal for a number of reasons—one of the most important was that raw materials were available on the company's land.

The soil was adobe dirt. This was blended with hardpan, which was three feet below the surface. To this mixture was added 10 percent binding clay which was shipped in from Lincoln, California. This local adobe soil, when burned in the kiln, turned red. When lighter colors were needed, the amount of Lincoln clay, which contained iron sulfate, could be varied to create colors like buff, rose, or peach.

In 1915, C. J. Craycroft died and the ownership of the company passed to his son, Frank Craycroft.

Employee Ed Sohm standing in front of the large bee-hive kiln at the Craycroft Brick Company on Bel-mont Avenue in the spring of 1936. It is in the kiln (pronounced kill) that the bricks are fired.
*Courtesy of Gary and Cathy Craycroft.*

This is another bee-hive kiln at the Craycroft Brick Company. Note the six chimneys. Photo taken the the the late 1920s or early 1930s.
*Courtesy of Gary and Cathy Craycroft.*

One of the benefits of the Belmont Avenue site was that it was close to the railroad. This view (late 1920s or early 1930s) shows a steam locomotive pulling cars into the brickyard. *Courtesy of Gary and Cathy Craycroft.*

The brick office building at Craycroft Brick Company. *Couresty of Earl and Beverly Knobloch.*

Third generation owner Kenneth Craycroft stands beside one of his company's trucks. *Courtesy of Earl and Beverly Knobloch.*

# Craycroft Brick Company–Finale

Brick making is a craft that has been handed down since ancient times. A brick is a piece of clay that is burned in a kiln. It is often rectangular. There are five steps in the brick making process: The first is winning or extracting the soil; next, mixing the soil, clay, and water; next is extruding—the clay column is pressed through a die then cut, forming the bricks; then the brick is dried in the air; and, fifth, the brick is burned in a kiln at 1,850 degrees Fahrenheit.

The oldest brickyard in Fresno was owned by the Craycroft family. In the late 1880s and 1890s, Craycroft bricks were used to build the brick business buildings, known as "blocks," in downtown Fresno. They were also used to build the additions, or wings, to the Fresno County Courthouse.

During the decade of the 1910s, the face of downtown changed as skyscrapers were built on Fulton Street. Most of them, if not all of them, were constructed with bricks from Craycroft Brick Company.

Ownership passed from one family member to another as the years went by. In 1915, with the death of C. J. Craycroft, his son Frank became owner. When Frank died in 1929, his widow Mae ran the operation until her death in 1957. Their son Kenneth was president of the business until his death in 1985. His son Gary became president of the company.

The Craycroft Brick Company produced a range of burned clay products—common brick, face brick, fire brick, fire clay, roofing tile, hollow file, sewer pipe, drain pipe, cooling tile, pavers, and patio tile. Roofing tile was shipped nationally as well as to Puerto Rico, Guam and Japan.

On February 14, 1994, Gary Craycroft sent a letter to customers telling them that Craycroft Brick Company was suspending production. So much of the work at Craycroft's was still done by hand—an expensive process. Larger companies, with the latest in automated machinery, could create a cheaper product.

After one hundred and seven years, the company that truly had built Fresno closed. It was a sad day in the tales of our Valley.

# The Craycroft Home

On the west side of Palm Avenue, just north of Sierra Avenue, a large brick home sits nestled in an office complex. One might wonder how it came to be there in the middle of this development. It seems to be vacant. One might wonder what story it has to tell.

The Period Revival home was built in 1927 by Frank J. Craycroft, owner of Craycroft Brick Company. The architect was W. S. Coates. There is something unique about this house that is not apparent when one looks at it. One has to walk inside on a hot summer day or on a cold, foggy, winter day to learn what it is. The brick used in building this home was laid in such a way as to act as insulation. The outside walls were constructed using four-inch brick. After visiting the house, Fred C. Foy, writer for *San Joaquin Power Magazine*, said that inside the brick walls "is an inch and a half to two inches of air space where any heat that might penetrate the bricks can run around or lie down and cool off." Inside the air space is a six-inch wall made of hollow tile. In the summer, the house stays cool and, in the winter, the furnace brings warm air into the house that stays inside so the house is nice and warm. "In other words, outside heat can't get in and inside heat can't get out."

The home was lived in by the Craycroft family for many years until Frank's son, Kenneth, and his wife, June, moved to the Bay Area. It was vacant for a time—then the property was sold to Penstar developers.

It was the mid-1980s and the City of Fresno was without a Historic Preservation Commission. The Fresno Historical Society's Preservation Committee was Fresno's only preservation advocate group at the time. One of its members got an anonymous phone call saying the house was going to be torn down. Members of the committee got to work. They called Fresno Development Department director George Kerber and asked him to red flag the building so a demolition permit could not be issued. Then, in a historic move, the committee brought together Kerber and the owners of Penstar to begin a dialogue on ways the building could be saved.

Frank Craycroft,
son of C. J. Craycroft,
stands in front of the
brick home he built on
North Palm Avenue.
*Courtesy of Gary
and Cathy Craycroft.*

Thanks to the Preservation Committee's efforts and the willingness of Kerber and Penstar, the house was saved. It has now been purchased by a couple who plan to restore it. Listed on the Local Register of Historic Resources, the Craycroft home will continue to add beauty and history to the Fresno community.

# Mr. Stern Comes to Town

On the evening of February 24, 1960, the Roosevelt Auditorium began to fill with excited people. Ladies and gentlemen, dressed in their finest evening attire, walked down the aisles to their seats. Some young people could be seen in the crowd. This was going to be more than just a regular performance of the Fresno Philharmonic Orchestra for, on this night, one of the finest violinists in the world was going to perform—his name was Isaac Stern.

That morning Stern had gotten off an airplane at the Fresno Air Terminal carrying a newspaper under one arm and a $65,000 Guarnerius violin under the other. On his way into town, Stern spoke to *Fresno Bee* reporter James Bort, Jr. about "concert audiences, the economic restrictions faced by musicians, the importance of music in our relationship with other countries, the role of a virtuoso, [and] contemporary music." He said that until society realizes "that supporting cultural activities is not giving to charity but giving to its own civilization, there will always be an economic problem facing musicians."

An hour later, he was in rehearsal mode, playing with the orchestra in preparation for the evening's concert.

At precisely 8:30 P.M., the house lights dimmed, the curtains opened, and conductor Paul Vermel walked onto the stage to his platform. He raised his baton and the orchestra began to play Gluck's *Alceste Overture*. This was followed by Prokofiev's *Fifth Symphony* and the intermission. Fifteen minutes later, the house lights began to blink on and off, letting concertgoers know that the second half of the program was about to begin. This is what they had all been waiting for.

Isaac Stern, carrying his violin, walked onto the stage. Vermel lifted his baton. Stern began to play. All at once, bells began to ring crazily. Everyone gasped. Stern stopped and began to pantomime picking up a phone. Everyone burst out laughing. Stern and Vermel left the stage. Someone turned off the fire alarm that had been set off by accident.

Stern and Vermel returned to the stage. Once again, Vermel

lifted his baton; Stern lifted his bow. The first strains of the Braham's *Violin Concerto* could be heard. The glorious music filled every corner of the hall as Stern and the Fresno Philharmonic Orchestra swept the audience along on a magical ride with the sheer beauty of this masterpiece. It was an evening to be remembered forever in the tales of our Valley.

# Mr. Benny Charms Fresno

Excitement was in the air during the week of December 9, 1968. It had nothing to do with Christmas or presents or Santa Claus, but it had everything to do with a man who was probably one of the greatest comedians who ever lived. He was coming to Fresno, he was bringing his valuable Stradivarius violin, and he was going to play with the Fresno Philharmonic Orchestra—yes, indeed, as Mayor Floyd Hyde proclaimed—it was "Jack Benny Week" in Fresno.

From the moment of Benny's arrival at the Fresno Airport on December 10—he was greeted by the Edison High School Band, Convention Center officials, Philharmonic committee members, and a host of fans—the people of Fresno had a jolly good time.

The orchestra needed an acoustical shell for the Convention Center Theatre (today, the Saroyan Theatre)—it was going to cost $30,000. This benefit concert and a champagne supper afterwards, for those who paid fifty dollars a ticket, were to raise money for that purpose.

On the evening of December 11, the theatre began to fill with excited ticket holders. They knew they were in for an unusual musical experience, to say the least. They weren't disappointed. From the moment Jack Benny walked on stage, the audience was treated to some beautiful music and many moments of really bad playing. According to music critic James Bort, Jr. of *The Fresno Bee*, Benny "sawed his way through a passage in Mendelssohn's *Violin Concerto*…[and] threw in his theme song 'Love in Bloom.'" Benny said that a Boston critic compared him to the great violinist Jascha Heifetz by saying that "like Heifetz, he held the violin under his chin."

It was an evening of great merriment, Benny was at his best, and, at evening's end, the Fresno Philharmonic was $20,000 richer—it was a very good week, indeed, in the tales of our Valley.

# The Other Carnegie or What Might Have Been

For those of a certain generation memories of the long-gone Carnegie Library that once stood on Broadway can easily be called to mind. The stately brick structure, with six Ionic columns out front, was all that a library should be. It had a spacious, open, floor plan and housed two thousand books. Opened for business in 1904, it served the needs of the Fresno community until 1959, when a larger facility was needed, and the present Central Library was opened on Mariposa Street.

For all the memories that building evokes, it may be of interest to note that there was another design for the Carnegie that almost was built instead.

The other design was submitted to the board of trustees by the architectural firm of Burnham & Bliesner of Los Angeles. It was a larger building, designed in the Mission style and would be 140 feet long. (The plan that was accepted was 110 feet long). This would leave just seventeen and a half feet on each side of the building to the property line. The building would be built of brick covered with plaster. The roof would be finished with metal tiles. The floors would be cement laid directly on the ground. The reading rooms would be at each end of the building instead of in the center as in the plan that was accepted. There would be an auditorium on the second floor.

When the front door was entered, one's eye would go straight ahead through a long delivery area to the stacks at the back. The stack area curved in an arc, which lent interest to the design.

If this design had been accepted—some of the trustees preferred it—Broadway would have had an imposing library that would have looked very much like the Santa Fe depot. It may be interesting to ponder whether or not that design would have appealed more to the community and, perhaps, there would have been a concerted effort to preserve it.

# Michael Francis Tarpey

Farmer, manufacturer, explorer, politician, and president of the Fresno Irrigation District, Michael Francis Tarpey and his son were staying overnight in Modesto en route to San Francisco. Tarpey wasn't feeling well and, during the night of November 24, 1925, he died of a massive heart attack.

M. F. Tarpey was born in County Mayo, Ireland, in 1848. He came to Brooklyn, New York, with his parents in 1856. Three years later the family moved to San Francisco. He went to a little wooden schoolhouse on the site of the present-day Palace Hotel and later graduated from Saint Ignatius College.

In 1868, he tried his hand at silver mining in Nevada and then returned to California, engaging in stock raising in Stanislaus and Calaveras counties. In 1885, he bought one hundred sixty acres in Fresno County that he planted in vines. A grasshopper plague wiped out his vineyard, causing him to have to replant in 1888.

Tarpey got involved in California politics in 1886, running for lieutenant governor on the Democratic ticket. He did not win, but continued to be politically active with membership in both the Democratic state and national committees.

As his vineyards grew and began to bear fruit, Tarpey began buying up adjacent land. His holdings eventually totaled 1,200 acres. He grew both table and wine grapes. He planted a grove of orange trees and planted fruit trees along the streets of his ranch. He also experimented with cotton and found that it could grow in this area. His La Paloma winery produced some of the finest dessert wines in the Central Valley.

The last years of M. F. Tarpey's life were spent pursing the building of Pine Flat Dam, which he felt would "perfect irrigation for nearly a million acres on the Kings River." He died before his vision was realized.

# The Tarpey Ranch

After the death of M. F. Tarpey in 1925, his son A. B. Tarpey continued to run his father's Clovis ranch. Ever since his father's vineyard first came into production, the ranch was a showplace and was visited by viticulture experts from all over the world. It was noted for being one of the most productive vineyards in California. The Tarpeys always kept up with the latest equipment and methods of viticulture so the high quality of the product would be maintained not only in the present, but also through the years.

On the Tarpey's 1,200-acre vineyard the following varieties of grapes were grown: Thompsons, Missions, Malagas, Zinfandels, Grenache, and Petit Bouchets. It took a workforce of three hundred men, during the height of the season, to take care of the vineyards.

In addition to grapes, ten acres of navel oranges and forty acres of alfalfa were grown on the ranch. A new addition to the operation was the raising of fancy hogs. Four Hampshire sows and one Hampshire boar—all registered—and fifteen purebred Hampshire feeders were purchased from the Cowan-Sample herd of Fresno County. A. B. Tarpey was hopeful his hogs would win blue ribbons at the Fresno County Fair.

In 1930, when Prohibition was still the law, the ranch's La Paloma winery had been standing idle for some time. In pre-Prohibition days, the winery had produced some of the finest Muscat, Port, Angelica, and Claret in California. These wines were enjoyed by connoisseurs all over the country. The winery's machinery was intact and sitting ready to go, on twelve hours notice, should the law be changed.

Today, the Tarpey lands are housing developments. The old Tarpey station that sat on the Pollasky/Southern Pacific line—a shipping point for Tarpey's produce—has found a permanent home in Clovis. Restored, it proudly houses a visitor's center and, in this new millennium, is a reminder of one family that played a major role in the agriculture of Fresno County.

# Notes

ROEDING'S OLIVES
  Clough and Secrest, *Fresno County,* pp. 339-340.
  *The Fresno Morning Republican*, October 9, 1898.
  *The Fresno Morning Republican*, January 6, 1899.
WELLINGTON PILKINTON
  *The Fresno Morning Republican*, February 6, 1927.
LEMONADE & OTHER LIBATIONS
  *The Daily Republican*, July 6, 1889.
OUR RICH VALLEY
  No notes.
BASEBALL & BOBBY BONDS IN FRESNO
  McKay interview.
  *The Fresno Bee*, April 19, 1966.
  *The Fresno Bee*, June 18, 1966.
  *The Fresno Bee*, June 19, 1966.
  *The Fresno Bee*, June 26, 1968.
  *The Fresno Bee*, April 7, 1974.
  *The Fresno Bee*, August 24, 2003.
FRANCO'S
  Franco and Sandoval interview.
WILLIAM PARKER LYON
  Ainsworth, *Pot Luck*, pp. 5-79.
WILLIAM PARKER LYON—THE SAGA CONTINUES
  Ainsworth, *Pot Luck*, 1940, pp. 5-79.
  Walker, *The Fresno County Blue Book*, pg. 218.
WILLIAM PARKER LYON—THE SAGA ENDS
  Martin, *The Parker Lyon-Harrah's Pony Express Museum*, pp. 168-9.
  Reprint of Lyon obituary from the *Los Angeles Times*.
  *The Fresno Bee*, December 15, 1949, obituary.
  *The Fresno Weekly Republican*, February 11, 1898.
  *The Fresno Weekly Republican*, February 25, 1898.
ANOTHER SAD GOODBYE
  *Los Angeles Times*, August 29, 1911.
  *The Fresno Morning Republican*, August 29, 1911.
ADVERTISING—LYON'S WAY
  Ainsworth, *Pot Luck*, pg. 96.
  *Daily Evening Expositor*, February 14, 1894.
  *The Fresno Morning Republican*, April 5, 1902.
LYON'S LAST CHRISTMAS CARD
  Martin, *The Parker Lyon-Harrah's Pony Express Museum*, pg. 168.
  Reprint of Lyon obituary from the *Los Angeles Times*.
  *The Fresno Bee*, December 18, 1949.
THE PARROT OF THE DIAMOND PALACE
  Clough et al., *Fresno County in the 20th Century,* pp. 36-8.
  Thompson, *Official Historical Atlas Map of Fresno County*, pp. 112-3.
  *The Fresno Weekly Republican*, June 24, 1892.
  *The Fresno Weekly Republican*, January 25, 1894.

# Notes

THE FIRST AFRICAN-AMERICAN PIONEERS
   English, *Leaves from the Past*, pp. 16-20.
GABRIEL BIBBARD MOORE
   English, *Leaves from the Past*, pp. 20-21.
A HERO IS HONORED
   Rehart, *The Valley's Legends & Legacies*, pg. 103.
   *The Fresno Bee*, December 14, 1949.
   *The Fresno Bee*, December 16, 1949.
TENNYSON DAY
   *The Complete Poetical Works of Alfred, Lord Tennyson*, pg. 147.
   *The Fresno Weekly Republican*, November 25, 1898.
THURSDAY NIGHT AT THE BODEGA SALOON
   *The Fresno Weekly Republican*, September 9, 1898.
THE EVANGELIST'S BIG MISTAKE
   *The Fresno Weekly Republican*, March 27, 1896.
THE MAN WITH THE VERY LONG BEARD
   *The Fresno Weekly Republican*, August 4, 1893.
SHERMAN'S STORY
   *The Fresno Weekly Republican*, January 17, 1890.
A TEST FOR TEACHERS
   *The Fresno Weekly Republican*, June 15, 1899.
A TRADITION OF ACADEMIC EXCELLENCE
   *Fresno High School Centennial 1889-1989*, pp. 6, 16, 24.
   Rehart, *The Valley's Legends & Legacies V*, pg. 166.
   *The Fresno Weekly Republican*, June 15, 1899.
   Fresno High School website
A BRILLIANT BALL AT ARMORY HALL
   *The Fresno Weekly Republican*, April 22, 1892.
THE ROOTS OF A SYMPHONY
   Clough et al., *Fresno County in the 20th Century*, pp. 382-5.
KATHARINE CALDWELL RIGGS
   Winton, editor, *Fresno Musical Club 75th Anniversary*, pp. 26, 27, 33.
   *The Fresno Bee*, July 4, 1942, obituary.
FRESNO PHILHARMONIC ORCHESTRA
   Heagy, "The Vision That Became A Reality," *Fresnopolitian*, November-December, 1956.
   Fresno Philharmonic Orchestra office, promotional and archival materials.
THE EX-MAYOR AND THE EX-OUTLAW MEET AGAIN
   Martin, *The Parker Lyon-Harrah's Pony Express Museum*, pp. 98-99.
A FEDERATION OF CLUBS
   *The San Joaquin Valley Federation of Woman's Clubs*, program of Fifth Annual Meeting, April 2, 3, & 4 , 1902.
   *The Fresno Morning Republican*, April 3, 1902.
   *The Fresno Morning Republican*, April 4, 1902.
   *The Fresno Morning Republican*, April 6, 1902.

# Notes

REVEREND AND MRS. T. O. ELLIS
Elliott, *History of Fresno County California*, pg. 230.
Wardlaw, *The Early History of Fresno County*, pp. 79-80.

S. ADISON MILLER
Clough and Secrest, *Fresno County*, pp. 130, 131, 144, 316.
Walker, *The Fresno County Blue Book*, pg. 45.
Wardlaw, *The Early History of Fresno County*, pp. 131-2.

DR. BRADLEY WAYMAN DOYLE
Wardlaw, *The Early History of Fresno County*, pp. 48-52.

THE STRANGE DISAPPEARANCE OF PHINEAS LOUCKS
English, *Leaves from the Past*, pp. 26-27.

A REFORMED MR. DALTON COMES TO TOWN
*The Fresno Morning Republican*, March 30, 1931.

GEORGE HEALY TONDEL
Author's memories.
*The Fresno Bee*, November 14, 1988, obituary.
Reeves, "He had only one fault—neglecting himself," *The Fresno Bee*,
November 22, 1988.

THE ROEDING-THORNE NUPTIALS
Rehart, *The Valley's Legends & Legacies IV*, pg. 138.
*The Fresno Weekly Republican*, December 17, 1897.

FLAG DAY
Heck, "A History of Our Flag."
"The History of Flag Day."

THE PARLOR LECTURE CLUB
"Remembrance of Things Past."

A BASKET SOCIAL
*The Fresno Morning Republican*, April 15, 1904.

AN UNFORTUNATE DRINK OF WATER
*The Fresno Morning Republican*, April 2, 1931.

BICYCLES BOUND FOR YOSEMITE
*The Fresno Morning Republican*, June 15, 1904.
*The Fresno Morning Republican*, June 22, 1904.

A PICNIC AT CLARK'S BRIDGE
*The Fresno Morning Republican*, June 14, 1904.

THE CALL OF THE KLONDIKE
Morse, The Klondike Gold Rush: Curriculum Materials.
*The Fresno Morning Republican*, August 8, 1899.

THE SECRETARY OF AGRICULTURE PAYS A VISIT
*The Fresno Morning Republican*, August 8, 1899.

LET'S STOP THE GAMES FOREVER
*The Fresno Morning Republican*, May 31, 1904.

GRADUATION NIGHT IN EASTON
*The Fresno Morning Republican*, May 29, 1904.

JUDGE E. W. RISLEY
*Fresno County Centennial Almanac*, pg. 55.

# *Notes*

Vandor, *History of Fresno County California*, Vol. I & II, pp. 540, 1669.
*The Fresno Morning Republican*, December 16, 1918, obituary.
DR. OSMER ABBOTT
  Vandor, *History of Fresno County California*, Vol. I, pg. 515.
  *The Fresno Morning Republican*, November 24, 1917, obituary.
JAMES RIGGS WHITE
  Rehart, *The Valley's Legends & Legacies*, pg. 182.
  Vandor, *History of Fresno County California*, Vol. I, pg. 544.
  *The Fresno Morning Republican*, May 7, 1907, obituary.
JULY 4, 1917
  *The Fresno Morning Republican*, July 3, 1917.
  *The Fresno Morning Republican*, July 4, 1917.
  *The Fresno Morning Republican*, July 5, 1917.
UNION FOREVER
  *The Fresno Morning Republican*, September 21, 1899.
  *The Fresno Morning Republican*, September 27, 1899.
CHARLES O'NEAL
  Kean, *Wide Places in the California Roads*, Vol. IV, pg. 154.
  *The Fresno Morning Republican*, March 1, 1923.
THE TIES THAT BIND
  *The Fresno Morning Republican*, February 9, 1930.
LIFE IN WASHINGTON COLONY IN 1874
  Clough and Secrest, *Fresno County,* pg. 187.
  *The Fresno Morning Republican*, March 28, 1926.
THE RIVER OF MERCY
  Cabezut-Ortiz, *Merced County the Golden Harvest*, pg. 18.
  Smith, *Garden of the Sun*, pp. 55-62.
MERCED COUNTY IS CREATED
  Cabezut-Ortiz, *Merced County the Golden Harvest*, pp. 28-31.
  Clark, *History of Merced County*, pp.4-5.
  Smith, *Garden of the Sun,* pg. 217.
ROBERT JOHNSON STEELE
  Cabezut-Ortiz, *Merced County the Golden Harvest*, pg. 78.
  Elliot, *History of Merced County*, pp. 115-116.
  Radcliffe, *History of Merced County*, pg. 200.
  "The Late Robert Johnson Steele."
  Robert Johnson Steele biographical information.
ROWENA GRANICE STEELE
  Cabezut-Ortiz, *Merced County the Golden Harvest*, pg. 78.
FROM THE ARGUS TO THE SUN-STAR
  Lim, information provided on dates of Merced County newspapers.
  Radcliffe, *History of Merced County*, pg. 200.
  "The Late Robert Johnson Steele."
  Robert Johnson Steele biographical information.
  University of California Merced news website.

# Notes

SNELLING
> Elliot, *History of Merced County*, pg. 115-117.
> Kean, *Wide Places in the California Roads*, Vol. IV, pp. 193, 194.

CRACKALOO
> Boessenecker, *Gold Dust and Gunsmoke*, pg. 196-197.
> *San Joaquin Republican*, January 26, 1858.

THE VENDETTA CONTINUES
> Boessenecker, *Gold Dust and Gunsmoke*, pg. 196-197.
> *San Joaquin Republican*, January 26, 1858.

HOPETON AND PLAINSBURG
> Elliot, *History of Merced County*, pg. 118.
> Kean, *Wide Places in the California Roads*, Vol. IV, pp. 101, 165.

THE FOUNDING OF MERCED
> Elliot, *History of Merced County*, pg. 111.
> Radcliffe, *History of Merced County*, pp. 107-113.
> Smith, *Towns Along the Tracks*, pg. 123.

SNELLING OR MERCED—THE GREAT DEBATE
> Radcliffe, *History of Merced County*, pp. 114-117.
> Smith, *Towns Along the Tracks*, pg. 123.

A GRAND COURTHOUSE FOR MERCED
> Bare, *Pioneer Genius Charles Henry Huffman*, pg. 36.
> Lim, *Greetings from Fountain City*, pg. 40.
> Radcliffe, *History of Merced County*, pp. 117, 188, 121.

THE STATE ARCHITECT
> Bishop, tour of Merced County Courthouse Museum.
> *The California Architect and Building News*, June, 1884, pg. 105.

THE MERCED COUNTY COURTHOUSE
> Bare, *Pioneer Genius Charles Henry Huffman*, pg. 37.
> Bishop, tour of Merced County Courthouse Museum.
> Lim, *Greetings from Fountain City*, pp. 40-41.

THE MERCED COUNTY COURTHOUSE MUSEUM
> Bishop, tour of Merced County Courthouse Museum.

EL CAPITAN HOTEL
> Elliot, *History of Merced County*, pp. 114, 115.
> Lim, *Greetings from Fountain City*, pp. 8, 35.
> Bare, *Pioneer Genius Charles Henry Huffman*, pg. 57.

WAR AND FROZEN FEET
> *The Fresno Morning Republican*, January 13, 1929.

WILLIAM THOMAS RIGGS
> *The Fresno Morning Republican*, March 12, 1912.

CIVIL WAR STORIES
> *The Fresno Morning Republican*, January 6, 1929.

THE WATCHMAKER
> *The Fresno Morning Republican*, January 6, 1924.

LYON—FRESNO'S HOT TAMALE CHAMPION
> *The Fresno Morning Republican*, June 21, 1904.

# Notes

A GATHERING OF PIONEERS
  *The Fresno Morning Republican*, June 21, 1904.
  *The Fresno Morning Republican*, June 25, 1904.
DR. ROWELL REMINISCES
  *The Fresno Morning Republican*, June 25, 1904.
THE MISSING WINE AND THE TALL, WHITE HAT
  *The Fresno Morning Republican*, June 25, 1904.
FIRST CHINESE BAPTIST CHURCH—THE MISSION YEARS
  *First Chinese Baptist Church 100th Anniversary*, pp. 8-10.
FIRST CHINESE BAPTIST CHURCH—THE YEARS OF MINISTRY
  Chinn interview.
  *First Chinese Baptist Church 100ᵗʰ Anniversary*, pp. 10-12, 28.
  Jack interview.
JOSIAH ROYCE HALL
  Matlosz, "Pretty in Purple."
  Reyes interview.
  Temple interview.
GUSTAV EISEN'S DATES
  Rehart, *The Valley's Legends & Legacies III*, pg. 126.
  *The Fresno Morning Republican*, August 2, 1912.
ALBERT DOWNING OLNEY
  *The Fresno Morning Republican*, January 31, 1926.
  *The Fresno Morning Republican*, April 9, 1927.
A FLOOD ON A SPRING NIGHT
  *The Fresno Morning Republican*, February 27, 1927.
CARRY AMELIA NATION
  Carrie Nation, biography, website
  Carry A. Nation, biography, website
  Grace, *Carry A. Nation*, pp. 2, 20-24, 268, 274.
THE WOMAN WITH THE HATCHET COMES TO TOWN
  *The Fresno Morning Republican*, March 28, 1903.
  *The Fresno Morning Republican*, March 31, 1903.
CARRY NATION AT ARMORY HALL
  *The Fresno Morning Republican*, March 31, 1903.
  *The Fresno Morning Republican*, April 1, 1903.
THANKSGIVING 1894
  *Fresno County Centennial Almanac*, pg. 54.
  *The Fresno Weekly Republican*, November 30, 1894.
THANKSGIVING—A NATIONAL HOLIDAY
  *The First Thanksgiving Day Observance*, website
  Rumela's Web, website
  Jerry Wilson, website
A STAR OF HONOR
  *The Fresno Morning Republican*, December 10, 1921.
ANGUS MARION CLARK
  Clough, *Madera*, pp. 48-49.

# *Notes*

Vandor, *History of Fresno County California*, Vol. I, pp. 948-949.
*The Fresno Morning Republican*, December 3, 1907, obituary.
THE CHINESE AT MILLERTON
Clough and Secrest, *Fresno County*, pp. 63, 64, 85, 88.
English, *Leaves from the Past*, pp. 20-24.
A SAD NEW YEAR'S EVE
"Proceedings had at a meeting of the Citizens of Millerton on December 30 & 31, A.D. 1867"
FRESNO'S CHINATOWN—THE FIRST CHAPTER
Clough and Secrest, *Fresno County*, pg. 138.
Grimes, "Chinese Contributed to Color, Progress of Early Period."
FRESNO'S CHINATOWN—CHAPTER TWO
Grimes, "Chinese Contributed to Color, Progress of Early Period."
Patton, "Strange Lure Is Found in Chinatown Old Customs and New Now Mingle."
*The Fresno Bee*, May 22, 1962.
A FIRE ON CHINA ALLEY
*The Fresno Morning Republican*, August 17, 1908.
A CHRISTMAS TREE FOR FRESNO
Winchell, "Christmas in the Seventies."
FRESNO'S FIRST GENERAL ELECTION
Elliott, *History of Fresno County California*, pg. 96.
Winchell, "Fresno Memories: First General Election in Fresno."
*The Fresno Expositor*, August 25, 1875.
*The Fresno Expositor*, September 1, 1875.
*The Fresno Expositor*, September 8, 1875.
A DODGE CITY CHRISTMAS
*The Fresno Expositor*, December 22, 1875.
*The Fresno Expositor*, December 29, 1875.
A NEW YEAR'S BALL AT MAGNOLIA HALL
*The Fresno Expositor*, December 30, 1874.
*The Fresno Expositor*, January 6, 1875.
LAURA WINCHELL'S MINCE PIE
Winchell, "Fresno Memories: The Mince Pie."
FANCY EQUIPAGES IN 1880s FRESNO
Winchell, "Fresno Memories: Equipages of the Eighties."
WEST PARK COLONY
Anonymous, "Some Statistical History of West Park School."
*Washington Union High School Centennial 1892-1992*, pp. 31, 34.
Kearney, *Fresno County California and the Evolution of the Fruitvale Estate*, pg. 24.
Rehart, *The Valley's Legends & Legacies IV*, pg. 198.
Thompson, *Official Historical Atlas Map of Fresno County*, pg. 67.
WEST PARK THURSDAY CLUB
"West Park Thursday Club"
Bixler, Blackburn, Burleigh, Harden, Holgate, McCullough, and

# Notes

McNeil interviews.
Easton Historical Society. *Washington Union High School Centennial 1892-1992*, pg. 176.
Hart letter

A LITERARY AFTERNOON IN WEST PARK
"Constitution and By-laws of the West Park Thursday Club," pg. 6.
"West Park Thursday Club 1899-1900," pg. 3.
"West Park Thursday Club 1913-1914," pg. 5.

JOHN EPHRAIM BUGG
English, *Leaves from the Past*, pp. 86-88.
*The Fresno Morning Republican*, March 26, 1922.

JONESVILLE TALES
English, *Leaves from the Past*, pp. 86-88.
*The Fresno Morning Republican*, March 26, 1922.

MOSES MOCK
English, *Leaves from the Past*, pp. 99-100.
Winchell, "Fresno Memories: Moses Mock."
Winchell, "Fresno Memories: Mock's Steam Engine."

MOSES MOCK'S STEAM WAGON
Clough and Secrest, *Fresno County*, pg. 103.
English, *Leaves from the Past*, pp. 99-100.
Winchell, "Fresno Memories: Moses Mock."
Winchell, "Fresno Memories: Mock's Steam Engine."

RELIGION AND THE CENTRAL SCHOOL
Clough and Secrest, *Fresno County*, pp. 129, 135.
Rehart, *The Valley's Legends & Legacies*, pg. 24.
Winchell, "Fresno Memories: In the White Schoolhouse."

CHRISTMAS IN FRESNO STATION, 1872
Ballard, "Fresno Yuletide's Change, First Postmaster Reviews Life, Holiday Mail Light in 1872"
Rehart, *The Valley's Legends & Legacies V*, pg. 251.
Vandor, *History of Fresno County California*, Vol. I, pg. 317.

THE FOG OF WINTER, 1874
*The Fresno Expositor*, December 1874.

ABE LINCOLN TEACHES SUNDAY SCHOOL
*Fresno Morning Republican*, February 12, 1928.

THE PRESIDENT'S LAST ADDRESS
*Fresno Morning Republican*, February 13, 1927.

ARNE NIXON
Eash interview.
Eash, "The philosophy of Arne Nixon as reflected in the Center."

THE ARNE NIXON CENTER
Carpenter interview.
"Lewis Carroll Society to meet in Fresno,"
"The Arne Nixon Center for the study of children's literature."

# *Notes*

A FLAG RAISING
  *Washington Union High School Centennial 1892-1992*, pg. 25.
  *The Fresno Weekly Republican*, April 1, 1892.
THE DASHAWAY LITERARY ASSOCIATION
  Clough and Secrest, *Fresno County*, pg. 137.
  *The Fresno Expositor*, November 18, 1874.
PARTY POLITICS IN 1892 FRESNO
  *The Fresno Weekly Republican*, April 1, 1892.
MARTHA ANN HUMPHREYS
  Rehart, *The Valley's Legends & Legacies II*, pg. 272
  Rehart, *The Valley's Legends & Legacies V*, pg. 216.
  *The Fresno Bee*, April 20, 1940, obituary.
A SCHOOL BY MANY NAMES
  Winchell, "Fresno Memories: The White Schoolhouse."
  *The Fresno Morning Republican*, December 4, 1921.
SAINT PATRICK'S DAY, 1923
  *The Fresno Morning Republican*, March 15, 1923.
  *The Fresno Morning Republican*, March 16, 1923.
GOOD FRIDAY, 1923
  *The Fresno Morning Republican*, March 15, 1923.
SARAH JANE ELLIS DAVIS
  Rehart, *The Valley's Legends & Legacies V*, pg. 21.
  Winchell, "Fresno Memories: A Pioneer Woman of Spirit."
THE HEDGES HOME
  Winchell, "Fresno Memories: The Hedges House."
A JOYOUS 50TH ANNIVERSARY
  Author's memories of stories her grandmother told her about the A.T.
  Stevens' home.
  *The Fresno Morning Republican*, June 9, 1900.
A MOST ROMANTIC LOVE STORY
  *The Fresno Morning Republican*, January 12, 1900.
MORE BOOKS FOR THE LIBRARY
  *The Fresno Morning Republican*, June 5, 1900.
FRESNO HIGH ALUMNI
  *Fresno High School Centennial 1889-1989*, pp. 27, 33.
  *The Fresno Morning Republican*, May 26, 1900.
  *The Fresno Morning Republican*, June 1, 1900.
  *The Fresno Morning Republican*, June 7, 1900.
  *The Fresno Morning Republican*, June 9, 1900.
THE SENIOR CLASS IS ENTERTAINED
  *The Fresno Morning Republican*, May 13, 1900.
THE STORY OF TWO SALOONS
  Clough and Secrest, *Fresno County*, pp. 286-7.
  Winchell, "Fresno Memories: Fresno's Early Amusement Halls."
  *The Fresno Weekly Republican*, July 29, 1882.

# Notes

FIRE ON A SUMMER AFTERNOON
  Winchell, "Fresno Memories: Fresno's Early Amusement Halls."
  *The Fresno Weekly Republican*, July 29, 1882.
PACIFIC BIBLE INSTITUTE
  *Heritage Fresno Homes and People*, pg. 47.
  Enns, "The U.S. Mennonite Brethren Board of Education, 1954-
  1979," pp. 5-6.
  Hofer, "Report of the Board of the Pacific Bible Institute," pp.1-2.
FRESNO PACIFIC UNIVERSITY
  Enns-Remple interview.
  *California Mennonite Historical Society Bulletin*, vol. 31, pg. 9.
  Toews, editor, *Mennonite Idealism and Higher Education*, pp. 1-11.
  Wiebe interview.
  Wiebe, "Retrospect and Prospect," pp. 6-7.
LADIES WHO LOVE LEARNING
  *The Fresno Morning Republican*, May 29, 1900.
SARAH ELIZABETH McCARDLE
  *Heritage Fresno Women and Their Contributions*, pg. 70.
  Parker, *History of the Fresno County Free Library 1910-1970*, pp. 15, 18, 44.
  *The Fresno Morning Republican*, September 28, 1931.
THE MAYOR OF CHINATOWN
  *The Fresno Morning Republican*, November 27, 1921.
THE ANTICS OF THE ANNEX
  *The Fresno Morning Republican*, February 24, 1900.
PADEREWSKI AT THE BARTON
  The New Encyclopaedia Britannica, Micropaedia, Vol. VII, pg. 669.
  *The Fresno Morning Republican*, March 21, 1900.
  *The Fresno Morning Republican*, April 5, 1900.
  *The Fresno Morning Republican*, April 8, 1900.
HERMANN'S HANFORD SALOON
  *The Fresno Morning Republican*, February 17, 1900.
THE BACHELOR'S SEND-OFF
  *The Fresno Morning Republican*, January 31, 1900.
WILLIAM JENNINGS BRYAN
  Morison, *The Oxford History of the American People*, pp. 798-9, 809, 842.
  William Jennings Bryan website.
BRYAN AT THE BARTON
  *The Fresno Morning Republican*, April 1, 1900.
  *The Fresno Morning Republican*, April 7, 1900.
  *The Fresno Morning Republican*, April 8, 1900.
WILLIAM WALTER SHIPP
  Rehart, *The Valley's Legends & Legacies II*, pg. 36.
  Vandor, *History of Fresno County California*, Vol. II, pg. 2289.
  *The Fresno Morning Republican*, January 17, 1900, obituary.
ROBBERY AT THE FRENCH BAKERY
  *The Fresno Morning Republican*, June 19, 1904.

# Notes

A GRAND PARADE
*The Fresno Morning Republican*, October 6, 1896.
MR. SPRECKELS' RAILROAD COMES TO TOWN
Eaton, *Vintage Fresno*, pg. 106.
*The Fresno Morning Republican*, October 6, 1896.
THE FESTIVITIES CONTINUE
*The Fresno Morning Republican*, October 6, 1896.
THE SANTA FE DEPOT
*The Fresno Weekly Republican*, November 9, 1899.
*The Fresno Morning Republican*, June 21, 1900.
SYCAMORE
Clough and Secrest, *Fresno County*, pg. 63.
Winchell, "Fresno Memories: Sycamore"
CONVERSE FERRY
Winchell, "Fresno Memories: Converse Ferry"
Vandor, *History of Fresno County California*, Vol. I, pg. 98.
REDHEADS RULED THE DAY
*The Fresno Morning Republican*, March 16, 1916.
*The Fresno Morning Republican*, March 18, 1916.
A MAN AND HIS ADS
*The Fresno Weekly Republican*, December 2, 1898.
*The Fresno Morning Republican*, February 23, 1902.
*The Fresno Morning Republican*, March 19, 1903.
THOMAS W. PATTERSON
*Davis' Commercial Encyclopedia of the Pacific Southwest*, pg. 470.
Streit, *Fresno's Pioneer Banks and Savings and Loans*, pp. 101-103.
T. W. PATTERSON BUILDING
Streit, *Fresno's Pioneer Banks and Savings and Loans*, pg. 101.
*The Fresno Morning Republican*, March 18, 1923.
APRIL TIDBITS—1900 STYLE
*The Fresno Morning Republican*, April 15, 1900.
JOSEPH DOBBINS DAVIDSON
Rehart, *The Valley's Legends & Legacies IV*, pg. 61.
*The Fresno Morning Republican*, December 7, 1908.
BURNS' NIGHT—1892
The Fresno Daily Evening Expositor, January 27, 1892.
WILLIAM WALKER PHILLIPS—THE EARLY YEARS
Phillips, "A Narrative of My Life."
WILLIAM WALKER PHILLIPS—A JOYOUS WELCOME
Phillips, "A Narrative of My Life."
WILLIAM WALKER PHILLIPS—THE FRESNO YEARS
Streit, *Fresno's Pioneer Banks and Savings and Loans*, pg. 38.
*The Fresno Bee*, January 21, 1935, obituary.
Phillips, "A Narrative of My Life."
ELIZABETH PRESSLEY PHILLIPS
*The Book of Common Prayer*, pg. 469.

# Notes

*The Fresno Morning Republican*, March 17, 1916, obituary.
*The Fresno Morning Republican*, March 18, 1916.
THE BURIED TREASURE HOAX
*The Fresno Morning Republican*, July 20, 1900.
WHEELING PARTIES AND MELON SOCIALS
*The Fresno Morning Republican*, July 21, 1900.
MIDSUMMER IN COURTHOUSE PARK
*The Fresno Morning Republican*, July 21, 1900.
A SEPTEMBER SUNDAY AT MILLERTON
*Weekly Merced Herald*, September 30, 1865.
CULTURE AND ELEGANCE COME TO FRESNO
Eaton, *Vintage Fresno*, pg. 85.
*Daily Evening Expositor*, September 30, 1890.
CHURCH'S VISION FOR FRESNO
*Daily Evening Expositor*, September 30, 1890.
THE SINKS OF DRY CREEK
Winchell, "Fresno Memories: The Sinks of Dry Creek."
THE FIRE WHISTLE
Rehart, *The Valley's Legends & Legacies*, pg. 27.
*The Fresno Morning Republican*, March 25, 1896.
ATWATER
Cabezut-Ortiz, *Merced County the Golden Harvest*, pg. 58.
Smith, *Garden of the Sun*, pp. 290, 380.
MR. CEARLEY CLEARLY CAN'T SING
Rehart, *The Valley's Legends & Legacies*, pg. 160.
*The Fresno Weekly Republican*, December 17, 1897.
WEDNESDAY CLUB'S EIGHTH OPTIONAL
*The Fresno Weekly Republican*, May 14, 1897.
THE THIMBLE CLUB
*The Fresno Morning Republican*, March 11, 1896.
WOMEN'S SUFFRAGE TAKES CENTER STAGE
*Fresno Morning Republican*, March 21, 1896.
History of Women's Suffrage website.
THE SAN JOAQUIN VALLEY MEDICAL SOCIETY
Eaton, *Vintage Fresno*, pg. 4.
*Fresno Morning Republican*, March 24, 1896.
J. W. FERGUSON
*The Fresno Morning Republican*, July 27, 1900, obituary.
A MOST INCREDIBLE CONCERT
Briggs, "Six-Piano Ensemble Feature of Music Week Concert At College."
THE VISITING SHERIFF
*The Fresno Morning Republican*, April 1, 1896.
NEEDLEWORK IN THE 1880s
Winchell, "Fresno Memories: Art in the Eighties."
Quilt Bus website.
Root, Redwork Embroidery Primer website.

# Notes

A BICENTENNIAL SPECTACTULAR
Rose, "Pageant Brings Out the 'Patriot' in All of Us."
*The Fresno Bee*, July 2, 1976.
*The Fresno Bee*, July 3, 1976.
*The Fresno Bee*, July 4, 1976.
*The Fresno Bee*, July 5, 1976.
PATRICIA MARION BAKER FEY
Ellen Fey interview.
"In Celebration of the life of Patricia Marion Baker Fey," funeral
memorial program.
Sarah Fey interview.
*The Fresno Bee*, May 27, 1998, obituary.
Author's memories.
CITRUS, CITRUS EVERYWHERE
*The Fresno Morning Republican*, January 3, 1896.
*The Fresno Morning Republican*, January 4, 1896.
THE FIRST EVER CITRUS FAIR
*The Fresno Morning Republican*, January 3, 1896.
*The Fresno Morning Republican*, January 4, 1896.
ALMA'S BIRDCAGE
*The Daily Republican*, July 21, 1889.
RUSSELL HARRISON FLEMING
Clough and Secrest, *Fresno County*, pp. 121-2.
*The Fresno Morning Republican*, April 11, 1920.
*The Fresno Morning Republican*, December 15, 1928, obituary.
THE TILE LAYER'S LAMENT
Eaton, *Vintage Fresno*, pg. 113.
*Fresno Daily Evening Expositor*, May 19, 1892.
*Fresno Daily Evening Expositor*, April 8, 1893.
*Fresno Daily Evening Expositor*, September 16, 1893.
THE DOMES OF THE COURTHOUSE
Eaton, *Vintage Fresno*, pg. 112-114.
*Fresno Daily Evening Expositor*, July 30, 1895.
THE HIDEOUS GREEN DOME
*The Fresno Weekly Republican*, June 25, 1897.
THE MIGHTY DOME
Rehart, *The Valley's Legends & Legacies*, pg. 72.
*The Fresno Morning Republican*, March 22, 1898.
HAROLD ZINKIN—THE MUSCLE BEACH ERA
Hearn-Hill and Dunn, "Highlights of Harold Zinkin's Athletic & Fitness
Career."
Hearn-Hill and Dunn, "Harold Zinkin."
Zinkin with Bonnie Hearn, *Remembering Muscle Beach*, pp. 9-11.
HAROLD ZINKIN—THE FRESNO YEARS
Hearn-Hill and Dunn, "Highlights of Harold Zinkin's Athletic & Fitness
Career."

# Notes

Hearn-Hill and Dunn, "Harold Zinkin."
CRAYCROFT BRICK COMPANY—THE EARLY YEARS
Coyle, "Craycroft Brick Co. to shut its doors."
Cathy Craycroft interview.
Gary Craycroft interview.
Mae Craycroft, undated letter.
Laughnan, "Craycroft Brick Co.—A Fresno Pioneer."
Rehart, *The Valley's Legends & Legacies III*, pg. 55.
*Fresno Business Journal*, January 5, 1988.
CRAYCROFT BRICK COMPANY—FINALE
Coyle, "Craycroft Brick Co. to shut its doors."
Cathy Craycroft interview.
Gary Craycroft interview.
Mae Craycroft, undated letter.
Laughnan, "Craycroft Brick Co.—A Fresno Pioneer."
Rehart, *The Valley's Legends & Legacies III*, pg. 55.
*Fresno Business Journal*, January 5, 1988.
THE CRAYCROFT HOME
Author's memories of the Preservation Committee's work on the
Craycroft Home.
Fox, "Home Comforts in Brick."
MR. STERN COMES TO TOWN
Bort, "Stern Declares Government Will Have To Subsidize Music."
Rea, "Isaac Stern Performance Is Termed 'Rare Treat.'"
*The Fresno Bee*, February 25, 1960.
MR. BENNY CHARMS FRESNO
Desa Belyea, "Note-Able Men Aid WSL."
*The Fresno Bee*, December 1, 1968.
Bort, "It's 'Love in Bloom'—Benny, Violin, Audience."
Wylie, "After 48 Years Jack Benny Comes Back To A Split Week in
Fresno."
THE OTHER CARNEGIE OR WHAT MIGHT HAVE BEEN
Rehart, *The Valley's Legends & Legacies*, pg. 132.
*The Fresno Morning Republican*, January 44, 1902.
MICHAEL FRANCIS TARPEY
*Davis' Commercial Encyclopedia of the Pacific Southwest*.
*The Fresno Morning Republican*, November 25, 1925, obituary.
THE TARPEY RANCH
Keyes, "Pioneer Tarpey Vineyard Still Heavy Producer."

# Bibliography

Ainsworth, Ed. *Pot Luck*. Hollywood: George Palmer Putnam, Inc., 1940.

American Association of University Women. *Heritage Fresno Homes and People*. Fresno: Pioneer Publishing Co., 1975.

American Association of University Women. *Heritage Fresno Women and Their Contributions*. Fresno: Pioneer Publishing Co., 1987.

Anonymous. "Some Statistical History of West Park School." Original manuscript. Provided by the members of the West Park Thursday Club.

Anonymous. "West Park Thursday Club." Handwritten early history. Original manuscript. Provided by the members of the West Park Thursday Club.

"Arne Nixon Center for the study of children's literature." Informational brochure.

Ballard, Berton. "Fresno Yuletide's Change, First Postmaster Reviews Life, Holiday Mail Light in 1872." *The Fresno Morning Republican*, December 1923.

Bare, Colleen Stanley. *Pioneer Genius Charles Henry Huffman*. Merced: Merced County Historical Society, 2003.

Belyea, Desa. "Note-Able Men Aid WSL." *The Fresno Bee*, November 11, 1968.

Bishop, Zoe, docent coordinator, Merced County Historical Society. Tour of Merced County Courthouse Museum, May 21, 2004.

Bixler, Helen, Ida Blackburn, Harriet Pervier Burleigh, Eleanor Harden, Harriett Harkness Holgate, Mary Jane Burleigh McCullough, and Nancy McNeil, members of the West Park Thursday Club. Interviews, June 17, 2004.

Boessenecker, John. *Gold Dust and Gunsmoke*. New York: John Wiley and Sons, 1999.

*Book of Common Prayer, The*. New York: The Seabury Press, 1979.

Bort, James, Jr. "It's 'Love in Bloom'—Benny, Violin, Audience." *The Fresno Bee*, December 12, 1968.

Bort, James, Jr. "Stern Declares Government Will Have To Subsidize Music." *The Fresno Bee*, February 24, 1960.

Briggs, Mitchell P. "Six-Piano Ensemble Feature of Music Week Concert At College." *The Fresno Bee*, May 5, 1931.

Bryan, William Jennings. www.u-s-history.com/pages/h805.html

Cabezut-Ortiz, Delores J. *Merced County the Golden Harvest*. Northridge: Windsor Publications, Inc., 1987.

*California Architect and Building News, The*. June 1884.

*California Mennonite Historical Society Bulletin*. Vol. 31, December 1994.

Carpenter, Angelica, curator of the Arne Nixon Center. Interview and tour of center, November 30, 2004.

Chinn, Dr. Dennis. Interview and tour of First Chinese Baptist Church. June 30, 2004.

Clark, George W. *History of Merced County*. Merced, 1955.

Clough, Charles W. et al., *Fresno County in the 20th Century: from 1900 to the 1980s*. Fresno: Panorama West Books, 1986.

Clough, Charles W. and William B. Secrest, Jr. *Fresno County: The Pioneer Years.* Fresno: Panorama West Books, 1984.

Clough, Charles W. *Madera.* Madera: Madera County History Society, 1968.

*Complete Poetical Works of Alfred, Lord Tennyson, The.* New York: Harper & Brothers, 1884.

"Constitution and By-laws of the West Park Thursday Club."

Coyle, Wanda. "Craycroft Brick Co. to shut its doors." *The Fresno Bee,* March 10, 1994.

Craycroft, Cathy. Interview. May 14, 2005.

Craycroft, Gary. Interview. May 14, 2005.

Craycroft, Mae. Undated letter.

*Davis' Commercial Encyclopedia of the Pacific Southwest.* Oakland: Ellis A. Davis, 1915.

*Davis' Commercial Encyclopedia of the Pacific Southwest.* Oakland, Ellis A. Davis, 1918.

Eash, Maurice, Ph.D., trustee of the Arne Nixon Center and professor emeritus, University of Illinois at Chicago. Interview. December 15, 2004.

_____. "The philosophy of Arne Nixon as reflected in the Center." *The Magic Mirror,* newsletter of the Arne Nixon Center Advocates (ANCA). Angelica Carpenter, editor. Number 5. Fresno, April 2004.

Easton Historical Society. *Washington Union High School Centennial 1892-1992.* Fresno: Easton Historical Society, 1992.

Eaton, Edwin. *Vintage Fresno.* Fresno: The Huntington Press, 1965.

Elliott, Wallace W. *History of Fresno County California.* San Francisco: Wallace W. Elliott & Co., 1882.

Elliot, Wallace W. *History of Merced County.* San Francisco: Elliot & Moore, 1881. Reprinted by California History Books, Fresno, 1974.

English, June. *Leaves from the Past.* Fresno: The Fresno County Library, The Fresno County Genealogical Society, 2001.

Enns, Peter. "The U.S. Mennonite Brethren Board of Education, 1954-1979: A Ten-year Retrospect." *California Mennonite Historical Society Bulletin,* Vol. 31. Fresno, December 1994.

Enns-Remple, Kevin. Interview. August 16, 2004.

Fey, Ellen. Interview. April 30, 2005.

Fey, Sarah. Interview. April 30, 2005.

*First Chinese Baptist Church 100th Anniversary.* Centennial history. Fresno, May 16, 19, 20, 1984.

Fox, Fred C. "Home Comforts in Brick." *San Joaquin Power Magazine.* Vol. XI, No. 3. March 1929.

Franco, Seferina and Rosalie Franco Sandoval. Interview. October 8, 2003.

*Fresno County Centennial Almanac.* Fresno: Fresno County Centennial Committee, 1956.

*Fresno High School Centennial 1889-1989.* Fresno: Centennial Committee, 1989.

Fresno Philharmonic Orchestra office. Promotional and archival materials.

Grace, Fran. *Carry A. Nation*. Bloomington: Indiana University Press, 2001.

Grimes, Ward. "Chinese Contributed to Color, Progress of Early Period." *The Fresno Bee*, April 18, 1956.

Hart, Davadella. Letter outlining early history of the West Park Thursday Club. Original manuscript. Provided by the West Park Thursday Club.

Heagy, Mrs. Clarence. "The Vision That Became A Reality." *Fresnopolitian*. November-December 1956.

Heck, Rose Marie, New Jersey assemblywoman. "A History of Our Flag." Reprint of an editorial. http://www.hasbrouchheights.com/news01/wtc5.shtml

Hearn-Hill, Bonnie, and Ed Dunn. "Harold Zinkin." Media bio. "Highlights of Harold Zinkin's Athletic & Fitness Career." Provided by Ed Dunn, Dunn Marketing.

"History of Flag Day, The." http://www.usflag.org/flag.day.html

Hofer, J. D. "Report of the Board of the Pacific Bible Institute." *California Mennonite Historical Society Bulletin,* Vol. 31. Fresno, December 1994.

"In Celebration of the life of Patricia Marion Baker Fey." Funeral memorial program.

Jack, Reverend Danny, minister of First Chinese Baptist Church. Interview, June 30, 2004.

Kean, David W. *Wide Places in the California Roads*. Vol. IV. Sunnyvale: The Concord Press, 1996.

Keyes, M. J. "Pioneer Tarpey Vineyard Still Heavy Producer." *The Fresno Bee*, June 29, 1930.

Kearney, M. Theo. *Fresno County California and the Evolution of the Fruitvale Estate*. Facsimile edition. Fresno: Fresno City and County Historical Society, 1980.

Laughnan, Woody. "Craycroft Brick Co.—A Fresno Pioneer." *The Fresno Bee*, April 27, 1969.

"Late Robert Johnson Steele, The." *San Joaquin Valley Argus*, February 8, 1890. Submitted by Priscilla Stone Sharp. www.columbiagazette.com/steele.htm

"Lewis Carroll Society to meet in Fresno. *Magic Mirror*, newsletter of the Arne Nixon Center Advocates (ANCA). Angelica Carpenter, editor. Number 6. Fresno, October 2004.

Lim, Sarah, director, Merced County Historical Society. Information provided regarding dates of Merced County newspapers. May 10, 2005.

_____. *Greetings from Fountain City*. Merced: Merced County Historical Society, 2002.

Martin, Greg. *The Parker Lyon-Harrah's Pony Express Museum*. San Francisco: Chrysopolis Press, 1987. Reprint of Lyon obituary from the *Los Angeles Times*.

Matlosz, Felicia Cousart. "Pretty in Purple." *The Fresno Bee*, November 10, 2003.

McKay, Robert W. Interview, August 25, 2003.

Morison, Samuel Elliot. *The Oxford History of the American People*, New
York: Oxford University Press, 1965.

Morse, Kathryn. University of Washington Department of History. The
Klondike Gold Rush: Curriculum Materials for the History of the
Pacific Northwest in the Washington Public Schools.
http://www.washington.edu/uwired/outreach/cspn/curklon/
main.html

Nation, Carrie. Biography. http://www.fact-index.com/c/ca/
carrie_nation.html

Nation, Carry A. Biography. http://www.ku.edu/kansas/medicine/
carry.html

New Encyclopaedia Britannica, The. Micropaedia. Vol. VII. Chicago:
Encyclopaedia Britannica, Inc., 1984.

Parker, Mary Ann. *History of the Fresno County Free Library 1910-1970*.
Master of arts thesis. California State University, Fresno, August 1977.

Patton, Dorothy. "Strange Lure Is Found in Chinatown Old Customs and
New Now Mingle." *The Fresno Bee*, July 5, 1931.

Phillips, William Walker. "A Narrative of My Life." Unpublished manuscript. Courtesy of David Phillips.

"Proceedings had at a meeting of the Citizens of Millerton on December
30 & 31, A.D. 1867." Copy of original manuscript. California History
and Genealogy Room, Fresno County Free Library.

Radcliffe, Corwin. *History of Merced County*. Merced: Arthur H. Crawston,
1940.

Rea, Alan. "Isaac Stern Performance Is Termed 'Rare Treat.'" *The Fresno
Bee*, February 25, 1960.

Reeves, Scott. "He had only one fault—neglecting himself." *The Fresno Bee*,
November 22, 1988.

Rehart, Catherine Morison. *The Valley's Legends & Legacies*. Fresno: Word
Dancer Press, 1996.

_____. *The Valley's Legends & Legacies II*, Clovis: Word Dancer Press, 1997.

_____. *The Valley's Legends & Legacies III*. Clovis: Word Dancer Press, 1999.

_____. *The Valley's Legends & Legacies IV*. Clovis: Word Dancer Press, 2001.

_____. *The Valley's Legends & Legacies V*. Sanger: Word Dancer Press, 2004.

"Remembrance of Things Past, A History of the Parlor Lecture Club 1894-
1994."

Reyes, Robert, principal of Fresno High School. Interview and tour of
Royce Hall. January 8, 2004.

Rose, Gene. "Pageant Brings Out the 'Patriot' in All of Us." *The Fresno Bee*,
July 4, 1976.

*San Joaquin Valley Federation of Woman's Clubs, The*. Program of Fifth
Annual Meeting. Fresno, April 2, 3, & 4 , 1902.

Smith, Richard Harold. *Towns Along the Tracks*. Dissertation written in
partial fulfillment of doctor of philosophy degree requirement. Los
Angeles: University of California Los Angeles, 1976.

Smith, Wallace. *Garden of the Sun A History of the San Joaquin Valley, 1772-*

*1939*. Edited and revised by William B. Secrest, Jr. 2nd edition. Fresno: Linden Publishing, 2004.

Streit, Edwin. *Fresno's Pioneer Banks and Savings and Loans*. Fresno, 1999.

Temple, J. Martin. Interview. February 5, 2004.

Thompson, Thos. H. *Official Historical Atlas Map of Fresno County*. Tulare: Thos. H. Thompson, 1891.

Toews, Paul, editor. *Mennonite Idealism and Higher Education*. Fresno: The Center for Mennonite Brethren Studies, 1995.

Vandor, Paul E. *History of Fresno County California*. Volumes I & II. Los Angeles: Historic Record Company, 1919.

Walker, Ben R. *The Fresno County Blue Book*. Fresno: Arthur H. Crawston, 1941.

Wardlaw, Muriel Emery. *The Early History of Fresno County*. Edited by Jessica A. Crisp and William B. Secrest, Jr. Fresno: Fresno County Genealogical Society, 2001.

"West Park Thursday Club 1899-1900." Program book. Provided by the West Park Thursday Club.

"West Park Thursday Club 1913-1914. " Program book. Provided by the West Park Thursday Club.

Wiebe, Arthur J. Interview. August 16, 2004.

_____. "Retrospect and Prospect." *California Mennonite Historical Society Bulletin*. Vol. 31. December, 1994.

Winchell, Ernestine. "Fresno Memories: Art in the Eighties." *The Fresno Morning Republican*, September 18, 1927.

_____. "Fresno Memories: A Pioneer Woman of Spirit." *The Fresno Morning Republican*, February 23, 1930.

_____. "Fresno Memories: Christmas in the Seventies." *The Fresno Morning Republican*, December 25, 1927.

_____. "Fresno Memories: Converse Ferry." *The Fresno Morning Republican*, September 12, 1926.

_____. "Fresno Memories: Equipages of the Eighties." *The Fresno Morning Republican*, January 24, 1925.

_____. "Fresno Memories: First General Election in Fresno." *The Fresno Morning Republican*, no date.

_____. "Fresno Memories: Fresno's Early Amusement Halls." *The Fresno Morning Republican*, March 16, 1924.

_____. "Fresno Memories: In the White Schoolhouse." *The Fresno Morning Republican*, September 29, 1926.

_____. "Fresno Memories: Mock's Steam Engine." *The Fresno Morning Republican*, April 4, 1926.

_____. "Fresno Memories: Moses Mock." *The Fresno Morning Republican*, March 28, 1926.

_____. "Fresno Memories: Sycamore." *The Fresno Morning Republican*, May 8, 1927.

_____. "Fresno Memories: The Hedges House." *The Fresno Morning Republican*, July 7, 1929.

_____. "Fresno Memories: The Mince Pie." *The Fresno Morning Republican*, November 22, 1925.

_____. "Fresno Memories: The Sinks of Dry Creek." *The Fresno Morning Republican*, June 16, 1929.

_____. "Fresno Memories: The White Schoolhouse." *The Fresno Morning Republican*, September 20, 1925.

Winton, Ruth, editor. *Fresno Musical Club 75th Anniversary*. Fresno, 1982.

Wylie, Deane. "After 48 Years Jack Benny Comes Back To A Split Week in Fresno. *The Fresno Bee*, December 11, 1968.

Zinkin, Harold, with Bonnie Hearn. *Remembering Muscle Beach*. Santa Monica: Angel City Press, Inc., 1999.


*Daily Evening Expositor*. September 30, 1890.

_____. January 27, 1892.

_____. May 19, 1892.

_____. April 8, 1893.

_____. September 16, 1893.

_____. February 14, 1894.

_____. July 30, 1895.


*Los Angeles Times*. August 29, 1911.


*San Joaquin Republican*. Stockton, January 26, 1858.


*Fresno Business Journal*. January 5, 1988.


*The Daily Republican*. July 6, 1889.

_____. July 21, 1889.


*The Fresno Bee*. January 21, 19435. Obituary.

_____. April 20, 1940. Obituary.

_____. July 4, 1942. Obituary.

_____. December 15, 1949. Obituary.

_____. December 14, 1949.

_____. December 16, 1949.

_____. December 18, 1949.

_____. February 25, 1960.

_____. May 22, 1962.

_____. April 19, 1966.

_____. June 18, 1966.

_____. June 19, 1966.

_____. December 1, 1968.

_____. June 26, 1968.

_____. April 7, 1974.

_____. July 2, 1976.

_____. July 3, 1976.

_____. July 4, 1976.

\_\_\_\_\_. July 5, 1976.
\_\_\_\_\_. November 14, 1988. Obituary.
\_\_\_\_\_. May 27, 1998. Obituary.
\_\_\_\_\_. August 24, 2003.

*The Fresno Expositor.* November 18. 1874.
\_\_\_\_\_. December 1874.
\_\_\_\_\_. December 30, 1874.
\_\_\_\_\_. January 6, 1875.
\_\_\_\_\_. August 25, 1875.
\_\_\_\_\_. September 1, 1875.
\_\_\_\_\_. September 8, 1875.
\_\_\_\_\_. December 22, 1875.
\_\_\_\_\_. December 29, 1875.

*The Fresno Morning Republican.* April 1, 1896.
\_\_\_\_\_. January 3, 1896.
\_\_\_\_\_. January 4, 1896.
\_\_\_\_\_. March 11, 1896.
\_\_\_\_\_. March 21, 1896.
\_\_\_\_\_. March 24, 1896.
\_\_\_\_\_. March 25, 1896.
\_\_\_\_\_. October 6, 1896.
\_\_\_\_\_. March 22, 1898.
\_\_\_\_\_. October 9, 1898.
\_\_\_\_\_. January 6, 1899.
\_\_\_\_\_. September 21, 1899.
\_\_\_\_\_. September 27, 1899.
\_\_\_\_\_. August 8, 1899.
\_\_\_\_\_. April 1, 1900.
\_\_\_\_\_. April 5, 1900.
\_\_\_\_\_. April 7, 1900.
\_\_\_\_\_. April 8, 1900.
\_\_\_\_\_. February 17, 1900.
\_\_\_\_\_. February 24, 1900.
\_\_\_\_\_. January 12, 1900.
\_\_\_\_\_. January 17, 1900.
\_\_\_\_\_. January 17, 1900. Obituary.
\_\_\_\_\_. January 31, 1900.
\_\_\_\_\_. July 20, 1900.
\_\_\_\_\_. July 21, 1900.
\_\_\_\_\_. July 27, 1900. Obituary.
\_\_\_\_\_. June 1, 1900.
\_\_\_\_\_. June 7, 1900.
\_\_\_\_\_. June 5, 1900.
\_\_\_\_\_. June 8, 1900.
\_\_\_\_\_. June 9, 1900.

_____. June 21, 1900.

_____. March 21, 1900.

_____. May 13, 1900.

_____. May 26, 1900.

_____. May 29, 1900.

_____. April 3, 1902.

_____. April 4, 1902.

_____. April 5, 1902.

_____. April 6, 1902.

_____. February 23, 1902.

_____. January 24, 1902.

_____. March 28, 1903.

_____. March 31, 1903.

_____. April 1, 1903.

_____. March 19, 1903.

_____. April 15, 1904.

_____. May 29, 1904.

_____. May 31, 1904.

_____. June 14, 1904.

_____. June 15, 1904.

_____. June 19, 1904.

_____. June 21, 1904.

_____. June 21, 1904.

_____. June 22, 1904.

_____. June 25, 1904.

_____. May 7, 1907. Obituary.

_____. December 3, 1907. Obituary.

_____. August 17, 1908.

_____. December 7, 1908.

_____. August 29, 1911.

_____. March 12, 1912.

_____. August 2, 1912.

_____. March 16, 1916.

_____. March 17, 1916. Obituary.

_____. March 18, 1916.

_____. July 3, 1917.

_____. July 4, 1917.

_____. July 5, 1917.

_____. November 24, 1917. Obituary.

_____. December 16, 1918. Obituary.

_____. April 11, 1920.

_____. November 27, 1921.

_____. December 4, 1921.

_____. December 10, 1921.

_____. March 26, 1922.

_____. March 1, 1923.

_____. March 15, 1923.

_____. March 16, 1923.
_____. March 18, 1923.
_____. January 6, 1924.
_____. November 24, 1925. Obituary.
_____. January 31, 1926.
_____. March 28, 1926.
_____. March 8, 1927.
_____. February 6, 1927.
_____. February 6, 1927.
_____. February 13 1927.
_____. February 27, 1927.
_____. April 9, 1927.
_____. December 15, 1928. Obituary.
_____. February 12, 1928.
_____. January 6, 1929.
_____. January 13, 1929.
_____. February 9, 1930.
_____. March 30, 1931.
_____. April 2, 1931.
_____. September 28, 1931.

_The Fresno Weekly Republican_. July 29, 1882.
_____. January 17, 1890.
_____. April 1, 1892.
_____. April 22, 1892.
_____. June 24, 1892.
_____. August 4, 1893.
_____. January 25, 1894.
_____. November 30, 1894.
_____. March 27, 1896.
_____. June 25, 1897.
_____. May 14, 1897.
_____. December 17, 1897.
_____. December 2, 1898.
_____. February 11, 1898.
_____. February 25, 1898.
_____. September 9, 1898.
_____. November 25, 1898.
_____. November 9, 1899.
_____. June 15, 1899.

_Weekly Merced Herald_. September 30, 1865.

# Bibliography

William Jennings Bryan. www.u-s-history.com/pages/h805.html

Fresno High School. http://www.fresno.k12.ca.us/schools/s092/sch092hp.htm

History of Women's Suffrage. http://www.rochester.edu/SBA/history.html

*The First Thanksgiving Day Observance.* http://earlyamerica.com/earlyamerica/firsts/thanksgiving/

Quilt Bus. http://www.quiltbus.com/redwork.htm/

Rissa Piece Root. Redwork Embroidery Primer. http://www.prettyimpressivestuff.com]

Rumela's Web. http://www.rumela.com/events/events_november_thanksgiving.htm

Robert Johnson Steele, biographical information. www.cnpa.com/CalPress/hall/cmurphy.htm

University of California Merced news website. www.ucmerced.edu/news.articles

Jerry Wilson. http://wilstar.com/holidays/thankstr.htm.

# Index

# *About the Author*

Cathy Rehart's mother's family arrived in Fresno Station in 1873, the year after the town was founded. She was born in the Sample Sanitarium on Fulton Street, is a third generation graduate of Fresno High School and a second generation graduate of Fresno State College with a BA in English and history. She is the mother of three grown children.

During the years her children were in school, her involvement in their activities resulted in service on several PTA boards, the Fresno High School Site Council and the Cub Scouts. Later she served as first vice-chairwoman for the Historic Preservation Commission for the City of Fresno; as a member of the board of directors of the Fresno City and County Historical Society; as chair of the Preservation Committee of the FCCHS; and a president of the La Paloma Guild, the FCCH's auxiliary.

From 1986 to 1994, she held the position of education/information director for the FCCHS.

Her work as a freelance writer includes writing the KMJ Radio scripts for "The Valley's Legends and Legacies" —from which this book is derived—and other writing projects on local history.

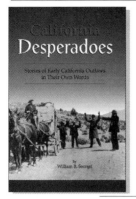